The New Narrative
of Mexico

The New Narrative of Mexico

Sub-Versions of History in Mexican Fiction

Kathy Taylor

Lewisburg
Bucknell University Press
London and Toronto: Associated University Presses

Associated University Presses
440 Forsgate Drive
Cranbury, NJ 08512

Associated University Presses
25 Sicilian Avenue
London WC1A 2QH, England

Associated University Presses
P.O. Box 338, Port Credit
Mississauga, Ontario
Canada L5G 4L8

The paper used in this publication meets the requirements
of the American National Standard for Permanence of Paper
for Printed Library Materials Z39.48-1984.

Library of Congress Cataloging-in-Publication Data

Taylor, Kathy, 1950–
    The new narrative of Mexico : sub-versions of history in Mexican
fiction / Kathy Taylor.
        p.   cm.
    Includes bibliographical references (p.   ) and index.
    ISBN 0-8387-5266-7 (alk. paper)
    1. Mexican fiction—20th century—History and criticism.
2. Historical fiction, Mexican—History and criticism.
3. Literature and history—Mexico.   I. Title.
PQ7155.T39   1994
863—dc20   92-56605
                                                                CIP

PRINTED IN THE UNITED STATES OF AMERICA

To Peter, Jordan, and Anika,
who love stories
and to Mexico,
where the past is always present

Contents

Acknowledgments

I would like to express my gratitude first to Professor Adriana Méndez Rodenas of the University of Iowa for her support and encouragement in all aspects of writing this book. I owe her a lot for the initial inspiration and ideas that launched this project, as well as for the care and enthusiasm with which she read and edited the manuscript. I would also like to recognize my debt to Professor Diana Vélez of the University of Iowa, who first introduced me to the genre of testimonial narrative. It was in classes and discussions with her that the beginnings of this book began to take shape. Professor Charles Hale of the University of Iowa gave me valuable suggestions and the perspective of an historian, so that I wouldn't invent too much of my story. I also owe a great debt to another historian. Professor Peter Taylor, my husband, has helped me more than he could know by listening to my stories, making suggestions, and always being ready to explore new ideas.

The practical aspects of this project were supported initially by the University of Iowa, in the form of the Ada Louisa Ballard Dissertation Year Fellowship. This award made possible a year of intensive work. I would also like to express appreciation to Earlham College and the Joyce Foundation for giving me a term of leave to finish working on the book. During that time I revised and translated the book (originally written in Spanish) into English.

Finally, I would like to thank my good friend Federico Campbell for his help and encouragement in publishing this book.

The New Narrative
of Mexico

1

Introduction: The Beginning of the Story

> The Hispanic American writer recognizes that his most acute
> challenge is in the institution of history, and that the most
> formidable rival of poetic invention in Hispanic America is
> historical invention.[1]

From its beginnings in the time of the Conquest to the most contemporary works, Latin American narrative has been born of the
inseparable embrace of literature and history. The conquistadors
and chroniclers arrived in the New World with their vision already
preconditioned by prevalent mythology and by the literary *topoi*
of Renaissance Spain. In their letters and chronicles they narrated
their observations and interpretations of America from the external perspective of the Old World; limited, as are all writers, by
their own linguistic and cultural experiences. Angel Rosenblat describes the setting:

> In this way, the names of things and places and the very vision the
> conquistador had of America represent a projection of European
> mentality. The discoverers and settlers made the American reality fit
> into the molds of the words, names and beliefs of Europe. In other
> words, they adjusted it to their own mental architecture. They pro-
> jected onto the American world not only the tangible reality of their
> European world, but also its literary, mythological and religious tra-
> dition.[2]

The wonders of this "New World" ("new" from the European
perspective) dazzle these narrators on the one hand, but on the
other hand they are compatible with their European mentality
and the expectations of finding an exotic land or even an earthly
paradise. According to Manual Durán, "The whole endeavor of
the conquerors, chroniclers and historians was to find the true
Dulcinea, to disenchant the peasant woman—to invent an

America worthy of being compared to the beautiful descriptions of the classical world and the original world."[3] In this way literary and mythological imagination condition not only the style with which they represent what they encounter, but the observations themselves, as Tzvetan Todorov shows in his discussion of Christopher Columbus: "Columbus believes not only in Christian Dogma, but also (and he is not alone at the time) in Cyclops and mermaids, in Amazons and men with tails, and his belief, as strong as Saint Peter's, therefore permits him to find them."[4]

In spite of the "literary" aspect common to these first Latin American writings, they don't all belong to the same category of writing, as Roberto González Echevarría points out. The collection of texts we call 'the Chronicles' represents many different rhetorical types: the relation, histories, letters, memorials, commentaries, and so forth.[5] And from these varied forms evolve the modern categories of narrative which we include under the name "history" or "literature." The implicit model for the chronicler was that of the humanist historiographer of the sixteenth century—González Echevarría explains—"which gave a prominent place to the aesthetic value of history . . . of organizing the facts in a coherent and harmonious way. . . ."[6] The relation, on the other hand, was a legal document in which "he gave a firm account of his person and of the facts pertinent to the case—the contact of an 'I' with the surrounding reality."[7] While the histories dealt with the high points of political and military movements, the relation narrated incidents from daily life, and "from there [derived] its anthropological and historical value in the modern sense of the word. But from there also comes its possible literary value, also in a modern sense."[8] As strange as it might seem, it is the relation which has had more influence on Latin American literature while the history led to poetics.[9]

If the testimonial value of the relation and its interest in documentation are added to the aesthetic value of history, we get a model for the Latin American tradition of testimonial literature. The chroniclers' texts were literary creations as well as historical testimonies. Enrique Pupo Walker shows the similarities between the narrative structure of many historical relations and fictional prose, as for example, between the anonymous text *Amadis de Gaula* and Alfonso el Sabio's *Crónica general*.[10] In addition to recording a reality in order to communicate it to those in the Old World, these early historians wanted to give an account of their situation and to justify their own actions. To do this they had to "organize the facts in a coherent and harmonious way" to the

point of "fictionalizing" themselves as protagonists of their accounts. The indigenous chroniclers also recognized the power of
the written word and they directed it defensively,[11] as did their
European counterparts, to the reader of the Old World, above all
to the Spanish Crown. They adopted in their histories many of
the cultural and literary references as well as the language of the
conquerors. Thus this first writing, whether it be literature or
historiographic discourse, is defined by an outsider's perspective—the view of the conqueror. The written word becomes an
instrument for convincing, and the form, point of view, and language of the texts are established as lasting proof of the Conquest.[12]

Perhaps the first truly "Latin American" writer, that is, of the
first mestizo generation, is El Inca Garcilaso de la Vega. His consciousness of being mestizo is very apparent in his work: "seeing
myself obliged to both nations, because I am the son of a Spaniard
and an Indian. . . ."[13] Garcilaso narrates the events of the explora-
tion of Florida as told to him by Hernando de Soto and other
firsthand witnesses. He also incorporates what he has read in the
manuscripts and relations of others. La historia de la Florida, which
was written in the same year as the Quijote, is literature as well as
history. It reflects, along with the great work by Cervantes, the
crisis of historical discourse toward the end of the sixteenth century.[14] Although La Florida was written as history, that is, as an
authentic testimony to an historic reality, and also in order to
convince Spain to settle Florida, the author himself confesses his
intention to write literature. Let's examine this mestizo character
of La Florida, not only in the cultural sense of the word, but also
in matters of genre. Hugo Rodríguez Vecchini lists some characteristics common to both the novel and an historical relation of
this type:

1. the irruption of the testimonial "I"
2. the elusivity of the author implicated in a process of self-
   referentiality
3. the opening of a space in which writing dramatizes its own
   creation[15]

The rhetorical techniques that Garcilaso uses to convince the
reader of the authenticity of his history, are the same ones that
reveal the literary character of the text. "And let this suffice that
you may believe that we are not writing fictions. . . ." "Without the
authority of my author, I have the responses of two other soldiers,

first hand witnesses. . . ." "Because the truth of the story obligates us to tell of the great feats done by Indians as well as those done by Spaniards."[16] Other phrases are more openly literary: "Returning to Juan Ortiz, whom we left in grave danger of death. . . ." and "Returning to our story a little farther back than where we were. . . ."[17] And so, from the impulse to give testimony to a reality that is marvelous in its strangeness, along with the consciousness of the creative role of writing, we see a new tradition being born. Garcilaso's work exemplifies the fertile symbiosis of history and fiction in which Latin American literature is rooted, and where the seeds of contemporary narrative are already visible.

The first novel of the Hispanic New World, *El Periquillo Sarniento,* was written by the first professional journalist in Mexico, José Joaquín Fernández de Lizardi.[18] Lizardi took his own experiences and incorporated novelistic elements or techniques to create his works.[19] Mary Ellen Kiddle comments on Lizardi's writing and his place in the literary tradition.

> It is noteworthy that Lizardi witnessed many of the events and people he describes in his works. In stressing his personal familiarity with the "*historia verdadera*" [true (hi)story] that he portrayed, Lizardi continued a tendency in Mexican literature that was first established in the *crónicas* of Díaz and Cortés and which would surface periodically in the future, most notably in the narratives of personal memoirs by Mariano Azuela, Martín Luís Guzmán, José Rubén Romero and other novelists of the revolution, and in the writings of several authors of the *novela testimonial.*[20]

Many novels of the Mexican Revolution, by continuing this testimonial tradition in Mexican literature, also fall into a hybrid category of narrative.[21] The writer as reporter, historian, and novelist adds to his observations of the events, the organization, interpretation, and style appropriate to his individual sensibility, the social context in which he writes, and the corresponding effect that he hopes to create. The resulting mixture of history and fiction, of reportage and invention, leads to a debate on the generic classification of the work. Kiddle explains:

> Many critics have concluded that the novels of the Revolution, for the most part, are a collection of personal memoirs of the authors, some more fictionalized than others, which feature more autobiographical

and documentary elements and less invention and artistic reorganization than is usual in novels.[22]

Other critics connect *El águila* [*y la serpiente*-by Martín Luís Guzmán] to the *crónicas*, noting that if indeed this and other books about the Revolution are not novels, then they took the place of novels, just as the *crónicas* served as the "novels" of the early Colonial Period.[23]

On studying these narrative works of the Revolution, one becomes aware of the inexact nature of the terms *history* and *fiction* or *novel*. We either have to admit the imprecision of the boundaries between the categories, or they should be redefined according to a changeable frame of reference.

The twentieth century has brought an intensified consciousness of history and our place in it. As Edward Hallett Carr notes: "The present age is the most historically minded of all ages. Modern man is to an unprecedented degree self-conscious and therefore conscious of history."[24] Latin American literature of the twentieth century reflects this growing interest in history and identity. The novels of the 1950s have as their main theme the search for identity and origin, seen, for example, in *Los pasos perdidos* (1953) by Alejo Carpentier, or in *Pedro Páramo* (1955) by Juan Rulfo. In the 1960s this search is intensified with the so-called boom of the novel.[25] Many works focus not only on history and origin, but also on the language and drama of writing itself. Language is no longer seen as merely a vehicle for the expression of a reality that is independent of it; it is, rather, a fundamental part of that reality. It is not a question of language as "merely a dimension of man, but man as a verbal being, as a dimension of language."[26] A new type of novel appears, influenced first by the prose of Borges, in which there is a search for an authentic Latin American language. Carlos Fuentes comments on this transition. "The final meaning of Borges' prose—without which there simply would not be a modern Hispanic American novel—is to testify that, first of all, Latin America is in need of a language and, consequently that it should construct one."[27] Following the way opened by Borges, Octavio Paz expressed, in his famous essay in 1961, the need to "invent our own reality" in literature. "Our literature is the response of the real reality of the Americans to the utopic reality of America. Before we had any existence of our own, we began by being a European idea. . . . Our name condemned us to be the historical projection of a foreign conscience: the European one."[28] "Our portion of a new world was an old closed up house, half convent and half barracks." Paz reiterates the need to understand the past, to search for it, and to rewrite history in terms of "our own reality." "Hispanic American literature is a returning and searching for a tradition. By searching for it, we invent it. But invention and discovery are not the most appropriate terms for its purest creations. . . . [Rather] The will of incarnation, literature of foundation."[29]

To forge a new literature means to invent a language, express reality in other terms, and rewrite history from the beginning. "To invent a language is to say everything that history has silenced," says Fuentes. "Our language has been the product of uninterrupted conquest and colonization; a conquest and colonization whose language revealed a hierarchical and oppressive order." "The new Hispanic American novel presents itself as a new foundation of language against the calcified extensions of our false and feudal foundation of origin and its equally false and anachronistic language."[30] Gabriel García Márquez invents such a language with the foundation of the mythical Macondo in his master work, *Cien años de soledad* (1967). This novel "reinvents" the history of Latin America in its "dream of reestablishing an original reality."[31] García Márquez not only founds a mythical place where history can be rewritten with a genealogy to represent it; he also creates a space in his text where the writing can be dismantled and deciphered while it is being written and rewritten. The room of Marquez's wizard-prophet Melquíades, an image of the library-archive of Borges,[32] represents "a relentless memory that disassembles the fictions of myth, literature and even history"[33] and at the same time serves for others as the repository for the chamber pots and residues of history. This double function of writing, of being both historical archive and mirror of its own creation, leads to a continuous refounding of literature. "Self-reflexivity"—says González Echevarría—"is a way of disassembling the mediation through which Latin America is narrated."[34]

The new Latin American literature while contemplating its own creation, brings about a fusion of a moral problematic and an aesthetic one, as Fuentes suggests, and this fusion tends to produce a critical literature.[35] The moral problematic is a natural result of the social position of writers in Latin America and the moral responsibility that they inherit. Fuentes refers to an "urgent literature" which is written "in our part of the world [where] . . . we have too many things to say." "There is a lot to say"—Fuentes continues—"and there is no other way to say it than this way, paradoxical and fragile among other things. We write books for people, the majority of whom don't know how to read and we propose words and ideas in societies in which at times it is not possible to distinguish the shouts of oratory from the screams of torture.[36]

Latin American writers fill multiple roles in society, given that they feel

> the obligation to assume many functions; a critical, informative, clarifying one, a function of perspective and also of immediacy, of debate, of defense and a voice for those who suffer injustice and silence . . . and to be, too, a legislator, journalist, philosopher, Father Confessor, leader of the workers, savior of Indians, social surgeon and champion of more or less lost causes.[37]

The aesthetic problematic is manifest above all in metafiction, that is, narration which refers to the process of narration. This type of self-conscious narration opens the way to experimentation with form as well as philosophical inquiry into the logical meaning of any literary discourse.[38] These concerns are not necessarily separated, however, from the moral preoccupation of many writers. In the words of John Brushwood:

> The focus on the act of narrating emphasizes the creative aspect of the literary endeavor. When this occurs in a society which, unfortunately, represses the creative inclination of the human being, it causes an opening or possibly a break in conventional experience. In this sense metafiction is valued as another facet of social change. . . .[39]

The aesthetic experimentation in the narrative of the 1970s, the period known as the "postboom," is expressed in parodic forms or "subliteratures" that "subvert the model of the novel established by the great narrators of the preceding period."[40] Adriana Méndez Rodenas summarizes the context.

> If García Márquez founds the prototype of the epic-mythic novel in *Cien años de soledad,* framing the narration of the story (history) in legend and myth, the new narrators of the seventies reject the totalizing impulse of undertaking the whole history of our continent in a great narrative enterprise. Quite the contrary, the narrative of the "post-boom" is engaged in creating a fragmented novel, or fragment of a novel, and the attempt to debunk the heritage of the "boom", that is, the postulate that, directly or indirectly, fiction mediates history.[41]

The textual fragmentation, aesthetic plurality, and the influence of other literary and extraliterary genre contribute to a narrative that is revolutionary in its form while at the same time refashioning an old tradition of Latin American literature, that of testimonial literature. González Echevarría discusses the dilemma of a revolutionary literature in Latin America. "The modern tradition is or proclaims itself to be revolutionary, so how can literary tradition be subverted to mark a new beginning without reasserting the tradition of subverting tradition?"[42]

If this revolutionary literature aims to undertake a rewriting of history or "the story" *(la historia),* it must first examine its beginnings or basic theoretical "principles" *(principios).* What is history? This is the implied question which has defined the historiographic canon and inspired the probings of the philosophy of history. The answer to this question requires continual cultural, philosophical, and even literary redefining of what is accepted as history. Hayden White defines the historical work as

> a verbal structure in the form of a narrative prose discourse. Histories (and philosophies of history as well) combine a certain amount of "data", theoretical concepts for "explaining" these data, and a narrative structure for their presentation as an icon of sets of events presumed to have occurred in times past.[43]

Another question almost as difficult as the first is: Why or for what purpose do we write history? Why is it important to write about the past, to explain the events of other times in narrative form? If writing is a way to record and preserve the human experience, then history gives it meaning and context. As a reflection of a culture, it helps at the same time to create the collective experience which gives that culture its identity. On narrating the past, the historian situates the present moment in a temporal continuum that structures our conception of reality. Erich Kahler comments on this process.

> As man becomes more aware of the coherence of what he does and what happens to him, in like measure he gives it meaning and makes it into history, not only theoretically, as a concept, but actually, as reality. . . . History, then, appears to be an ever widening process of intercreation between conscious comprehension and material reality.[44]

But historical discourse is not just the written result of the confrontation of people with their surrounding reality, nor of historians with their documents and data. History is a process of investigation and inquiry. "The initiative in history does not belong to the document"—says Paul Ricoeur—"but to the question posed by the historian. This question takes logical priority in historical inquiry."[45] Paul Hernadi suggests that the role of the historian includes the task of translation.

> All documents at his disposal, as well as the very work he is engaged in writing, are translations . . . they are *verbal* accounts of the largely *nonverbal* fabric of historical events. To the extent that the historian succeeds in communicating thoughts, things, and images as words, names, and signs, he translates—from the idiom of events, forever past, into the idiom of continually present discourse.[46]

If historians are considered objective investigators of the past, their discourse manages to be, at best, a partial translation of what "really happened."[47] If we accept Friedrich Schlegel's designation of a "prophet turned backwards" *(rückwärts gekehrter Prophet)*, historians would be, in the words of Hernadi, "long-sighted men who, in the twilight of the past, discern What Shall Be Remembered. In short, they will emerge as translators of events into myths."[48] As translators and scientific creators of myths, historians convert "the untold dramas of history" into intelligible stories."[49] In a sense, they turn them into literature.

For White, in all historiographic discourse there is a metahistorical element that is essentially poetic or literary. From a deep level of consciousness historians choose their conceptual strategies to explain or represent the data. This includes a deep structure of their discourse that "serves as the precritically accepted paradigm of what a distinctively 'historical' explanation should be."[50] Historical thought remains captive in the linguistic mode in which it is expressed and, according to White, the modes in which historical explanations are constructed are literary.[51]

Although Aristotle distinguished historical truth from poetic truth, history and literature have not always been seen as mutually exclusive fields. Lionel Gossman notes that

> for a long time the relation of history to literature was not notably problematic. History was a branch of literature. It was not until the meaning of the word literature, or the institution of literature itself, began to change, toward the end of the eighteenth century, that history came to appear as something distinct from literature.[52]

Djelal Kadir explains it in a different manner. He distinguishes literature from history by their origins.

Literature has its origins in language and the possibilities of language, that is, in the constellations of our secondary word . . . history and the historical originate in events—events which depend on language and its possibilities for their concretion. . . . For our civilization and its dependence on the written word, literature and history intersect and interplay in the arena of writing. The novel utilizes the historical event and history uses linguistic emplotment [the structuring of a narrative that proceeds from a past towards a present].[53]

History and literature share a dependence on narrative form. In contrast to science, which generally comprises prediction, narrative is based on "retrodiction," as Wallace Martin shows. "It is the end of the temporal series—how things eventually turned out—that determines which event began it: we know it was a beginning because of the end. . . . Thus history, fiction and biography are based on a reversal of cause-effect relations."[54] Hernadi contributes to this idea of retrodiction the concept of the double perspective of narrations, both historical and fictional. There is a balance created, generally, between a retrospective point of view (of what happened) and a prospective vision (of the intentions and expectations of those who participate in the events). As a result, Hernadi explains, "The reader of both historiography and narrative fiction is invited to comprehend time, as Louis Mink suggestively put it, 'in both directions at once'. . . ."[55]

After focusing our attention on the unity of narrative writing in general, it has become more difficult to determine the boundaries between the various classes of narrative. The distinction between history and fiction, for example, has become more problematic. David William Foster discusses this problem in contemporary Latin American writing.

Most readers who have any experience with contemporary writing accept that the boundaries between "literature" and other forms of cultural writing have become hopelessly blurred . . . not only does this blurring phenomenon allow us to expand considerably the frontiers of what we are going to call literary production in Latin America, but it is precisely these works in which we find the most original contributions of Latin American writers. It is for this reason that such works overlap so notably with the general sociopolitical concerns of intellectuals in Latin America as part of a continuous fabric of cultural writing.[56]

The new novel, with its flexibility of form and a tendency to self-reflection, not only narrates its version of "cultural writing," but also questions it. This questioning can lead to a theoretical deconstruction of the conventions of historiography as well as literature, as J. Hillis Miller explains.

> Insofar as a novel raises questions about the key assumptions of storytelling, for example about the notions of origin and end, about consciousness or selfhood, about causality, or about gradually emerging unified meaning, then this putting in question of narrative form becomes also obliquely a putting in question of history or of the writing of history. . . . Insofar as a novel "deconstructs" the assumptions of "realism" in fiction, it also turns out to "deconstruct" naive notions about history or about the writing of history.[57]

The new narrative of Mexico is characterized by a variety of forms and themes, from testimonial literature and its rewriting of an old tradition, to the extremes of textual experimentation. Margo Glantz distinguishes two trends within this literary group which she calls *onda* (literally wave) and *escritura* (writing).[58] The works of *la onda* (Gustavo Sainz and José Augustín, for example) concentrate on social protest and on the rebellion of a generation of adolescents in the context of the culture of the sixties. The narrative of this trend exhibits a strong interest on the part of the authors in the social dialectics of the youth culture of that time. The category of *la escritura* is more difficult to define. Glantz introduces her discussion by recognizing the amplitude and ambiguity of the designation. "To talk of *'escritura'* can mean many things or perhaps it's just a pointless digression.[59] Then she refers to the many tendencies in Mexican narrative with special focus on writing; a new "explicit attitude, tendencies whose point of convergence would be the essential preoccupation with language and structure."[60] This definition, although useful, seems rather vague, and for that reason we will now turn to Roland Barthes's theory on writing.[61]

In Barthes's theory, "writing" (*écriture*) is a special kind of narrative. Narrative in general, according to Barthes, has lost its traditional identity and function through a process of alienation from its fixed meaning. The attempt to imitate a reality that is conceived as fixed and to write a fiction that reflects more or less directly an historical world, yields to a more introspective writing that examines its own creative process. The new narrative is a writing of absence, a process that refers to itself and expresses a *relationship* between artistic creation and society. When artists portray society they also portray themselves as part of that society. They reveal in their writing their class prejudices and assume, consciously or not, a position with regard to the social importance of art in general. In view of the fact that this new writing responds to a conception of reality very different than that of the era of the bourgeois novel, for example, it becomes, therefore, experimental in its form. Form and content unite to express a complicated reality, often including in the text itself a criticism of the genre.

"Novels are now problems," says Gustavo Sainz.[62] Following Barthes's theory, they are no longer simply creations of writers, instruments to express their ideas and genius and to become part of the literary canon or great Tradition. Now the novel is also a testimony to the process of writing and the relationship of authors to their work. It is in a sense a negation of itself that questions the very meaning of the novelistic genre or of narrative in general.[63] Sainz continues:

> The preocupation with "writing well" characteristic of Martín Luís Guzmán or Salvador Novo now has an opposition: those who no longer believe in literary ceremonials. If to write is to enter a *templum* which imposes on us . . . an implicit religion, . . . to write is also to want to destroy the temple even before building it; it is at least to ask oneself before crossing the threshhold about the servitudes of such a place, about the original sin that the decision to shut oneself in there will constitute.[64]

This *gesto interrogante* (questioning gesture)[65] of writing permeates the whole gamut of new narrative. In testimonial literature, on the one hand, there is an implicit questioning in the genre itself, a genre which through the nature of its own marginal status questions the very boundaries of literature. This "socio-literature," as Miguel Barnet calls it in his famous article on the testimonial novel,[66] represents a marriage between art and the social sciences. Out of this union there arise problems in classification; works that on the one hand carry on the tradition established by the chronicles, and on the other hand require the definition of new contemporary categories. In some cases we see modern literary and journalistic techniques applied to testimonial writing, as, for example, in *La noche de Tlatelolco* (1971) by Elena Poniatowska, in order to create new forms of historical documentation and artistic expression.

At the other end of the spectrum we find an introspective writing, that is, one obsessed by its own creation. It is a "superficial" or external writing (in the style of Severo Sarduy), a verbal game, even a sort of erotic play with words full of self-referentiality and re-creation of its own image. It undermines and profanes the sacredness of the text, which has been divorced from any fixed meaning or message. In *Farabeuf* (1965) by Salvador Elizondo, for example, writing is reduced to a sadistic game, a circular repetition of an instant. In *El grafógrafo* (1972) by the same author, it is more of a theoretical game, a collection of meditative fragments in which writing is emptied to the point of being pure graphics, that is, inert marks on the page. These empty marks are merely the residue of intellectual activity and the process of writing.

Between these two extremes, represented by the testimonial literature of Poniatowska and the ludic writing of Elizondo, there are many intermediate variations. We find satirical works (René Avilés Fabila, and Hugo Hiriart) and allegories (José Emilio Pacheco) for example. John Brushwood names as principal characteristics of the Mexican novel between 1967 and 1982, "metafiction" and the "consciousness" of Tlatelolco."[67] A number of works exhibit definitively the first characteristic (metafiction) such as, *Cambio de piel* (1967) by Carlos Fuentes, *Morirás lejos* (1967) by José Emilio Pacheco, *El hipogeo secreto* (1968) by Salvador Elizondo, *Tiene los cabellos rojizos y se llama Sabina* (1974) by Julieta Campos, and *Pretexta* (1979) by Federico Campbell. From the "invention of reality" in the works of Borges, Paz, and García Márquez, we pass to the "invention of the invention of reality"[68] or, in the words of Claude Fell, "the fascination of the creation creating itself."[69] In the second category, that of the consciousness of Tlatelolco, the list is extensive. There are documentary novels such as *Tlatelolco, reflexiones de un testigo* (1969) by Gilberto Balam and *La noche de Tlatelolco* (1971) by Poniatowska, as well as more poetic novels like *Palinuro de México* (1977) by Fernando del Paso and *Si muero lejos de ti* (1979) by Jorge Aguilar Mora.

The purpose of this book, however, is not a comprehensive study nor even a panoramic view of the major works of each trend in the Mexican new narrative. Instead, we will examine four works that represent in different ways a characteristic that is more specific but also more basic to this literature; namely, the rewriting of history. Included in the new historical vision ("revision") of this narrative is an implicit and explicit criticism of the very act of narrating a history (story) whether it be "real" or fictitious. In Mexico, where the burdens of the past seem to dominate the present to the point of obsession, the creation of a work becomes for many writers a question of how to write history. Our cultural identity depends on history and our understanding of it is derived

from the narrations we have. Against the backdrop of Tradition
the new stories are written, a rewriting of past history translated
for the present. "To do literature in Mexico means to inherit a
great national tradition of the historical novel—the canonized
'novel of the Mexican Revolution'. It also requires that you assimi-
late the rewriting of this tradition launched by Carlos Fuentes in
La muerte de Artemio Cruz (1962), mythically purged in Rulfo's
Pedro Páramo (1955)."[70] Like Borges's Pierre Menard, who wanted
to rewrite *El Quijote*,[71] Mexican writers dedicate themselves to rewriting their literary and historical heritage. Although the original story and the rewritten version may be "verbally identical,"
that is, texts about the same events and themes, the effect of the
new story is very different.[72] This phenomenon, according to Borges's story, has to do with a new technique of reading "of deliberate anachronism and erroneous attributions."[73] We always see with
new eyes, and our vision is colored not only by the time that has
passed since the moment being observed, but also by what has
been written in the meantime interpreting that moment, thereby
becoming assimilated into the tradition that defines our perspective. Let us examine briefly our four examples of this Mexican
"new reading" in which a privileged reader participates in the
recomposition and reinterpretation of the past, while at the same
time being witness to the very process of writing.

La noche de Tlatelolco (1971) by Elena Poniatowska has been
called "documentary fiction" as well as "testimonial literature" and
even "oral history." It is a novelistically structured recounting of
an historical event, the massacre of hundreds of people at the
Plaza de las Tres Culturas in Mexico City. As a culminating point
in the student movement of 1968, this historical moment had a
great impact on Mexican consciousness and literature. Poniatowska functions as a journalist-historian by collecting testimonies
and documents, and she weaves the written and oral fragments
into a verbal tapestry in order to re-create the story. An apparently spontaneous chorus of voices (but actually skillfully orchestrated by the author) narrates the terrible story to which the
reader becomes a witness. This work by Poniatowska, so important
because of its literary innovation as well as its contribution to the
disinterment of a period of history that had been covered by
official silence, marks a new era in Mexican narrative.

Testimonios sobre Mariana (1981) by Elena Garro is a work of
pure fiction; that is, it does not refer to any historical event. By
making use of the testimonial form to create her fiction, Garro
inverts the relationship between text and reality that is found in

testimonial literature. Instead of portraying the "real essence" of a society and an historical era,[74] this novel reveals the "fictitious essence" of narrative and of any understanding of the past. Mariana is a woman who has been cruelly oppressed by her husband with the help of a vicious and hypocritical society. The novel is composed of the testimonies of three (fictitious) characters who knew Mariana and who try to recover and reconstruct the truth about her past and her final fate. The identity of Mariana which emerges from the fragmented vision presented to us seems to be only a fiction of words, formed by the limited perspectives and partial truths of the testimonies. Given that she never speaks for herself, the reader must assume the role of detective or judge to resolve Mariana's "case." In the search for Mariana's identity and the truth about her past, we learn much about fiction and history and the complex relationship between art and reality.

Morirás lejos (1967) by José Emilio Pacheco has been called "one of the most interesting experiments in Mexican narrative."[75] It is an allegorical work that not only deals with an historical theme (the persecution of the Jews in different periods of history), but it is also an exposition of the problematics of writing itself. This problematic includes the moral responsibility that the writer feels on choosing the theme of his story. How does one express the atrocities of human history so that they will not be forgotten? In Pacheco's story fragments of historical documents are intermixed with conjectures and criticism on the part of readers, narrators, and even hypothetical protagonists. Although this work was published in 1967, it inaugurates a trend that really belongs to the decade of the seventies. Ann Duncan comments on the importance of *Morirás lejos* in Latin American as well as Mexican narrative.

> This attempt to fuse two sorts of literature, usually thought of as incompatible—art that is committed and art for art's sake—is rare in Europe and was not conspicuous in Latin America before the publication of *Morirás lejos* . . . [and it] can therefore be seen as something of a pioneer work and one which still contains valuable suggestions for us as regards literary technique, as well as provoking us to a reconsideration of one of the basic moral issues of our time.[76]

Federico Campbell's *Pretexta* (1979) is a textual labyrinth of authorial masks and layers of fiction. It is a sort of "pretext," like a tapestry still on the loom. Similar to *Morirás lejos* it is a "prehistory" of writing, that is, the story of the writer in the act of writing. *Pretexta* belongs to a group of works that Adriana Méndez Rodenas identifies as a third trend (along with those of *onda* and *escritura* suggested by Glantz). This trend proposes, according to Méndez Rodenas,

> perhaps the most radical alternative: the fragmentation of the narrative format as traditional historiography is broken down into a series of texts lacking legitimacy. Heirs of Salvador Elizondo, this group of writers subordinates the obsession for writing to the questioning of the official (PRI-ist) version of modern Mexico.[77]

In Campbell's story, the protagonist is a writer contracted by the State to "rewrite" history, in this case a false biography of Professor Ocaranza, a leader of the student movement of 1968. His mission is to discredit the old professor, interweaving in his story the information which they provide him from the archive with the threads of his own invention. The reader watches this author-protagonist become entangled in the fictions of his own story as well as the story about the writing of his story and the story Campbell tells of his own writing. We are left with the paradoxical image of the text as not only end product of writing and of history, but also as a preliminary stage in their very formation. We witness also the dilemma of the contemporary writer in Mexico, as expressed by Carlos Monsiváis. "After 1968 the [only] possible roads seem to be the unconditional assimilation into the regime or marginalization with its forseeable consequences."[78]

In these four works that represent different tendencies in the new narrative of Mexico we can discover a common and central theme; that of the writing of history. Between the sense of urgency and the obligation to write of a journalist like Poniatowska and the paralysis and the impossibility of writing that Campbell portrays, we find the writer struggling with ethical dilemmas, philosophical questions, and a self-criticism of narrative in general. We watch the artist experimenting with the limits of form and language while the historian searches in the archives and in his own conscience for the truth about the past. These writers take on a serious task in their critical contribution to literature, although their sometimes parodic stance seems to corrode the "seriousness" of the story. They explore new ethical and aesthetic ground with their works, following in their own way the instructions of Horace that literature should "delight and instruct." While reflecting the reality of the postmodern world in which it is produced, this writing reveals, with its internal mirrors, the premises and structures with which we interpret and "invent" our surrounding reality. Latin American narrative was inaugurated and continues its new beginnings with the imaginative creation of the New World that was hoped to be discovered, at the same time as it repeats and reforms the tradition it has inherited. Invention and discovery, remembering and rewriting; that's how the story begins. We shall see how each of the works included in this study extends a little our understanding of the writing of fiction as it reveals the influence of the latter on historiographical writing.

2

Elena Poniatowska: Testimonial Tapestries

Here is the echo of the scream of those who died and the scream of those who remained. Here is their indignation and their protest.[1]

Although she identifies herself primarily as a journalist,[2] Elena Poniatowska has become renowned for her writing in other genres. Since 1954 she has published novels, short stories, a play, interviews, chronicles, and other innovative works that are not easy to classify. *La noche de Tlatelolco,* her timely work about the student massacre at Tlatelolco in 1968, exemplifies the propitious marriage between her journalistic talents and her skill as a writer of various literary genres. This work enjoyed such immediate success in Mexico[3] that the editions that were printed ran out quickly. Constructed from materials gathered from Poniatowska's interviews and investigations as a journalist along with her personal experiences, *La noche de Tlatelolco* is a collage of testimonies that could be placed just as easily on the bookshelves of history as on those of literature.

In accordance with a long testimonial tradition and a tendency toward a sometimes brutal realism in Latin American literature,[4] Poniatowska participates with *La noche de Tlatelolco* in the beginning of a new literary genre called "testimonial narrative." This new literature differs from the traditional testimonial genre that began with the chronicles of the Conquest, in its focus on the popular classes and the people "without history."[5] And the new realism is not a literary trend as was the bourgeois realism of the nineteenth century, but rather an attempt to register directly the human experience and to allow the "protagonists" of reality to speak.[6] In order to understand the literary and historical significance of Poniatowska's *La noche de Tlatelolco,* we should first examine the characteristics of this new genre, one which is still in the process of being defined.

A discussion of the testimonial genre cannot avoid certain confusion and ambiguity with regard to its definition. Victor Casaus points out a positive aspect of this ambiguity.

> Perhaps the greatest perspective and richness for us with this genre is expressed precisely in the difficulty we have in defining it, in classifying it. This resistance of the genre surely comes from its youth, but also, I believe, from its enriching flexibility for taking traits from other ways of narrating and expressing reality so (apparently) different from each other like narrative, graphics, film or journalism . . . (to produce) a new form of expression.[7]

This incorporating of other genres has always been a characteristic of the novel, according to Mikhail Bakhtin, as a part of the fundamental diversity and stratification of language (heteroglossia) of this literary form. "The compositional forms for appropriating and organizing heteroglossia in the novel, worked out during the long course of the genre's historical development, are extremely heterogeneous in their variety of generic types."[8] Thus for Bakhtin, the novel is an aggregate and polyphonic form. For Laura Rice-Sayre the testimonial genre is by definition pluralistic. "Testimony" can suggest "to testify" as a judicial term, "to affirm" or "witness to" in the religious sense, or according to natural laws, "to write biography or autobiography," or "to give hommage."[9] All of these semantic contexts can be projected onto testimonial narrative. Jorge Narvaez reaffirms the definition established by Miguel Barnet when he considers that testimony not only belongs to art but it also feels the influence of journalism and the social sciences, above all anthropology and sociology. As a literary genre it reflects a change in the field of communications in general, which has seen the "resurgence of a new democratizing agent in the arena of social communications, and in the process of the production of historical meaning."[10] In this way testimony not only goes across limits between literary genres, but also penetrates into other disciplines.

The most well-known theory on the new testimonial literature is that of Barnet. In his article, "La novela testimonio: socio-literatura," Barnet presents a "manifesto" of the genre, in which he explains and defends his theory with examples from his own two testimonial novels, *Biografía de un cimarrón* (1966) and *Canción de Rachel* (1970).[11] In Barnet's view, the writer has to be a scientist as well as an artist (an "artist-sociologist"), and above all he has to be a visionary. He should contribute to the knowledge of reality "taking the events that have most affected the sensibilities of a people and describing them through the mouth of one of its most representative protagonists."[12] By suppressing his own ego as a writer, the author tries to present in an authentic but at the same time artistic way the real essence of an epoch. Barnet wants to give voice to the people "without history," removing from the historical event the mask with which it has been covered by the prejudiced and classist vision.[13] Through his authentic representation of the past the artist-sociologist can contribute to a clearer and more just vision of the future.

Renato Prada Oropeza emphasizes in his outline of the characteristics of testimonial discourse, the predominance of the sociopolitical intention over the aesthetic one, of the truth of the narrated events over the beauty of their form.[14] This political function is consistent with Barnet's visionary thesis as well as the theories of other critics on the definition of this hybrid genre. Ariel Dorfman, for example, outlines the three primary functions of testimonies in their political context: in the name of the conquered or marginalized, of those who do not fit in the historical manuals, the testimony should *accuse* the torturers, *record* the suffering and epic stories, and *encourage* the other combatants in the middle of the struggle.[15] Nubya Casas lists the traits of authenticity, antiliterality, combativeness, and functionality as basic characteristics of the testimony, all of which point to its active political nature. Casas comments on the combative character of the testimony. "In general, the testimony has been a conflictive work. It combats the versions of the 'status quo'. It denounces what literature or history traditionally omit. It even dares to divulge what oral narrative can only allow itself to murmur."[16]

In addition to the sociological and political functions of the testimony, critics seem to agree on the importance of its historical function. According to Rice-Sayre one finds in testimonial narrative a union of literary, political, and economic history.[17] In all of these histories the testimony fulfills the role of uncovering the past and exposing it to the light of a new perspective.[18] It also serves to register and criticize the events of the present (history in progress) in its historical significance.[19] And finally, the testimony is charged to tell the truth, with the help of art, in the most authentic way possible. Barbara Foley offers a good summary of that mission: "The documentary novel aspires to tell the truth, and it associates this truth with claims to empirical validation . . . some specific and verifiable link to the historical world."[20]

In testimonial narrative, as Barnet has defined it, there is generally one voice that speaks for many. It is a collective discourse represented in the voice of an individual who wants to give a personal account of an historical event. This individual should be "a representative protagonist, a legitimate actor," in Barnet's words,[21] who functions as an historical memory of a people and an era. As Domitila Barrios de Chungara says in her testimony [*Si me permiten hablar . . . Testimonio de Domitila una mujer de las minas de Bolivia* (1977)]: "The story I am going to tell, I don't want you to interpret it for a moment as just a personal problem. Because I think that my life is connected with my people. What happens to me, could have happened to hundreds of people in my country."[22] The representative protagonist is a kind of collective character type[23] who gives an identity to the nameless masses.[24]

In Poniatowska's *La noche de Tlatelolco* it is not the voice of a representative protagonist nor a collective character type who narrates the story. It is the collectivity itself that speaks, a multitude composed of individuals, each with a name and an identity. In order to understand the reality of which the testimonies in this book give account, as well as the testimony the author gives in writing it, we should first study the historical context of Mexico in that time period.

The year 1968 was one of protests and demonstrations in the universities of many countries.[25] In Mexico the student movement became visible in the summer of 1968, during the months which preceded the Olympic Games. According to Octavio Paz the student movement and the celebration of the Olympics were complementary events: both were signs of the relative development of the country.[26] Mexico had enjoyed rapid economic progress in the years since the Revolution, which had been accompanied by a long period of political stability. In 1968, under the administration of President Gustavo Díaz Ordaz, the country was entering the world of the developed nations.[27] As proof of this, Mexico was chosen as the center for the Olympic Games of that year. Paz comments, "As a kind of international recognition of its transformation into a modern or semi-modern country, Mexico requested and was granted [the honor] to have its capital be the center for the Olympic Games in 1968."[28] Proud of the great honor, the government spent billions of pesos to construct the Olympic City in preparation for the games. At the same time it increased the repression of any discordant voice that might stain the image that they wanted to present to the world. Paz explains the origin of the student movement under a government that wouldn't accept public criticism, much less so during its moment of international exposure.

> The student movement began as a street skirmish between rival bands of adolescents. The police brutality united the kids. Afterwards, as the rigors of the repression increased and the hostility of the press, radio and television grew, almost totally sold out to the government, the [student] movement became stronger, more extensive and acquired a consciousness of itself. In the course of some weeks it became clear that the students, without having expressly intended it, were the spokesmen of the people.[29]

The student demonstrations, which were supported to a large extent by the people, grew during August and September of 1968 until the great "silent demonstration" to which it is calculated that almost four hundred thousand people came.[30] On the second of October the students were having a meeting (Paz emphasizes that it was a meeting and not a demonstration) at the Plaza of Tlatelolco.[31] "At the moment in which the meeting was over and those gathered were ready to disperse, the Plaza was surrounded by the army and the massacre began."[32] Hundreds of people died.[33] There were innumerable injuries and more than a thousand people were imprisoned. The experiences of terror and disbelief that the witnesses and survivors of Tlatelolco tell are recorded in *La noche de Tlatelolco* and in many subsequent works. We will probably never be able to know the whole truth about what happened during that episode. But there is no question that it was a key event in the history of Mexico.[34]

In the literary history of Mexico the year 1968 stands out as a key point of reference. "In literature, we can now speak of authors writing before or after Tlatelolco," says Luis Leal in his article "Tlatelolco, Tlatelolco."[35] Leal concludes:

> The most important consequence of Tlatelolco, in literature, is the deep impression it left in the minds of the intellectuals and creative writers. All of them agree that the year 1968 marks a break with the past, a break with the period characterized by changes brought about by the Revolution of 1910–1917. . . . The literature of Tlatelolco revealed that the ideals of the Revolution, so strongly defended by the party in power, had become empty.[36]

John S. Brushwood refers to "the spectral presence" *(la presencia espectral)* of Tlatelolco as a characteristic of the contemporary Mexican novel. It appears not only as a theme in many works, but it also becomes a filter for commenting on Mexican reality. . . . "In other words, what happened at Tlatelolco engenders, by the mere fact of being evoked, a complex set of reactions that can truly alter the effect of any other event."[37]

Apart from its importance as an historical moment, literary theme or focus, the tragedy of Tlatelolco generated a kind of subgenre in the Mexican novel, which Leal named "the novel of Tlatelolco."[38] These "novels" included documentary works, chronicles, and testimonies as well as fictive and historical novels.[39] In the middle of so much artistic production (there were also many poems and dramas published, not to mention essays and articles), Poniatowska's *La noche de Tlatelolco* is the work that gained the most attention from the public. It was a great and immediate success and an extraordinary number of editions have been printed.[40] Let's examine now this important work.

La noche de Tlatelolco (testimonios de historia oral) was born of Poniatowska's journalistic investigating. Based on interviews, documents, letters, newspaper clippings, tapes, poems, speeches, photos, banners, and posters, this work took shape to tell the story of the event of 2 October 1968, which had such an enormous impact on the Mexican people. The subtitle, already a bit problematic since it refers to a *written* work, perhaps should be revised to say, "testimonies of oral and visual history." If a picture is worth a thousand words, as the saying goes, the photographs included at the beginning of *La noche de Tlatelolco* present a strong testimony to the events of those months of 1968 that would become a critical point in the history and literature of Mexico. Accompanied by captions, often words taken from the actual testimonies of the book, the photos sketch the history of the student movement and its final tragedy. On the cover of the book we see a photo of young people marching, happy, even joyous, with their posters and their enthusiasm. If one didn't know the story, one might think perhaps that "the night of Tlatelolco" was some sort of festival or celebration, giving the cruel shock of the tragedy that follows even greater impact. This is how the story begins in Poniatowska's book, re-creating for the reader the experience of the witnesses who contribute to it.

The first words of the text reflect, in turn, the story evoked in the photographs. Through the author's eyes, which have already seen the whole tragedy, we see first that innocent jubilation of the students. "They are many. They come on foot, laughing as they go. They have come down Melchor Ocampo, Reforma, Juárez, Cinco de Mayo [names of streets], young men and women students who march arm and arm through the demonstration with the same joy as when they were going off to the fair a few days earlier" (13).[41] This image that we see in the author's memory is clouded by the bitter vision of experience from a future point which is the moment of narration: "carefree young people who don't know that tomorrow, within two days or four days they will be lying there swollen under the rain, after a fair in which they will be the targets . . ." (13).[42] From the first page of the book the students begin their march and we hear their voices and see them advance (alive or already dead) throughout the text, just as Poniatowska sees them in her memory. "I see them through a fog, but I hear their voices, their footsteps, pas, pas, pas, paaaaas, paaaaaas, like in the silent demonstration, my whole life I will hear those steps that keep advancing" (14).[43] She (the author), who will never be able to forget those steps of the student "movement," also writes her own testimony so that we will never forget either. And at the end of this short dedication the author seems to join the students' march, adding her voice to their chorus: "Mé-xi-co, Li-ber-tad, Mé-xi-co, Li-ber-tad . . ." (14).

At first glance, *La noche de Tlatelolco* seems to be a chaotic collection of fragments lacking the structure or coherence that are traditionally associated with a literary work. Many different people speak; some anonymous, others are identified but they are never presented as "characters." It is a *pastiche* of testimonies, experiences, documents, and inscriptions, of voices that seem to speak for themselves, without any authorial mediation. But on reading the book carefully, it becomes clear how skillfully the apparently spontaneous chorus of voices has been orchestrated.[44] One notes that there is indeed narrative coherence to the work, both structural and thematic.

The structure of this work, which has been called a "documentary novel" or "journalistic fiction," is found in the blank spaces on the page. The absent or perhaps invisible author-narrator is hidden there in the pauses between the testimonies. Her presence can almost be perceived as the interviewer in the silent but implied questions which give form to the "responses" of the speakers. This is not to say that the written segments are purely fragments of interviews (in reality the material comes from many and varied sources), nor that there is a formal journalistic structure. But Poniatowska's presence is felt on several levels; her dedication as a journalist-historian, her poetic sensibility as a writer, and her pain and indignation as a human being and an actor in the historical drama. Bakhtin, who always emphasizes the heterogeneous linguistic nature of the novel, addresses the true position of an author of a novel: "The author (as creator of the novelistic whole) cannot be found at any one of the novel's language levels: he is to be found at the center of organization where all levels intersect."[45] Michael Foucault also concerns himself with the problem of the function of the author. For him, the author is, besides being the real person who created the work, "a certain functional principle by which, in our culture, one limits, excludes, and chooses. . . ."[46] In *La noche de Tlatelolco* Poniatowska plays with this role of structuring the work, of giving it focus and grouping the themes. She is the organizational center (which is then replaced by the reader) toward which all of the voices speak. She is the center which then leaves the stage so that others may speak.

The book consists of three parts in addition to the photographic introduction. The two sections which constitute the body of the narrative mosaic tell the history of the student movement and the events which culminated in the massacre of Tlatelolco and the heavy repression which followed. The first part, which is titled "Taking to the Streets," presents the political and social climate in Mexico City during the months that preceded the Olympics of October 1968. By means of many testimonies and other "oral" and written fragments, we get to know the "characters," the stage, the themes, and the audience of this real drama. We see the students and their supporters "taking to the streets" (and to the microphone) with their bigger and bigger demonstrations, protesting government repression and intolerance of criticism. We listen to the opinions of diverse groups and individuals on political and social topics, including the student movement and the Olympic Games. The counterpoint between this "discussion" of themes and the telling of what happened at Tlatelolco creates a narrative tension that gives unity and structure to the work.

The second part is called "The night of Tlatelolco," an echo of the title of the book. In this section we see presented and commented upon the events of the massacre of 2 October in the Plaza de las Tres Culturas (Plaza of the Three Cultures), generally known as the Plaza of Tlatelolco. We also "hear" testimony to the repercussions of the massacre and the resulting repression by the government. Many fragments of writing appear: poems, documents, speeches, official statements, journalistic excerpts, as well as the testimonies of the people interviewed by Poniatowska. A poem by Rosario Castellanos ("Memorial de Tlatelolco") opens the second part. It was written specially for this book and establishes the tone of memorial and protest for this section. It begins with a dramatic image of the setting:

> The darkness engenders violence
>
> and violence needs darkness
>
> to carry out the crime.
>
> That's why the second of October waited until night
>
> so no one would see the hand that gripped
>
> the weapon, but only its lightning effect.
>
> (163)[47]

In the brief prologue to this section Poniatowska reveals a little of the history of the writing of the work. "The majority of these testimonies were collected in October and November of 1968. The students in prison gave theirs over the course of the following two years. This story belongs to them. It is made of their words, their struggles, their errors, their pain and shock" (164).[48] And then, before leaving the stage as the mistress of ceremonies, the author presents her unfortunate actors with this emotional dedication: "Here is the echo of the screams of those who died and the screams of those who remained. Here is their indignation and their protest. It is the silent scream that stuck in thousands of throats, in thousands of eyes opened wide from fright on October 2nd, 1968, on the night of Tlatelolco" (164).[49]

The third part is a chronology "based on the events to which the students refer in their testimonies of oral history" (275).[50] It begins with the 22nd of July and continues until the 13th of December of 1968, including in its short scope, descriptions of the important events of the period. Much like the series of photos introduced at the beginning of the book, this minimal chronical at the end only sketches the outline of a story. The chronological and "objective" focus of the events narrated contrasts with the thematic organization of the two narrative parts, which emphasize more the intense human experience of Tlatelolco.

La noche de Tlatelolco is a more complex work than it might seem at first glance. Although it is generally classified as documentary literature (and it does function as such), it also has a "novelistic texture," as David William Foster has pointed out.[51] The true story of what happened is in a sense too incomprehensible and unreal for a purely documentary narrative. By the same token, to tell it in the form of a novel would deny the weight of reality and the impact that it could have on the reader. Poniatowska testifies to the difficulty and the urgent necessity of trying to interpret the horror of Tlatelolco. "The sad night of Tlatelolco—in spite of all its voices and testimonies—continues being incomprehensible. Why? Tlatelolco is incoherent, contradictory. But death is not." Then she says, "No chronicle can give us a complete picture" (170).[52] In spite of the impossible task of reconstructing the reality, of recomposing the puzzle of the past, Poniatowska has tried to give us a "complete picture" by means of a collage of voices and texts, a tapestry of testimonies organized in novelistic form. The technique of mosaic hides the artistic architecture of the narration but at the same time creates a coherent image of the artistic "object." This can be seen, for example, in the presentation of the testimonies by the informant-characters. The author doesn't allow them to give their testimonies in full and all at once without interruption, as in a legal deposition. She is not interested in the legal case of the situation. The important thing here is the human experience of individuals trapped in a collective nightmare.[53] For this reason, we read loose fragments of the testimonies of one person or another in an apparently spontaneous chorus, as if all were talking almost at the same time. This integrative technique creates to a certain degree a novelistic world: a coherent textual "reality" in which the many and varied voices of a society speak.[54]

One function of literary criticism has been that of classifying the work it analyzes. *La noche de Tlatelolco* presents a problem for classification in traditional categories while at the same time serving as a model for new narrative forms. Whether it is called a "documentary novel," "nonfiction novel," or "testimonial novel," it represents a fusion and confusion of genres. For example: Is the book history or fiction? Is it (written) oral history or historical fiction? Foster addresses the problem and suggests that this ambiguity is part of the richness and cultural value of the work.

Although *Noche* has a place in a bibliography of contemporary Mexican social history, critics read it as an important contribution to the contemporary Latin American novel. To read *Noche* as more novel than document does not detract from its quality as documentary testimonial. Rather—as is true for all recent documentary and historical fiction in Latin America—such a reading testifies to the continuity of fiction and reality in that culture. . . .[55]

The analysis of the problem must include an examination of the very definitions of history and fiction. We have already seen earlier some definitions of history, emphasizing for our study the importance of narration and story as components of history. Lionel Gossman expresses well the narrative essence of history.

> The simplest of events, after all, is itself a story, the interpretation of which involves a larger story of which it is a part, so that history could be envisaged as a complex pattern of stories each of which contains another complex pattern of stories, and so on without end. There seems to be no outside of stories, no point at which they stop being stories and abut on hard particles of "facts".[56]

Hayden White points out not only the narrativity of history but also the importance of "invention" in the writing of this narrative.

> It is sometimes said that the aim of the historian is to explain the past by "finding", "identifying" or "uncovering" the "stories" that lie buried in chronicles; and that the difference between "history" and "fiction" resides in the fact that the historian "finds" his stories, whereas the fiction writer "invents" his. This conception of the historian's task, however, obscures the extent to which "invention" also plays a part in the historian's operations. The same event can serve as a different kind of element of many different historical stories. . . . The historian arranges the events in the chronicle into a hierarchy of significance by assigning events different functions as story elements in such a way as to disclose the formal coherences of a whole set of events considered as a comprehensible process with a discernible beginning, middle and end.[57]

If we accept the literary nature of historical narrative, where, then, do we situate fiction? What historical validity can a fictional story have besides being an object of art or a cultural artifact? What can it contribute to the historical archive? Gossman suggests that the opposition literature/history could be understood as one of "fictional narrative" (or "fictional history") versus "historical narrative."[58] The adjective "fictional" refers more to the *conscious intention* of invention than to the truth or veracity of the narrative. Barbara Foley says that the documentary novel is a clear example of a hybrid genre between history and fiction.[59]

> From the most meticulous naturalism to the most far-flung fantasy, fiction renders knowledge of the world by means of analogous con-

figuration . . . factual particulars may enter the text in a variety of ways to suit a variety of ends, but they frame and highlight the text's generalized propositions. The documentary novel's insistence that it has a particular truth to tell thus reinforces rather than undermines fiction's distinct status as a means of telling the truth.[60]

"Fiction" (from the Latin *fictio,* p.p. of *fingere:* to form, mold, or invent) is a text that is formed, molded, or invented according to artistic criteria. The raw material can be events that are real or analagous to reality (history/fiction), or a mixture of the two.

La noche de Tlatelolco is a text formed according to artistic criteria and based on real events. It is also composed of fictions, some invented in order to express the truth (poems or literary fragments) and others in order to hide it (the official rhetoric of the government with regard to what happened at Tlatelolco). It is both history and literature. The testimonies of oral history have been written down, or rather, transcribed in the book.[61] By being selected, edited, structured, and juxtaposed in an artistic plan of signification, they are turned into literature. But this literature doesn't stop being history. It exists on that borderline between the two fields, if indeed it is necessary to separate them, as a bridge of transition.[62] It can also serve to question the conventions of the two disciplines. In the words of Gossman again:

Fictional writing is constantly questioning existing fictional conventions, and for centuries it did so by appealing to history. But historical writing operates in the same way: every attempt to devise an order different from that of pure chronicle involved an appeal to the order of art—of fictional narrative or of drama. And correspondingly, when the intention was to reject a highly structured model of historical narrative, emphasis was again placed on the syntagmatic, and on the historian's task as simple reporter or eyewitness.[63]

In this case, Poniatowska's work, as fiction, never loses its authentic contact with historical experience. As history, it appeals to the art of fiction to give coherence to the narrative, but it never abandons its role of eyewitness and reporter.

La noche de Tlatelolco has also been called "journalistic fiction," thus suggesting another marriage of genre. Not only was it born of Poniatowska's journalistic investigations, but it also has the stamp of journalism in its form, style, and above all in the urgency of the writing. The focus of the text is on a present moment, or at least a present which has recently passed. It is a chronicle of the present that can in some future time function as an historical document. In that sense it is more journalism than literature or history. Roberto González Echevarría notes that

> the desire to chronicle the present leads inevitably in the direction of journalism . . . a desire to bypass literary entrapments or to dissolve the literariness of the narrative by turning to its sources." And then: "Journalism leads away from literature and aims at immediacy. . . . Journalism also tends to diffuse the question of authorship (and) . . . forces the illusion that incidents write themselves into history.[64]

The immediacy of journalistic writing gives us the sense of authenticity of the story and intensity of action. It creates the illusion of objectivity; the reader has the sensation of almost seeing the events happen, of hearing the voices of the participants. If history attempts to re-create and explain *how it was*,[65] journalism tries to record and transcribe *how it is* or *how it has just been*.

Many who have studied the so-called New Journalism[66] say that it not only tries to communicate the facts about a situation but also an understanding of it and a broader truth. The writers attempt to place the reader in a specific world of experience. To do so they often make use of the techniques and forms of fiction. John Hellmann comments on this. "The new journalists seek to merge the sophisticated and fluid forms provided by fiction with the facts sought in journalism."[67] For Hellmann, this new journalism should be considered a literary genre which has aesthetic form and purpose.[68] It is not a matter of "contaminating" the objective truth of the facts with fiction (in the sense of falsehood), but rather of representing and explaining it in the complex context of reality. As Norman Mailer said, "There is finally no way one can try to apprehend complex reality without a 'fiction.'"[69] This peculiar combination of fictional form and technique with real content and journalistic sources is common in the works of the era of Tlatelolco.

The journalistic character of *La noche de Tlatelolco* becomes particularly obvious in the introduction to the second part of the book. Following a brief prologue in which the author refers to the gathering of the testimonies (her role as journalist), we read the headlines of the principle Mexico City daily newspapers from Thursday, 3 October, 1968, one day after the massacre at Tlatelolco. These fragments are important not only as an historical record of the events (they represent the recognition, at least, that something did happen), but also because they illustrate different ways of interpreting (or inventing), "the facts."[70] Let's compare, for example, the difference between *El Universal* which read:

> Tlatelolco, Battlefield.
> For Several Hours Terrorists and
> Soldiers in Rough Combat.
> 29 Dead and more than 80 Injured from
> Both Groups; 1 000 Detained.
>
>   (165)[71]

And *El Sol de México* which read:

> Foreign Hands Endeavor to Ruin
> Mexico's Image.
> The Objective: To Jeopardize the XIX Games.
> Sharpshooters opened fire against the
> Troops at Tlatelolco.
> Wounded: One General, 11 Soldiers; 2 Soldiers and more than 20
> civilians dead in the worst skirmish.
>
>   (165)[72]

Following the headlines are testimonies from reporters (including the author) and fragments of the stories that came out in the newspapers. The reporters' testimonies are interwoven with the other "voices" of the second part. To the journalistic foundation of this work is added a literary perspective on journalism itself, a kind of "metajournalism," that is, a journalistic account that comments on the experience of its own creation.

Another aspect of the journalistic character of *La noche de Tlatelolco* is a form of hybridization[73] which I call *periosia* (poetry-journalism).[74] This category has two parts: (1) the poetic use of journalistic fragments—brief descriptions, with allusive or symbolic images, artistically placed to have a great emotional impact on the reader; inversely, (2) the journalistic use of poetic fragments—fragments of poems intermixed with the other voices of the text, thus appealing to the authority and validity of art as a testimony to reality.

The journalistic selections serve a poetic function when they are read interspersed in the poignant drama. Their dispassionate style intensifies the pathetic tone of the text as a whole. For example, after a brief testimony in which a student is talking about a classmate who "had been feeling happy that day" because they had chosen her to be *edecán*[75] (with the implication that she would later be one of the victims of the massacre), comes the following fragment from *Excélsior,* 3 October 1968:

> The Red Cross reported 46 wounded, almost all of them by bullets and some of them critically. They also informed that four people who were injured died in the hospital. They have not been identified. (255–56)[76]

There is no direct connection with the girl of the preceding fragment but the *effect* is to make the reader identify her as one of the dead. By means of such syntagmatic associations of fragments, Poniatowska structures and gives meaning to the narrative.

Other fragments of testimonies stand out as if they were verses of poetry: "The woman was sobbing her heart out" (240).[77] And "Beneath the placards, the rain-soaked banners, there were two bodies" (241).[78] The words of one mother only need to be rearranged on the page to be turned into poetry:

> We've never cried so much, we women, as we did in those days. It was as if we wanted to wash clean with our tears all of the images, all the walls, all the corners, all the stone benches stained with the blood of Tlatelolco, all the traces of the bodies bleeding in the corners. . . . But it's not true that the images are washed clean with tears. They are still there in your memory. (268)[79]

Let's see the effect of arranging the same words in poetic form. For example:

> We've never cried so much
> we women, as we did
> in those days.
> It was as if
> we wanted to wash away
> with our tears
> all the images,
> all the walls,
> all the corners,
> all the stone benches
> stained with the blood of Tlatelolco,
> all the traces of the bodies
> bleeding in the corners. . . .
> But it's not true
> that the images are washed clean
> by tears.
> They are still there
> in your memory.

This woman expresses spontaneously her pain, narrating with the rhythm and intensity of poetry. It is not a poem (at least that was not the intention) but it is a lament with great poetic strength.

In addition to revealing the poetic power of journalistic discourse, Poniatowska shows the journalistic function of poetry. A poem by Juan Bañuelos seems to take material from the news and create an artistic image in poetic form.

> A barefoot woman
> head covered with a black shawl
> waits for them to hand over her dead one.
> 22 years old, Polytechnic:
> red hole in his side
>   made by a
>   regulation M–1.
>
>   (256)[80]

The poets who wrote about Tlatelolco also give their testimonies in the work. Lines from poems appear as other sources of information and interpretation. These fragments of literature form part of the "chorus of voices" that Poniatowska is orchestrating. From a poem by José Carlos Becerra we read: "They took away the dead to who knows where. / They filled up the jails of the city with students" (230). And from the same poet:

> Behind the church of Santiago Tlatelolco
> thirty years of peace plus another
> thirty years of peace,
> plus all of the steel and cement used for the
> fiestas of this phantasmagoric country,
> plus all of the speeches
> came out of the mouth of the machine guns.
>
>   (233)[81]

And from the poet Octavio Paz, some lines of poetry that could serve as headlines for a newspaper: "The Municipal / employees wash away the blood / at the Plaza of the Sacrifices" (268).[82] To these contemporary voices from literature, are added some from the past in a few lines by the Cuban poet José Martí:

> And it's just that in America
> a new kind of people has arisen
> who ask for prose with substance
> and verse with context

and they want work and reality
in their politics
and literature.

(158)[83]

There are even Nahuatl indigenous texts which refer to another
tragedy at Tlatelolco in other times. Included on pages 158–59,
are selected texts from *Visión de los vencidos* translated from post-
Conquest texts in Nahuatl.[84] These verses lament the capture of
Cuauhtémoc and the massacre that took place in Tlatelolco in
Aztec times. Paz notes:

> It was an instinctive repetition which assumed the form of a ritual of
> expiation; the correspondence with the Mexican past, especially with
> the Aztec world, is fascinating, frightening, repugnant. The massacre
> of Tlatelolco reveals to us that a past which we believed to be buried
> is still alive and irrupts among us.[85]

The verses of the past resound in the text as witnesses to the
present, accentuating the feeling of the repetition of the history
of Tlatelolco.

To the immediacy of journalism, which responds to the urgency
of a present reality, we have added the expressiveness and con-
densed nature of poetry. Taking into account the testimonial value
of both (journalism and poetry) together with the reflection and
analysis of historical narrative and the technique and structure
of fictional narrative, this work by Poniatowska begins to form a
complex hybrid entity. Whether it is a testimonial novel, documentary history/fiction, journalistic fiction, or poetry, *La noche de Tlatelolco* is a work that accuses as well as observes, interprets as well
as records, and creates (invents) while it preserves a record of
the past.

The discussion of definitions and genre leads in the end to the
problematics of narration in general. If we consider the narrative
essence of history (history not in the sense of *res gestae* but in
the sense of *res gestarum*,[86] we can examine some theoretical and
practical problems which history and fiction share. In historiography (the history of historical writing and thought) and in literary
history we find a continual evolution of the philosophies and conventions which influence writing in the respective disciplines. The
authors (of history or of fiction) assume different positions of
"authority" with regard to the narration of their work. These
different narrative perspectives reflect the philosophies of each

era with regard to the nature and function of history and of art.[87] Epistemological, ideological, and aesthetic values condition the perception and the representation of reality in writing. Writers direct their work, whether consciously or not, toward the image of an archetypal reader and according to the relationship which they (perceive that they) should have, as historians or artists, with that reader. Even when history and fiction have leaned toward the "objectivity" of science, they have not lost these narrative elements which they have in common.

The sometimes parallel, sometimes transverse evolution of history and fiction has often been noted.[88] Gossman comments on the contemporary situation as follows:

> In our own time there appear to be correspondences between developments in historiography and certain developments in modern fiction—among them the repudiation of realism, the collapse of the subject or character as an integrated and integrating entity, and an increasingly acute awareness of the fundamental logic or syntax of narrative and of the constraints and opportunities it provides.[89]

The dialectic objectivity/subjectivity (often associated with that of history/fiction) becomes complicated with an intensified consciousness of the functioning of language and of narrations. González Echevarría cites Paul de Man to distinguish, in terms of language, historical narrative from fictional narrative:

> The historian, in his function as historian, can remain quite remote from the collective acts he records; his language and the events that the language denotes are clearly distinct entities. But the writer's language is to some degree the product of his own action; he is both the historian and the agent of his own language. The ambivalence of writing is such that it can be considered both an act and an interpretive process that follows after an act with which it cannot coincide. As such, it both affirms and denies its own nature or specificity. Unlike the historian, the writer remains so closely involved with action that he can never free himself of the temptation to destroy whatever stands between him and his deed, especially the temporal distance that makes him dependent on an earlier past.[90]

History, then, is in a certain sense more objective than fiction because the emphasis is more on the "object" narrated (the past) than on the narration itself. Fiction, on the other hand, is more subjective because the emphasis is on the "subject" of the narration (the writer) and his art of narrating. But this is a question of emphasis, since as we have seen, history is also subjective and fiction has objective value.

The question of the degrees of objectivity/subjectivity is most pertinent to any type of writing. The contract between author and reader is rooted in the function of the narrator and his credibility for the reader as a teller of truth.[91] In *La noche de Tlatelolco* Poniatowska rejects the traditional convention in narrative (both historical and fictional) of a central narrator. The voices represented here narrate their own hi(story). Each one tells a story, his or her version of "*the* story." But these narrators are not creations of the author: neither fictitious characters nor fictionalized historical figures. They are real people who belong to the "object" being studied, that is, the real story, the true history. These same people are also subjects, ones who narrate the story (collage of stories) that appears in Poniatowska's book. The author, by choosing, transcribing, and organizing the testimonies together with the many other elements of her text, converts the totality into *historia (rerum gestarum)*, which can then assume a place in human history and literature.

Why has Poniatowska opted for this technique apparently lacking in narrative unity? Why does she limit her presence to that of editor of texts and renounce the creative power of fiction? Perhaps it is for the same reason given in a note to another novel about Tlatelolco (*La Plaza* by Luis Spota[92]) which says that a novel about such a monumental topic could not be written by one person. It needs the collaboration of many writers and many voices.[93] Ronald Christ discusses the role of the author as editor in this book, concluding that the work achieves its tremendous importance precisely because it elevates the narrator to the position of editor. Christ also compares the narrative style of *La noche de Tlatelolco* to the cinematographic technique of montage. Like in a movie, the book is presented in staccato "takes" and more developed sequences, "each one of which in accordance with the fundamental principles of montage, grows and reverberates dialectically by its placement in relation to what precedes it and what immediately follows it."[94] This narrative technique, which imitates the rapid movement of the camera and the superimposition of scenes characteristic of cinematographic montage, reflects and re-creates for the reader the chaotic and unreal experience of the massacre. Foster refers to a "strategy of disbelief" in which the narrative reveals gradually a reality that is incredible for the participants and witnesses as well as for the readers of the text.[95] In a process of losing our innocence we have to "suspend disbelief,"[96] not in

order to enter into a fantasy of fiction but to accept an unbeliev-
able reality. Foster comments on this:

> Poniatowska's narrative derives its force from the incredulity of the
> reader, mirrored in the statements of the individuals Poniatowska in-
> terviewed, that such events could happen in Mexico, a country that
> in the twentieth century has claimed to be above the human-rights
> infringements characteristic of Latin America.[97]

This political aspect of the work (in the broad sense of the word
"political") leads us again to testimonial narrative and its role of
telling the "other hi(stories)," the sub-versions (and subversions)
of the official hi(story). The testimonies of Poniatowska's book,
which according to Jean Franco are generated out of the official
silence,[98] allow those who suffered the repression of the government to speak. Those "without history" (that is, the faceless
masses, the sectors of society which find themselves marginalized)[99] now enter into the story. They enter not only as "objects"
of the narrated story but also as "subjects" who narrate their own
story. It is this second role, when the objects of history rise up to
become subjects, that most subverts the official (hi)story.

The impulse of the marginalized of society to "speak," to participate in the discourse of the present and influence the history
of the future, gave strength to the student movement. In the
words of one student:

> This has come to pass I believe because the peasant young people
> [*campesinos*], the workers and the students have few decent options in
> life, because the sources of work are created for the benefit of individ-
> ual interests and not for the whole of society. They say to us continu-
> ally: "You are the future of the country." But they systematically deny
> us any opportunity to act and participate in the political decisions of
> the present. . . . We want and are ABLE TO participate now, not when
> we are sixty years old. . . . (18)[100]

But at times words don't have the communicative force that is
needed, especially when directly confronting power. "I no longer
believe in words" (69) says one disillusioned voice in the text.
Words have to be turned into actions and the actions speak. The
announcement of the Great March of Silence (which some three
hundred thousand people would join) ends with this invocation:
"The day has come in which our silence will be more eloquent
than the words which were silenced yesterday by the bayonets"
(60).[101] And so it happens, according to the testimonies which tell

us of a marvelous scene in which thousands of young people pass by in absolute silence, some even with their mouths taped shut to insure their silence (60). The image of the students marching, presented to us by the author at the beginning of the book, is brought to life again. Our attention is focused again on their footsteps, and we forget for a moment the "voice" that is narrating the sequence to us.

> Only the sound of their footsteps could be heard. . . . Steps, steps on the asphalt, steps, the sound of many feet marching, the sound of thousands of feet advancing. The silence was more impressive than the crowd. It seemed like we were trampling on all the verbosity of the politicians, all of their speeches, always the same, all the demagogy, the rhetoric, the piles of words which the facts never backed, the stream of lies; we went sweeping them away under our feet. . . ." (60)[102]

The students and other groups that supported them were asking for dialogue with the government—public dialogue. "Dialogue, dialogue, dialogue" chants a chorus in the demonstrations (30). They complain of the eternal monologue of the government that doesn't accept criticism. "For fifty years now the government has carried on a monologue with itself" criticizes one student (30). "The government believes that in Mexico there is only one public opinion: the one which applauds it, which ingratiates itself to it. . . ." says another. "But there is another one: the one which criticizes, which doesn't believe in anything they say . . ." (53).[103] Franco comments on the struggle of writers against the monologue of the State:

> Up to the mid-sixties, Mexican writers had typically defined their relationship to society as a relationship to the state. One of their main problems was how to evade or postpone immolation in its monolithic structure. Symbolized as a pyramid by Octavio Paz in *Posdata*, the Mexican State allowed no room for dialogue or heresy and seemed to have presented the same hierarchical order from pre-Columbian times to the present.[104]

Carlos Fuentes, in a severe critique of the government, summarizes the situation in the following manner: "And how could it respond with intelligence and generosity, a system lulled to sleep by thirty years of self-praise, monolithism, monologue with itself and myths riveted by self-deception: national unity, political equilibrium, economic miracle?"[105] The dialogue which the students finally won was short and definitive. The answer came in the Plaza of Tlatelolco and the government had the last word.

What Poniatowska offers in *La noche de Tlatelolco* is a break with that monolithic and monologic structure of Tradition, both literary and historical as well as political. Her work is more than a dialogue; it's a "polylogue."[106] As testimonial narrative, it is a collective vision. But it is not just one voice that speaks for many; rather, they are many voices that form a chorus: a (hi)story of many (hi)stories. It is not only the *narration* of a story by one voice, but the *representation* of many actor-narrators in the act of telling their stories. It is in this sense a drama.

Herbert Lindenberger presents the notion of the theater as a metaphor for the operations of history.[107] In other words, human history is a type of real-life drama. A rather obvious distinction between narrative and theater is that the former *narrates* the story (real or fictional) and the latter *represents* it. Lindenberger cites Friedrich Schiller who said of these forms: "All narrative forms turn the present into past; all dramatic forms turn the past into present."[108] According to Lindenberger, it is a question of distance. "Narrative works to create a distance, both temporal and physical, between us and the personages it depicts, while drama seeks an immediacy of effect which succeeds in giving its personages a direct power over us."[109] A play gives us the impression of being there *in* the story or historical moment, observing it in the moment of creation and even participating in it.

We have already discussed the influence of journalism on Poniatowska's narrative and the effect of temporal proximity that is created. Let's examine now some dramatic aspects of *La noche de Tlatelolco*, which also contribute to the sense of immediacy in the narrative. Among the narrated testimonies are some scenes of dialogue, some of them re-created through the memory of an eyewitness, others recovered directly from the voices recorded in the moment represented. Since those who speak are real people, the representation of these scenes takes us to the edge of the stage of real-life history, and the original moment of the actions.

The following scene appears without any introduction, a scene recorded from a conversation between a student imprisoned after Tlatelolco and his grandmother. It is presented as conventional drama, even with stage directions.

 —I brought you some fabada. . . .
 —Oh, grandmother, my stomach is bothering me!

(Gilberto Guevara enters with a wool cap which according to Luis and Raúl and Saúl el Chale, he never takes off. His grandmother extends her arms to him.)
—My Guevara!
She hugs him for a long time. She is the classic grandma of children's stories; plump, sweet, white hair, a little ball of tenderness.
—You were saying that your stomach is bothering you Raúl? . . .

$$(154)^{110}$$

Another purely verbal scene (off stage) of anonymous voices:

"Stop! Stop firing! Stop!" (Voices from the crowd)
"I can't! I can't take any more!" (Woman's voice)
"Don't leave! Don't move!" (Man's voice)
"Surround them! Over here!" Over here! Surround them, surround them I say! (A voice)
"I'm wounded! Call a doctor. I'm. . . . !" (A voice)

$$(196)^{111}$$

The dramatic monologue that follows situates us in the middle of the massacre. A wounded reporter is talking into the microphone, recording at the same time a piece of history in action and his reactions to it.

I'm going to die. It hurts. I'm sure I'm going to die. . . . Here I am at Tlatelolco, today the second of October, I'm twenty-four years old. I'm losing a lot of blood. . . . How everyone is running! And I can't even drag this leg after me. I can't see a single blasted stretcher bearer, you can't hear anything with these machine guns. If I die he'll dedicate half of his column to me [reference to a columnist], probably the whole column. . . . Who will pass on my data to him? $(189)^{112}$

To whom is this young reporter speaking? To himself? To no one? To everyone? Like all writers-narrators, he directs his words to an audience unknown at the moment but which will become real in the future. We the readers of Poniatowska's work listen to his thoughts and fears as if he were a fictional character. But here it is not a literary trick that gives us the artificial privilege of entering into the mind of a character. It is the recorded voice of a real person who narrates the story to us while he is living it.

One drama with special significance in the text is the one about the Poniatowska family. The author lost a brother during this epoch, a fact that is mentioned in her book without any more attention than the other personal tragedies. Although limited to several inconspicuous fragments, the story of his death is framed by a simple dedication at the beginning of the text. "To Jan, 1947–1968." From this we know that he was a youth about twenty-one years old. On page 39 there is a dialogue between a student and his mother. The student (identified as Jan Poniatowska Amor) has come home late one night and explains to his mother that they went out to paint [graffiti] on the National Palace. When she scolds him, acting very worried, he responds—"We're immortal. . . ." The next fragment is a clipping from the daily newspaper *Excélsior*, 18 November 1968.

A student 19 years of age—Luis González Sánchez—lost his life at the hands of the police, November 17, 1968, for the crime of being surprised painting propaganda of the Movement on a wall, near the Periférico.[113]

This creates the same effect of syntagmatic association as the other example in this work. But in this case we find out, almost at the end of the text, that this young man (the author's brother) in fact did die. "On December 8, the day we took Jan to be buried . . ." (272).[114] we read in another fragment. This is not the voice of the author but the voice of Elena Poniatowska, another real person among the multitude who give their testimonies about the tragedy at Tlatelolco. Her testimony, not very apparent among the hundreds in the book, is only identified by the initials "E.P." at the bottom. The author, who has disappeared from the stage so that others may speak, has not left the theater. She allows herself to speak as a witness to the reality, leaving aside for a moment her creative role, thus emphasizing the authentic historical foundation of the work.

And finally, a fragment of a piece that appeared in the newspaper *El Universal* begins with the sentence, "The scenes of dramatism are unnarratable" (192).[115] It seems that at times horror paralyzes the imagination and impedes the narration and description of those scenes.[116] Other times the urgency to speak supersedes the narrator and the events seem to narrate themselves. The author creates the illusion of having placed a microphone in the middle of the crowd and the action so that we can experience history firsthand.

In addition to these small individual episodes on the great historical stage, there is another dramatic representation in *La noche de Tlatelolco*, namely, the drama of the writing itself. The voices of society speak directly in this work. They narrate their own history. The eyewitnesses appear on the stage as actors; not only actor-participants in the real historial drama but also actor-authors of the book itself.[117] Some of the people interviewed by Poniatowska are also writers who eventually come out with their own versions of the story.[118] Her text is on the one hand a narrated drama and on the other hand it is dramatized narration. It is both "history" in its most direct form, almost unmediated, and transparent narrative-drama which reveals its own workings. If the multiple narrators are not literary creations of the author, but actors in the real story, they are in a sense also authors of the text. They are, like Poniatowska, witnesses, reporters, and writers of *La noche de Tlatelolco*.

The questions of narration and representation brought up here suggest another problematic aspect of writing. Both history and fiction are based on the narration of human experiences. In the narrative these experiences are embodied in representative lives, whether they are historical individuals or literary characters. The creation of these lives in the text (fictional creation or historical re-creation) presents technical problems for the writer. How do you narrate these lives? What perspective will they have on their own (hi)story? Even real people are turned into literary characters when they become part of a text.

In Poniatowska's book there are no clearly drawn characters nor historical personages that stand out. The "voices" of the text seem to come from all directions, rhetorical fragments of all types orchestrated in a meaningful rhythm. Ronald Christ refers to "antiphonal choirs of many, alternating solos where the interval of their occurrence is augmented by the interval of the level of their diction."[119] The anonymous voices of the choruses and the brief inscriptions of the banners and placards form a staccato counterpoint for the more sustained "solos" of the personal testimonies. However, to continue the musical metaphor, this story is not a simple song. It is a whole symphony in which the musical themes surface and resurface out of the complex texture of the totality of the piece. Although each selection is marked with the name and identity of the author, it is difficult for a first-time reader of the text to distinguish and recognize the different voices. Nevertheless, some voices stand out because of their greater frequency.[120] As we read, we go along gathering the threads of these personal stories so that little by little the outlines of characters are drawn.[121]

The fragments of the testimony of Diana Salmerón de Contreras, for example, give her a certain shape as a character. She recounts her experience during the massacre, telling how she tried to escape with her younger brother from the shower of bullets in the middle of the plaza. We first "meet" her on page 183 when she begins to speak without introduction. "We lost sight of Reyes and I heard a shout from my brother: 'Don't let go of me!' We grabbed each other firmly by the hand. . . ."[122] Her story then gets lost in the midst of others until page 193. This technique of repeatedly interrupting her narration creates suspense and increases the intensity of the tragedy. The reader knows from the beginning that her brother is going to die. "If I had realized that Julio was already dying. . . ." Diana says in her testimony (185). With a mixture of temporal perspectives she recalls for us her own words and impressions during the confusion of the situation. "Little brother, what's wrong? Little brother, answer me! . . . (185). "A stretcher, please!" "the people who were lying all over the Plaza; the living and the dead together . . ." (186). "Little brother, why don't you answer me?" (187). And so she continues, more and more desperate when she begins to realize how seriously wounded her brother is. We follow the two of them to the hospital where Julio dies. Now narrating everything in the past, Diana reflects: "Julio was 15 years old, he was studying in the vocational school number 1 that is near the Tlatelolco housing complex. It was the second time he had [ever] attended a political meeting" (189). By the time we get to this point, the reader already recognizes Diana's voice even before reading her name at the bottom of each selection. She concludes her story: "My father died shortly after Julio. As a result of the shock he had a heart attack. He [Julio] was his only son, the youngest. He would often repeat: 'But why my son? . . .' My mother went on living, who knows how" (193). Then we lose sight of Diana among the crowd in the text. But before disappearing from the stage she has already developed some dimension as a character.

Another dramatic sequence is developed over several pages. In imitation of the Rashomon technique,[123] a story is narrated from the perspectives of different testimonies. It is the story of Margarita Nolasca, an anthropologist who is looking for her son who has not returned home that fatal night in October. We have already seen fragments of her testimony scattered throughout the text by the time the scene of her search for her son begins.[124] She begins to seem familiar to us after having recounted her personal trauma of being at Tlatelolco during the massacre. She tells that on returning to her house she discovers that her son has not come home, having gone to the Tlatelolco Movie Theater that night

(222). And then: "I opened the door of the house. —And Carlitos? —He hasn't come home. We don't know anything. —Then the worst night of my life began" (236–37). She returns to Tlatelolco to look for him. "We began to knock on door after door: I would shout 'Carlos, Carlitos, Carlitos, where are you?'" (248).[125] From another perspective we read the testimony of a friend of hers who accompanied her. "And Margarita, out of her mind, went from door to door shouting: 'Carlitos, it's me! Open up!' It was Kafkaesque" (248).[126] And then from a third perspective the same episode is told. These are the words of a writer who lived in the building in which Margarita and her friend were searching: "And . . . a mother . . . a mother shouting: 'Carlitos!' through the halls and stairways, sobbing in search of her son and asking for him" (252).[127] In the end, this technique of allowing us to get to know Margarita from different perspectives gives her a certain depth as a character, in the same way as it does to the whole story of Tlatelolco.

What happened at Tlatelolco affected everyone. Many died; others were wounded. Some lost loved ones; others lost their freedom. Even those who came out of the experience without physical injury or tangible loss, felt profoundly touched by the tragedy. "I feel that after that date I am not the same as before: I couldn't be" (133),[128] says a voice in the text. Although external life might not have changed markedly, the internal change was unfathomable and irrevocable. Some even felt offended by the apparent normality of life after Tlatelolco: "It seemed incredible to me how everything returned to normal. It was as if Tlatelolco had not existed." "When I left Tlatelolco, everything was of a horrible normality, insulting. It wasn't possible that everything could go on calmly" (235).[129] The image recalls the incredulity of Don Quijote who, on coming out of the Cave of Montesinos, can't understand that others have not shared his intense experience. For many of the survivors of Tlatelolco, it was a profound spiritual experience in a negative sense, destructive but intense. And in spite of the unreal nature of the event, it was something that really happened, part of the historical reality of the times. The most difficult part of understanding the experience was first to accept that it really happened. Paz explains the disconcerting and contradictory reality of the story:

> As with all historical events, the story of what took place in 1968 in Mexico is a tangled web of ambiguous facts and enigmatic meanings.

These events really occurred, but their reality doesn't have the same texture as everyday reality. Nor does it have the fantastic self-consistency of an imaginary reality such as we find in works of fiction. What these events represent is the contradictory reality of history—the most puzzling and the most elusive reality of all.[130]

The reader (or at least an unprepared reader) enters into the experience of the book as innocently as the people who were at Tlatelolco had to confront the reality. Along with the "characters" of the story and the author herself, the reader of the work has to participate in a sort of conversion experience.[131] It is not a religious conversion as such, but it is an abrupt and profound change in the perspective from which we interpret reality. The reader, in a double role of "witness" to the story re-created by the testimonies and audience for the drama represented here, cannot help but experience a radical change of consciousness. As one of the authors of a testimony says, "At least this serves to create a consciousness, a national consciousness" (139).[132]

Poniatowska explains in an interview[133] her own experience of conversion.

In August of 1968 they began to tell me some things about the demonstrations, which I didn't attend because I had just had Felipito. On the third of October three women came to my house: María Alicia Martínez Medrano, Margarita Nolasco, and Mercedes Oliver. Crying, they told me what had happened, what they had witnessed at Tlatelolco. I thought they were hysterical, all worked up. Of course, what had come out in the papers was in itself horrifying enough! They told me of piles of dead bodies lying in the plaza; of how they had run to get out of there. . . . Crazy with horror, the following morning I went to Tlatelolco and you could still see in the doors of the elevators, on the walls, the marks of the machine guns, of the gunshots, even blood on the floor. I began to collect the testimonies of the kids who wanted to talk, changing their names for them. Later, when the book came out, many students told me "I have things to tell you more terrible than the ones you wrote." That always happens, at first nobody wants to talk, then everyone wants to.[134]

Poniatowska gives her own impassioned testimony in the text and then remains quiet to allow others to speak. She also knows how to listen. Paz comments in the introduction to *Massacre in Mexico* (the English translation) on Poniatowska's unique ability as a writer and historian: "In *Massacre in Mexico* she uses her admirable ability to listen and to reproduce what others have to say to serve the cause of history. Her book is a historical account and at the same time a most imaginative linguistic tour de force."[135]

In her role as journalist, or chronicler of the present, Poniatowska records for us the voices of an era and the testimonies of a people. Paz describes her work as "a historical chronicle—but one that shows us history before the spoken word has become written text."[136] We, as reader-historians look for the truth in the documents that she has left us. In the fragments of her text we find the traces (including those of blood) of a past reality. And as historian-archaeologists we search in the strata of human experience for a truth beneath the surface of the narration. There isn't just one (hi)story. There are sub-versions of the official version, which tries to cover up and bury the past while maintaining smooth and calm the surface of the present. Like a "current that corrodes the pyramids,"[137] these other versions of history undermine the monolithic structures of power and the stone texts of Tradition. We have to excavate deeply in the past and in our consciences to discover, uncover the truth. A contemporary historian once said: "What is truth? Mighty above all things, it resides in the small pieces which together form the record."[138] And by disinterring the truth of Tlatelolco we exhume these small and terrible pieces of evidence inscribed in the text. We stumble across the reality of those who died. As if responding to an expression of disbelief, the following simple affirmation is repeated three times throughout the book: "They are bodies, sir. . . ."[139] The young people who before were marching so enthusiastically are now just figures of history, bodies of the text. Tlatelolco is incoherent, contradictory. But death is not.[140] These are the hard facts. From there we must begin to reconstruct the story.

3

Elena Garro: The Inversions of Fiction

People would sooner believe a lie than the truth.[1]

Elena Garro, like Elena Poniatowska, is a talented writer in several different arenas. In addition to her works of fiction she has written essays, interviews, literary criticism, and translation. During the early years of her artistic production she was known for her plays, some of which have been translated and produced in the United States and Europe. Her first novel, *Los recuerdos del porvenir* (1963) anticipates the famous "magical realism" and has been called by John Brushwood "perhaps the best novel of 1963."[2] After several collections of short stories and a few other plays, Garro's second novel, *Testimonios sobre Mariana* was published in 1981.

While Poniatowska's *La noche de Tlatelolco* is a hybrid work of problematic genre, *Testimonios sobre Mariana* is situated in the realm of pure fiction. It is an invented world of imaginary characters and narrators. But the fictional parameters of this important work by Garro do not limit its access to the truth. Its fictive story comments on an historic reality, while the work itself illustrates symbolically that what we call reality is primarily an imaginative construct.

Testimonios sobre Mariana is in a sense an inversion of *La noche de Tlatelolco*. It is not a testimonial novel (testimony in the form of a novel) but rather a novel in the form of testimonies. The voices of *La noche de Tlatelolco* are of real people who give their testimonies about a series of events that really happened. In contrast, the narrators of *Testimonios sobre Mariana*, besides being fictitious themselves, give their testimonies about the fate of an even more "fictitious" character: Mariana exists within the text only through the narrations of others and her life is shrouded in mystery, almost invented by them in their attempts to understand and control her. Testimony is a narrative form which can communicate a sense of historical authenticity, of firsthand reporting about an event. But it can also reveal the "subjectivity" of the subjects and their limited vision in the interpretation of that reality. The "truth" has to take into account these two aspects of the testimonies in this story (and in fact of any testimony) and the reader must be the judge.

The text of *Testimonios sobre Mariana* consists of three parts which correspond to the testimonies of three people (character-narrators) who knew Mariana. In imitation of the Rashomon technique,[3] the story of Mariana is narrated through three different perspectives. The narrators each tell the story of their own relations with her, in the process revealing more about themselves than about Mariana. But at the same time these partial images of Mariana are all we have. There is no master narrative to unite the three parts. The novel seems to be comprised of three independent stories which begin from their own beginnings without intertextual references or apparent awareness of the other testimonies. This technique contributes to a fragmented vision of Mariana and her life, a kaleidoscope of impressions, rumors, and desires. As if in a poorly edited film, each testimony follows the story of Mariana, stumbling through great lapses of time and abrupt transitions. Small clues float in the apparent confusion of the text, like pieces of a puzzle that must be reconstructed little by little during the process of reading. The reader assumes the role of detective, trying to organize and interpret the information in order to solve the mystery.

Testimonios sobre Mariana deals with the story of a woman (Mariana) who has disappeared with her daughter, fleeing the cruel oppression of her husband (Augusto) and the stifling social environment of Paris in which she lived. The book reads like a mystery novel in which the reader-detective hears the testimonies and has to arrive at some conclusions about the mysterious history of Mariana. It is a complex work that poses indirectly a series of philosophical, psychological, and political dilemmas, all illustrated by Mariana's life and her relationships with others. There is a strong social criticism in the treatment of the character types of the French elite and even more of the group of Latin Americans in Paris who surrounded Mariana and Augusto. It is a world of hypocrisy and lies, great ironies, and above all of social struggle. On one level the whole work could be seen as a Marxist-feminist critique of a society in which the rich exploit the poor and men oppress women. But on another level the novel is much more complex and the categories become confused. Those who identify themselves as revolutionary Marxists are the same bourgeois "careerists" who exploit anyone to further their careers. And women appear as oppressors as well. A woman can reach a position of power by means of money or sex with which she can buy the allegiance of a man. We see some strange alliances of class enemies such as the old Russian aristocrat, Boris, and the Communist servant, Raymonde. André (the third narrator) once confessed that he no longer knows which are the enemies of class (333). These complications do not weaken the social criticism in the novel; on the contrary, they seem to give it more depth.

The book begins with testimony by Vicente, a South American, former lover of Mariana. He tells of his experiences with her, and through his memories Mariana's story begins to take shape. The first image we see of Mariana is a description by Vicente. "The first time I saw her was in a photograph that Pepe showed us on returning from Paris. . . . She was leaning against the trunk of a tree in the middle of a misty woods" (7). For the reader as well as for the narrator the first encounter with Mariana is from a photo, a static portrait almost erased by time and distance. "Mariana began in that woods softly blurred by the mist" (7).[5] Vicente says, reminding us inadvertently that she exists for us only within his narration. Her story is not a chronicle of events but rather a collage of impressions and experiences in which he tries to explain the mystery of Mariana. It's difficult for him to organize his story because the truth is not that coherent. "I'm not telling this in order," he confesses. "What is the order with Mariana?" (7).[6]

During Vicente's testimony we manage to find out very little about Mariana. We learn of certain "facts," basic information about her life and her problems. But the scenes are always partial and limited, a perspective filtered through the desire and frustration of Vicente. Although he is her lover, Vicente is never able to really know her. "He didn't know anything about her; she was the unforeseen traveler, the stranger with no past or future. . . . There was something artificial about her, as if she didn't really exist in a permanent sense. . . ." (22).[7] For the reader as well, in the first part of the book Mariana's image lacks dimension and history, seen only through the one-sided perspective of Vicente. And although he wants to help her escape her terrible situation, he always finds himself for one reason or another impotent to change her fate.

The second testimony is that of Gabrielle, a French woman of the lower classes who had fought in the French Resistance. Mariana's story begins again, but this time from the perspective of a woman, her accomplice and confidante. Gabrielle identifies with Mariana as another marginalized being, oppressed by her inevitable destiny. Gabrielle's economic situation is so desperate that she finds herself obliged to accept a job working for Augusto, Mariana's husband. This increases her sense of guilt and impotence with regard to Mariana's desperate struggle. Each impulse on Gabrielle's part to try to save Mariana is accompanied by resignation in the face of the futility of the struggle. "She's trapped, she'll never be rescued," Gabrielle says to herself. . . . "I'm taking useless risks trying to help her" (126).[8] In this way Gabrielle tries to justify her own cowardice in the face of her friend's difficulties. "My work obligated me to betray my friend. The word betrayal is unfair since to sacrifice myself for her would have been useless. Mariana was *déclassé*. She knew she was stuck in an extreme situation that would inevitably force her to take drastic measures. I couldn't save her" (127).[9]

Gabrielle's tale (the longest of the three) gives us more information about Mariana and her oppressors, although the perspective is not at all objective. We first see Mariana through Gabrielle's eyes not at the beginning of her testimony but later on in the text. Gabrielle remembers how, on meeting Mariana for the first time, she was already prejudiced about her due to the stories she had heard from others. In a similar way, we as readers see the new image that is presented to us by Gabrielle already influenced by the portrait painted of her in Vicente's testimony. Gabrielle tells us of her experience, "Romualdo took me to Mariana's house. Already beforehand the character had seemed disagreeable to me." But when she finally sees her, Gabrielle has a different impression than the image she had carried in her mind. "Suddenly Mariana appeared. She wasn't the femme fatale I had imagined. She wore her blond hair loose over her shoulders, and was dressed in slacks and some old ballet shoes" (139).[10] And so the testimony proceeds, maintaining a constant tension between what others say about Mariana and Gabrielle's actual experience with her.

Although Gabrielle never refers to Vicente's text, she does give us a view of him which colors retrospectively his testimony. She describes him as a "South American gigolo . . . a blond, athletic looking young man with a childish smile" who "possessed a poisonous power of seduction" (161).[11] The new perspective on Vicente interacts with what we are learning about Gabrielle and her prejudices. As readers we must readjust our vision of the truth to the constant change of lenses, while at the same time trying to maintain a sense of coherence for the story as a whole. It is not a passive role.

The third narrator, André, is a young Frenchman who meets Mariana through his cousin's acquaintances. His testimony (the shortest of the three) differs from the others in its more innocent perspective, one less tangled up in the complex relationships of the social group that surrounded Mariana. André is a young man of upper-class background who has not had much experience with women. His first encounter with Mariana is not loaded with preformed notions about her as was the case with Gabrielle. He describes her simply. "A young woman was smoking, seated on a velvet tabacco-colored canopy. She was wearing moccasins and she looked at me with self-assured eyes" (285).[12] The relationship that André has with Mariana is also more direct. He simply adores her and devotes himself to that adoration, even though he knows very little about her life.

By the time we get to André's testimony, short and direct as it may be, we have a third dimension added to the story of Mariana. André is able to surrender himself to his relationship with Mariana and his comments contribute to a more well-rounded image of her. "Mariana is not what you think,"[13] he says to his cousin Bertrand (331). We who have listened to the other testimonies can affirm that the truth about Mariana is in fact more complicated than even André suspects. Nevertheless, he is the only one who really manages to have an intimate relationship with her. He is also the one who discovers "the truth" about her life and ultimately tries to save her.

Through the testimonies of Vicente, Gabrielle, and André, Mariana's world begins to acquire dimensions of reality. The three give their testimonies in order to recover their memories of her, although "she" really has no existence other than in those memories. Those who re-create Mariana in their memories are three "subjects" in search of an objective reality, some common reference. They need to understand her or explain her in order to define themselves. Like the three sides of a triangle their narratives define a space where Mariana and her "true story" should be found. But that space on which their stories are focused is really empty. The "real" object (Mariana) to which they refer, has vanished or never even existed. At one point, Gabrielle comments on Mariana's ephemeral existence. "Sometimes I think that Mariana was only a dream that we all made up" (123–24).[14] This absent center of the text is part of our investigation here. Who is Mariana and what importance does her identity have for the interpretation of the text?

Before beginning the inquiry into the identity of Mariana, it would be useful to examine her role in the novel. What is her importance to the structure of the text? The central theme of *Testimonios sobre Mariana* is the identity and history of Mariana. She is the subject, the theme being discussed, the case which must be solved. Her symbolic importance can be subject to many interpretations about the meaning of the work, but that is an issue better left for later on. Mariana is also the subject-agent of the work, like the grammatical subject of a sentence. She is the one who evokes (although involuntarily) the giving of the testimonies and it is she who motivates the actions of the characters. If it is not she directly, it is at least the desires, the fears, or guilty conscience that she provokes in others. The third part of the subject triangle (to add to Mariana as subject-theme, subject-agent, . . .) is Mariana as victim. She is the subject-object, the one who is always "subject to" the action of others. This is the mystery and irony of her life: she has no control over her own destiny but she controls the lives of others. And so it is that she becomes the subject-theme of the testimonies. She is the disquieting question that haunts everyone.

Testimonios sobre Mariana is on one level a detective novel, the story of a woman who is persecuted and eventually killed.[15] The protagonist is absent: either dead or disappeared and she cannot give her own testimony. She is the central focus of the book but she is really outside of it. The text is not "Mariana" but rather the "testimonies about Mariana." It is not the story of the person herself nor a representation of her life, but rather the story of the attempt on the part of others to interpret the life of Mariana in order to shed light on their own experiences. This displacement of the focus of the writing from a "concrete" level (Mariana's life) to a discursive level (the stories about Mariana) changes Mariana into a metaphoric figure open to multiple interpretations. Therefore, one could classify *Testimonios sobre Mariana* as a detective novel on a more abstract level. The "case" to be solved would be not the life (and death) of Mariana but the meaning of the metaphor.

Who is Mariana? Her identity always seems to slip away from us like a shadow or a dream and all that remains is her "image transfigured by absence" (52–53)[16] in the words of her lover Vicente. She is the blank sign, a screen for the projections and inventions that surround her. She is a creation of fiction in several senses. The image that we have of her is a fiction because it is incomplete and subjective, a superficial image we might say. There is so much that we don't know about the "real" Mariana, the person behind our perceptions of her, a situation which lends itself to much speculation and invention. She says repeatedly, "You don't know anything at all."[17] Although this is directed toward another character in the book, the phrase resounds for the reader as well. Vicente recognizes intuitively that his memory of Mariana is not really Mariana herself. "If Mariana disappeared from my life she would be turned into an imagined Mariana . . . all that would remain would be her essence like a melancholy ochre colored shadow" (52). He also comments on the impossibility of capturing life in writing, which is a form of memory. "We can reflect our lives, sketching them on sheets of paper and it will never be our real lives. The paper cannot capture the tone of voice, the lightness of some footsteps, the intensity of suffering or the definitive sound of a door closing. . . ." (81).[18] In this novel Mariana is a phantom of words, not only in the platonic sense in which words are mere shadows of the real thing, but also because we know her only through the memories of others. She is only the memory of a memory. This discussion is somewhat ironic since all of the characters of the novel are literary figures, that is, verbal creations. Vicente seems to recognize this at one point. "I, too, thought that life was only a literary game" (53).[19] But even within the boundaries of fiction, Mariana is the creation of others. Her husband, Augusto, makes a fiction of her life. He refers to the "tales that she invents" (76)[20] and tries to discredit her at every turn. According to him, everything she says is a lie. He even invents lies for her. Augusto, in his imperial tyranny, wants to be the author of Mariana's life. Vicente recognizes bitterly the "authorial" power of Augusto: "Her husband had closed the chapter of our love" (74).[21] That is Mariana's existence. She is the topic for discussion, the blank page on which the others can write their own fantasies.

Mariana's identity, in its metaphorical function, points toward the universal problem of human identity. It is a problem with repercussions in the sciences as well as in the humanities. How is an individual formed or deformed? How is the identity of an individual defined in its social context? Is it possible to understand our existence from the perspective of that same existence? How can we understand the experience of others and record it by means of writing?

In Hegelian philosophy[22] a central determining force in the identity of the self is the struggle for self-consciousness. This presupposes an ironic conflict: in order to establish one's own self, one must destroy the other and its "otherness." The otherness of the other is a threat to one's identity. But at the same time that otherness is necessary to be able to define one's self. One can only affirm one's self by means of contrast with the other. Men are able to transcend this conflict by going out into the world. Man defines himself as an individual by inserting himself into the community and working for the universal. Women must stay at home and therefore are never able to reach that state of individual self-consciousness. Woman represents an unconscious ethical order, that of the family. This order is, for the community, a kind of necessary enemy, in conflict with conscious existence and its universal ethic but at the same time of fundamental importance to it. It is, in the words of Hegel, part of the "perpetual irony of the community."

In *Testimonios sobre Mariana* we see this Hegelian struggle especially in the character of Augusto. He wants to sacrifice everything for his career, his public life in which he defends eloquently the universal rights of the human being. He needs Mariana as a symbol of his respectable bourgeois life. As long as she remains in her "objective" (that of an object) position at the center of the family, he can use her as an ornament or as a scapegoat according to his needs. But Mariana is not willing to sacrifice herself completely. She is innocent and rebellious and doesn't follow the rules. She is a constant threat to Augusto's political image and he realizes that he must destroy her. "I'm going to tame Mariana!" he announces with frightening certainty (143).[23] Gabrielle asks herself if he really tamed her or if she died in the struggle. Later on she comments that "in order to destroy someone you first have to destroy her image" and "that was what little Mariana didn't realize. Sure of her steps, she moved about on the stage without knowing that someone had changed the lights of the reflectors in order to project on her light figure a black light that disfigured her. . . ." (143).[24] Even after Mariana's death, Augusto continues talking about her as if she were still alive, complaining about how she still persecutes him and ruins his life. He wants to destroy her but at the same time he still needs her in order to define himself.

The philosophy of Sartre[25] further develops Hegel's problem of the other. For Sartre, too, there is a conflict with the other in the definition of the self. The self is defined by the look of the other. My identity depends not only on the fact that the other looks at me, but also on the conception that that other has of me. Life is a struggle to transcend and liberate oneself from the look of the other. One must struggle to be the one who looks, to be the subject and refuse to be the object of the gaze. The state of transcendence consists of becoming a "perpetual center of infinite possibilities." According to Simone de Beauvoir, women have been subjected to being a permanent other; "otherness" is a feminine condition.[26]

Mariana's existence is defined by the look of others. She even says so once: "I feel looked at" (101).[27] She is the object of the gaze of everyone. They look at her not only for her beauty but also because of her vulnerability, her image of misfortune. Her passivity invites the looks of others. Gabrielle notes this when she comments, "My friend's life was not her own; it was determined by characters who would come close to her, leave their marks and disappear" (194).[28]

Woman as an object does not exercise her own will nor have her own opinions. When Mariana tries to protest or defend herself, the others all answer with such vehemence against her that she ends up worse than before. Augusto, who is passionately enamored of Sartre's philosophy, blames Mariana not only for being a woman-object but also for oppressing him with her state of submission and dependence. "The woman-object imprisons us and forces us to lead an artificial life. I for one would live in a garret devoted to love and my studies, but I'm not able to. Mariana and the girl have me chained to money, the daily routine and the artificial life" (292).[29] She is the scapegoat, the subject-object that cannot speak for herself. But Mariana, who has also read Sartre, says in another context, "Sartre's striving for consciousness is the philosophical explanation for the bourgeois will to acquisitive power" (133).[30] There is no doubt that she is referring to Augusto. He talks about freedom and transcendence of the self in order to rid himself of his responsibilities. At the same time he promotes himself as a hero of the oppressed in his farce as a socialist revolutionary, while living as a millionaire and taking advantage of his fame as a brilliant leftist. On another occasion, while discussing one of Sartre's books (La Question Juive) that was in vogue among Augusto and his admirers, Mariana declares "Ambiguous book. You might say that it justifies the crime." "I forbid you to speak!" (139).[31] Augusto orders in reply, returning Mariana to her position as object. An object is not supposed to speak. It only receives the actions of others.

Mariana, although clearly trapped as a woman-object, also functions as a subject, one who does the looking. In a sense she becomes the "perpetual center of infinite possibilities" of which Sartre spoke. By being the object of the gaze of all the others, she loses her identity and thereby gains a certain freedom. Ironically, by the very act of being a victim, she controls her oppressors. She looks at them as a reflection of their own gazes, a sort of guilty conscience, and thus leaves them always feeling uneasy. Her presence challenges the lies of her oppressors and they find themselves obliged to invent new lies, more and more extreme. They lose control of the situation and their actions become reactions to her.

In the formation of identity it is not only the look of others which defines us. From a psychological perspective equally important is the conception that an individual "I" has of him or herself. This is a neurological problem as well as a psychological one. A crucial component of the sense of self is, according to Dr. Oliver Sacks, an internal narrative that is the perpetual text of life:

> We have, each of us, a life-story, an inner narrative—whose continuity, whose sense, *is* us, our identities. . . . Each of us *is* a singular narrative, which is constructed, continually, unconsciously, by, through, and in us—through our perceptions, our feelings, our thoughts, our actions; and, not least, our discourse, our spoken narrations. . . . A man *needs* such a narrative, a continous inner narrative, to maintain his identity, his self.[32]

This narrative of the self depends on memory, a sense of the past in continuation to the present. If a person's past is continually denied, then that person's identity is fragmented. Dr. Sacks studies patients who suffer from a special kind of amnesia in which their memory lasts only a few seconds. In these cases the person has to "literally make himself (and his world) up every moment."[33] He lives in an eternal present.

Mariana leads such a fragmented life that she seems to be lost in an eternal present of repetition, as if she suffered from such an amnesia. "She was an intense present," Vicente says about her (22). "It seemed to me that she had a magnificent capacity for forgetting" (210).[34] Mariana forgets and the others forget and distort her past, all of which leaves her in a life without coherence or continuity. Gabrielle's description of Mariana makes note of this unfortunate state. "I seemed to see her reflected in a mirror smashed to pieces and she, too, contemplated her mutilated and multiplied image" (132).[35] André feels that his own life is falling apart in his unending search for Mariana, who represents for him the absent center of his life (as she does, also, for the story itself). "Every time I tried to get close to her something unforseen would make her untouchable and invisible" (334).[36] While Mariana has lost her past and wanders in a continually evanescent present, it seems that she also has no future. Vicente has a premonition of this in a dream: "I found her at the foot of a blank wall reading a book that was also blank. I knew then that our destiny was written there and that on those pages was not a single word" (56).[37] The future is not yet written. For Mariana the only future is a repetition of the past already written in the text, a past waiting to be reenacted with each reading of the work.

This motif of the repetition of the past in the future, a closed, predetermined future, appears frequently in Garro's writing. Adriana Méndez Rodenas has studied what Julia Kristeva calls "feminine time" in Garro's works. "In Elena Garro's short stories and novels, feminine time is a 'manifest destiny', where the past determines the future, a 'circular time identical to itself, like a mirror reflecting another mirror that repeats us.'"[38] "The past is written in time and is only the image of the future," says Mariana at one point (232).[39] On another occasion Gabrielle is sitting in her room contemplating an old electrical cord that hangs from the chandelier and she reflects on the division of time: "On one side was the past, on the other the future, exactly the same as the past, like a simple reflection of the first" (229).[40] This feminine existence of spacial and temporal enclosure is exemplified, as Méndez Rodenas shows, in the life of the prostitutes in Garro's *Los recuerdos del porvenir:* "forgotten women who represent the heritage with no way out, the tragic and repetitive destiny of women."[41] The identity of the prostitute is one which the others always try to impose on Mariana, thus reenforcing her imprisoned and degraded condition. This reaction on the part of others does not reflect any real tendency in Mariana. It is simply a judgment that all sexually free women are considered as such.

The image of the mirror, symbol par excellence of repetition, appears many times in *Testimonios sobre Mariana.* Mariana herself functions as a mirror for others. She is the blank sign that reflects the image of others; their desires, fears, and weaknesses. An acquaintance says the following with double meaning to her: "All the mirrors will break the moment you leave the city. . . ." (254).[42]

It is an allusion both to Mariana's beauty and to her function in the formation of the identity of everyone. She is like Narcissus's reflection in the water. They adore her because she is beautiful and she completes for them their own insecure images. Vicente confesses that even when they are separated by long distances she continues giving coherence to his life. "I would see her in dreams, in the streets, and in summer she would appear in the sea. At night she would call me and my friends were turned into incoherent forms. During my dreams, Mariana would appear to me underwater, looking at me with her eyes wide open, and I was above her and would wake up sweating. I would tell her about my nights visited by her and she became my distant conscience. . . ." (81). Mariana becomes part of Vicente, submerged in the waters of his subconscience. "I looked for her image in the mirrors and I found her calm in the bottom of the lakes from which she would send me signals" (83).[43] For Vicente, Mariana lives "underwater" in a pre-oedipal world. Her association with the sea suggests a spiritual and presocial depth for which the other empty and decentered characters like Vicente long. But at the same time they are threatened by the insubstantiality and constantly mutable form of water and similarly of Mariana's character. Vicente, on one occasion completely disillusioned with her, says: "I had made a mistake in my love for Mariana. The feelings were fleeting and illusory, like fireworks. Later, there was only the lonely night and I had entered into a dark dimension. When I arrived at the hotel I didn't recognize myself in the mirrors" (72).[44] Without being able to see his reflection in her, Vicente can no longer distinguish his own identity.

Even though the other characters adore Mariana's image, they also hate her. It is the dilemma of the imaginary state of which Jacques Lacan writes. In Lacan's theory, children discover by means of their perception of the image of another human being, a form *(Gestalt)*, a corporeal unity which they are lacking in this particular stage of their development.[45] This specular relationship of the subject with an image is both positive and negative; positive because it represents a normal stage in the psychological development of a "functional totality of the self," but on the other hand it embodies the fiction in which the subject is constructing himself.[46] From this relationship is generated a (false) image of unity where in fact there is discord, and from that results the alienation of the self.[47] According to Lacan, this "paranoic alienation of the ego through the mirror stage *(stade du miroir)* is one of the preconditions of human knowledge."[48] But "if the child doesn't manage to

escape the attraction of this alienated self, he can become em-
broiled in the pathological search of the lost object about which
Freud spoke."[49] All of the characters in this novel seem to be
trapped in a narcissistic state of psychological development. They
adore Mariana as an idealized projection of their own beings (or
at least a complementary image), and at the same time they hate
her for being unreal, that is, a product of their own fictions. Margo
Glantz[50] analyzes the struggle for self-awareness in the rebellion of
adolescents, and her observations are pertinent to our discussion.
Glantz quotes Octavio Paz in his discourse on the adolescent who
"cannot forget himself since on doing so he would cease to be
himself."[51] Glantz continues:

> This tragic paradox causes the adolescent to be at this stage in his life
> a Narcissus caught in the act of contemplating himself, a Narcissus
> incapable of recognizing his face, because the mirror that reflects it is
> fragmented before his image becomes clear, before he can manage to
> make out his features. Rebellion is the mirror broken before the un-
> veiling is completed.[52]

Mariana rebels against the society in which she lives and for
that reason she remains in a kind of permanent adolescence. Gabrielle once calls her "a grave historical error. She lived in an
imaginary dimension, refusing to see reality, and she would flee
like a schoolgirl instead of confronting the facts" (265).[53] Her
rebellion and alienation reach such an extreme that it causes fear
in the others. A friend of Mariana warns Gabrielle: "You can be
sure that she will end up committing suicide some day. She's just
a step away from schizophrenia and has closed off the channels
of communication with the outside world." And later Gabrielle
remarks to herself, "Mariana was incapable of externalizing; she
always talked about things that were not about herself" (92).[54]
Such isolation can lead to suicide or insanity. Augusto tries to
take advantage of both possibilities. He wants to have Mariana
committed to an insane asylum in order to get her off his hands.
In a rather ambiguous scene it seems that she has tried to kill
herself or that Augusto has tried to kill her. Whatever the case, it
is clearly a situation with no escape for her. Augusto is sure that
the attempted suicide will be evidence of Mariana's insanity and
that he only needs witnesses to be able to have her committed.
He calls Gabrielle so that she can be the third witness if necessary.
When Gabrielle enters the room, she sees Mariana first through
her reflection in an enormous mirror hanging on the wall. She

finds her so broken and traumatized that she thinks that she will remain "forever in the interior of that mirror" (151).[55] She also sees in the mirror the figures of Augusto and an accomplice. Soon Augusto's cook, who will also serve as a witness, enters the room. His name is Narciso (a name too opportune to be coincidence) and as his image approaches them in the mirror, he repeats his testimony of what happened. It is an exact repetition of what Augusto has said. Narciso is a sinister figure who has always been a witness against Mariana, thereby serving as a sort of duplication of Augusto. On leaving the house, Gabrielle sees Narciso's face covered in sweat "in spite of the cold that ran through the house" (157).[56] This reference to Narciso's strange sweat suggests associations with water, perhaps the water mirror in which the "august"[57] power of Mariana's husband is reflected. Augusto is the true Narcissus who always seeks in others the reflection of his own image.

The fragmented image of Mariana haunts the novel on many levels. She seems to be many people and yet she lacks identity. At times she gives the impression of having split apart or multiplied. She confounds her friends as well as her enemies. According to Vicente, "Nobody could trust her and it would end up being terrible for whoever loved her. I had the impression that there were two Marianas, a sweet one and a perverse one" (98).[58] Gabrielle alludes to the idea of a double in the relationship between Mariana and her daughter. "That night, while contemplating the mother and daughter, I had the strange sensation that the two were the same person and that one of them had invented the 'other' to make us believe that she enjoyed some company" (129).[59] André has the same impression on several occasions: "It was ten years after my first encounter with her, when I saw her and her double on the terrace of the Hotel Carlton in Cannes" (313). "I had the impression that Mariana had copied herself in her daughter and that they were the same person" (316).[60] Vicente and Mariana also seem like some sort of doubles according to Gabrielle. "Many times I had the strange impression of seeing superimposed on Mariana's blond face the blond face of the South American. I imagined that my friend's thoughts projected that far away face over her own to make her forget what was surrounding her" (216–17).[61] One of Mariana's Russian friends once explained to Gabrielle his theory on doubles: "There are no singular cases or unique people. Events and people are repeated in other events and people exactly alike, one is saved and the other is lost. God creates us, throws us into the same circumstances, one wanders off and gets lost and the other follows the tracks left by her angel and is saved" (241).[62] These words spoken by Vasily are ironic in their veiled allusion to Mariana. He pretends to be talking about a cousin of his, María, in order to protect Mariana, who has disappeared without a trace. However it is the very same Mariana to whom he is referring, the same person yet no longer the same.

The perpetually confusing circumstances of Mariana's life lead us to vacillate in our judgment of her. Was Mariana crazy? Or was it the society which surrounded her? The rebellious adolescent who rejects the rules of society becomes marginalized. At the same time, if that society is corrupt, doesn't it feel compelled to marginalize its critics? How else can we really see Mariana if not reflected in the social mirrors of her time and in the memories of those who narrate the story? How can we distinguish the "true" image of a person or an event from among other images distorted by the interests of power and presented as the "true story"? At the beginning of the second part of the novel Gabrielle summarizes the ending of Mariana's tragic fate.

> The hand that erased the image of Mariana in her friends' memories, like an image reflected in water, was the hand of Augusto her husband, who inexorably stirred up the water, disfiguring her face, her figure, until he had made her grotesque and distorted. In the end, when the waters had quieted, there was nothing left of Mariana! To change memory in order to destroy an image is a more arduous task than to destroy a person. (123)[63]

Who is/was Mariana? Is it possible to know her? How can we define her problematic identity? We have already seen that the identity of a person has many aspects. One's identity is a relationship of many factors: perceptions, actions, interpretations, circumstances. The look of others is important as well as our own perceptions, our social roles and individual experience. Our personal history is composed of our own internal narrative along with the interpretation and memory of others. In accordance with this model, the truth about Mariana would have to be complex as well. "Some day we will know the truth," says Bertrand, a cousin of André. André tells us his reaction to the statement by his cousin. "I looked at him sceptically, the truth has as many faces as does the lie" (319).[64] Would the truth about Mariana, then, have as many faces as all the lies invented about her?

Before continuing with this entangled, complicated investigation, we must remember that this novel is a work of fiction. Mariana is a creation of fiction, as are all of the other characters and narrators of the book. Why are we so concerned about the "truth" of a fictional invention? But if Mariana were real, how would the analysis proceed? Let's suppose that the story of Mariana is real, that she really existed and the testimonies about her have historical value as well. Then *Testimonios sobre Mariana* would be a collection of texts or historical "documents," testimonies like those that Poniatowska collected for *La noche de Tlatelolco*. Mariana would be the historical "object" we are studying, the *res gestae* of our history. It would be the reader's task to construct (mentally write) the biography of Mariana utilizing the three "documents" of the book. Let's now examine some of the problems that such a reader-historian might encounter.

How does one begin to write a history? First one must look for the hard facts. But if we are studying the past, how can we gather this information? Marc Bloch, one of the founders of modern social history,[65] addressed the problems that confront historians. According to Bloch, even direct evidence suffers distortion as a result of someone's observation. And we always depend on the observations of others. "A good half of all we see is seen through the eyes of others," Bloch notes.[66] But there are no reliable witnesses in an absolute sense, he adds; only testimonies that are more or less reliable.[67] "The truth is that the majority of minds are but mediocre recording-cameras of the surrounding world. Add that, since evidence, strictly speaking, is no more than the expression of remembrance, the first errors of perception run the constant risk of being entangled with the errors of memory. . . ."[68] The facts are not autonomous entities, but are, in the words of Octavio Paz, "tinted with humanity, that is, they are problematic."[69] By the same token, historical knowledge, which is based on the testimonies of others, is in the words of Henri Marrou "not a science properly speaking, but knowledge by faith."[70] Historians, like a detective or the reader of this novel, must first make a judgment about the origin of the evidence and the author of the testimony. This is not an easy task as Bloch notes, "Criticism of testimony, since it deals with psychic realities, will always remain a subtle act."[71] And for historians the task is even more arduous since many times they do not have access to the witnesses of the past events or phenomena, but only the "tracks" they have left behind, generally in the form of writing. Once again in the words of Bloch: "What do we really mean by 'documents,' if it is not a 'track'—the mark, perceptible to the senses, which some phenomenon, in itself inaccessible, has left behind?"[72] Similarly, if we the readers of *Testimonios sobre Mariana* propose to "track down" the truth about Mariana (in our game of reality), we have to study the tracks left by her life in the memories of her friends. At the same time, however, we must examine critically the "evidence" available, evidence which happens to be limited to the tales of others.

"History is not the past, any more than biology is life, or physics, matter," writes Oscar Handlin. "History is the distillation of evidence surviving from the past."[73] But even with the collection of evidence, of data about the events of the past, we still don't have (a) history. History is not "the past," nor the objects nor the "tracks" that that past has left us. It is a process, or many processes to which we give meaning. Erich Kahler explains the meaning of history in the following manner:

> History is happening, a particular kind of happening, and the attendant whirl it generates. Where there is no happening, there is no history. . . . To become history, events must, first of all, be related to each other, form a chain, a continuous flow. Continuity, coherence is the elementary prerequisite of history, and not only of history, but even of the simplest story.[74]

History is a story, not only the reproduction of the happenings of the past, but also the creation of a structure and a meaningful context to organize those happenings. Human perspective and interpretation are indispensable to the notion of history. Kahler concludes that the problem of the meaning of history is in effect the problem of the meaning of human life.[75]

History, then, is a verbal creation, at least in its narrative form available to us. It is in a sense a product of the imagination, though this notion might sound like heresy. Louis Mink[76] has studied narrative form in its function as a cognitive instrument which not only "narrates" a series of events, but also includes a complex process of ordering and combining of elements and relationships. "Narrative form in history, as in fiction, is an artifice, the product of individual imagination. Yet at the same time it is accepted as claiming truth—that is, as representing a real ensemble of interrelationships in past actuality."[77] Although no one doubts that there is an historical reality outside of historical narrative, it is not difficult to admit that our conception of the coherence and meaning of history comes primarily from written texts. Since we cannot see directly the events and objects of the past, we have to rely on their representation in texts. Lionel Gossman asserts that "history constructs its objects, and . . . its objects are objects of language, rather than entities of which words are in some way copies."[78] And so it seems that we end up right where we started with another commentary by Mink on the construction of historical narrative. "Events (or more precisely, descriptions of events) are not the raw material out of which narratives are constructed; rather an event is an abstraction from a narrative."[79] What has happened to our "hard facts" of history?

The difficulty we have in accepting historical narrative as a verbal creation is due in part to what Mink describes as the presupposition of a Universal History, the idea that "past actuality is an untold story and that there is a right way to tell it even though only in part."[80] The ideal history (though in reality impossible to write) would be a cumulative objective chronicle of everything that "really happened." Mink maintains that if we were to accept this notion of history, even as an ideal objective, narrative histories would have to be added on to more comprehensive narratives which in turn are part of one single complete history. But narrative, according to Mink, has by definition its own unity and one narrated history cannot simply be added to others.

> Narrative histories should be aggregative, insofar as they are histories, but cannot be insofar as they are narratives. Narrative history borrows from fictional narrative the convention by which a story generates its own imaginative space, within which it neither depends on nor can displace other stories, but it presupposes that past actuality is a single and determinate realm, a presupposition which, once it is made explicit, is at odds with the incomparability of imaginative stories.[81]

We shall see how this logical contradiction between narrative form and historical representation is exemplified in *Testimonios sobre Mariana*.

First let's return to the hypothetical situation of "if Mariana were real." She would then be part of that particular realm of the past which is to be represented in the narrative. As part of the "Ideal Chronicle" of a Universal History, the testimonies about Mariana ought to be repetitions or extensions of the same story, links of a great cumulative chain.[82] But these testimonies are not just repetitions or extensions of the same story. They are really different stories and in a sense about different Marianas. There is, for instance, the story of Mariana, Vicente's lover, as well as Mariana, friend of Gabrielle, and the other Mariana, friend/beloved of André. Each one of these stories is a fragmented reconstruction of many dimensions. The different perspectives and interpretations of the three narrators cannot be reduced to a linear chronicle, even less so because each one tells as well his or her own personal story.

The idea of a single universal history appears in *Testimonios sobre Mariana* as an instrument of absolute power. When Augusto declares something about Mariana, he will not accept any contradictory "history." The truth about the past must yield to the power of the present. Mariana asks Augusto once: "So the truth doesn't matter before the law?" He answers, "Mariana, the law *is* the truth" (176).[83] Augusto's friends are all in complete agreement with his statements, serving to reinforce an indisputable "truth." Even when an observation or interpretation arises that is contradictory to Augusto's dominant story, he merely assimilates or annuls its significance. He manages to convert any possible allies of Mariana into his own "best friends" who end up functioning as spies or police for him. In order to be able to describe the truth about Mariana, we have to get away from that dominant illusion of unity that either doesn't accept different perspectives or subsumes them so that they are lost and forgotten.

When we return to the fictitious Mariana, the "true" Mariana of our study, it is interesting to note the techniques of verisimilitude that are used in forming her character. The memories of her which the narrators present to us contain descriptions of objects, of fragments of conversations and personal observations; all recourses of traditional realism. The experience that we as readers have of constructing in our imaginations a coherent identity for Mariana from the fragments of "evidence" in the text is not very different from our experience in reality. Wallace Martin shows that, although fictitious characters might be purely imaginary constructs without any apparent relation to reality, our knowledge of them is formed in a manner similar to the experience we have with real people.

Yet the difference between fact and fiction is reduced when we consider the ways in which we put together our knowledge of people who exist. Fiction is like gossip. I hear verbal reports of the traits and acts of a person who circulates at the edge of my acquaintance. These I piece together with bits of personal observation. From all such fragments, I project a whole: what kind of person is she? A character in fiction or the character of a person in fact is a conjectural configuration. Often I can't quite make them out; they are neither flat nor round but three-dimensional polygons with some points undefined.[84]

Even the mimetic intention of literary realism, symbolized perhaps by the many references to photographs in the novel, comes
to us diluted and transformed by the perspectives of the narrators.
Vicente, when he is separated from Mariana, clings to the images
of her that he has in his photographs. "The miniature Marianas
of the photos had turned into real beings and some of them would
look at me sadly, while others would flash me happy bright smiles.
I spent long moments deciphering them. . . ." (82).[85] The photographs, certainly "realistic" reproductions of her, are no more
real nor less enigmatic for Vicente than the image of her that he
holds in his memory. By the end of the first part of the book,
Vicente realizes that he has lost Mariana and that she will no
longer be part of his life. He looks at his photos and sees the
images of Mariana begin to fade away (122). "Time erases everything," says Gabrielle on one occasion (247).[86] Mariana herself
seems to understand intuitively the fleeting nature of life. Like
the great sixteenth-century poet, she contemplates the river and
says: "It's slipping away from us. . . ." (286). "It will always slip
away. . . ." (294).[87] With the passing of time even the mimetic reproduction of a photograph fades and becomes distorted. Memories vanish as they lose their importance for the one who is
remembering. "If you leave, I will die," Mariana says to Vicente.
(81).[88] With this statement of double meaning Mariana points
ironically to her purely verbal existence. If Vicente (the narrator)
leaves, Mariana disappears, given that her existence (in the text)
depends entirely on his memories of her. And, as always, if the
reader leaves she in effect "dies" until another reader comes along
to resuscitate her.

The "fictitious" nature of fiction can be defined, according to
Barbara Herrnstein Smith, not by the irreality of the content of
the work (the characters, objects, events to which it alludes), but
rather in the irreality of the allusions themselves.[89] The lack of
existence or the falseness of things represented is not pertinent
to the definition of fiction, adds Martin. "By mutual agreement
of writer and reader, the language [in fiction] means just what it
usually means, except that in a peculiar sense it is empty, hollow,
void."[90]

This sense of the void behind fiction brings us back to the
problem of the identity of Mariana as the absent center of the
text. If the meaning of the work is not a fixed referent behind
the words but only an imaginative construct of language, then
fictions runs the risk of becoming lost in total relativity. A work
open to infinite possibilities of interpretation lends itself to free

exploitation and loses its autonomous identity. The text becomes a mere blank screen for the projection of everyone's favorite theories. This is what happens to Mariana, as Gabrielle tells us:

> I became a frequent visitor to Mariana's drawing room, where they fabricated literary, philosophical, sexual and sociological theories. Augusto would choose his wife to ilustrate the themes. In the presence of the girl they would discuss her education, her self-destructive tendencies, her sexual frigidity, her latent lesbianism, etc. . . . (140)[91]

These interpretations of Mariana's character, even when they were expressed in her presence, reveal more about the interests and imagination of the others than any reality about Mariana's life.

The treatment of Mariana as a text subject to the interpretations of others does not end with the application of theories. At times they try to "literally" turn her into a work of fiction. Her friend Gabrielle decides to write a novel about Mariana. She does it in order to help her, to give her an escape from her terrible life. "I remembered that nature imitates art and I decided to give her a happy ending, that would change her destiny." Like a detective, Gabrielle dedicates herself to solve through fiction the terrible enigma of Mariana's life. "I shut myself in to write, my character was complex, her life an inexplicable labyrinth, but I would lead her through that dark and treacherous ground to an unexpectedly luminous exit. It was the least I could do for poor Mariana" (209).[92]

Others try to "fictionalize" her in order to turn her into an object without a will of her own. Barnaby is Mariana's lover but he is also her oppressor and one of Augusto's co-conspirators. He, too, decides to write a novel about Mariana, or rather, he wants to *turn her into a novel*. Gabrielle relates that the situation had evolved to such a state that her friend's name "was an unpronounceable name. Only Barnaby dared to refer to her by her name and he published a book titled *Mariana*. The novel was a success among his friends, although the heroine was not at all sympathetic" (276).[93] Even though Barnaby's work is pure fiction as far as the "true" story of Mariana, in the public dominion of his power, his word is law. The fiction of those who rule can always overpower any pale truth. Barnaby utters and defines Mariana's name with the title of his novel. The signifier "Mariana" has two signifieds: the real person and the fictional story about her. For him, the woman and the novel are the same thing.

Although the examples we have examined are of deliberate attempts to create fiction (in the sense of falsification and lies), this danger exists on a more profound level of writing. Echevarría expresses this basic problem for the writer. "How can I reveal the other in my writing without turning him into literature and thereby falsifying him? By what means, in other words, can I become disentangled from writing to produce a sincere and authentic account of the other and of myself?"[94] Is writing itself a deception, a lie? If we accept the possibility of the fundamental deception of all writing, what can we say then about fiction? According to John Searle, fiction is a kind of honest deception. "Fiction is much more sophisticated than lying. To someone who did not understand the separate conventions of fiction it would seem that fiction is merely lying."[95] Wallace Martin adds that "fiction (pretending without intent to deceive) is, then, the child of lying, not the father of lies, as Plato said."[96] Perhaps this form of admitted pretending has a special access to the truth.

At times the truth is so terrible that we don't want to recognize it. Mariana complains to Gabrielle of this. "People would sooner believe a lie than the truth. If I lied to you right now you would believe me" (164).[97] Vicente senses Mariana's own fear of the truth. "She was hiding a truth that she didn't want to confess perhaps even to herself" (156).[98] And finally, André, who does not want to accept Mariana's tragic destiny, has to recognize the inescapable truth of her death. "There in the cemetery, in front of the abandoned grave of Mariana and Natalia, I learned that the truth is always terrible and that to know it destroys us" (352).[99] Frank Kermode suggests that fiction is necessary, that we create fictions in order to make some sense out of the chaos of our existence and to console ourselves.[100] Kermode examines the existentialist philosophy of Sartre (especially in his novel *La Nausée*) and the terror of the inescapable freedom of the human being. It is not a liberation of the constrictions of falsehood and lies, but rather being abandoned without consolation. For that reason we need art. In life "all ways are barred and nevertheless we must act. So we try to change the world; that is to live *as if* the relations between things and their potentialities were governed not by deterministic processes but by magic."[101] The function of art is then "to humanize the world's contingency ('the utter shapelessness and the utter inhumanity') by representing it—giving it form . . . the 'as if'."[102] Robert Alter also addresses this important role of fiction:

When things fall apart, ontologically and historically, where everything is "worn away, age after age", there are moments when artifice will seem not a reflection on or transformation of reality, but the only reality that one can count on, that one can humanly grasp. "No one is anything," unless artful consciousness makes him something, and even that identity is a moment suspended between twin eternities of dissolution.[103]

The vision of art as a human refuge, another reality, beautiful and coherent, is a leitmotiv of *Testimonios sobre Mariana*. When Gabrielle decides to write her novel about Mariana, she conceives it as "an entirety, a magic work, a masterpiece" (209–10).[104] She hopes to change the sad reality of her friend. For Mariana, art and above all ballet have always been very important. It is not just a beautiful diversion, an escape from crude reality; it is the secret center of her being, the expression of the identity she has lost. On marrying Augusto, Mariana finds herself forced to sacrifice her art. He forbids her to dance anymore. She tries to maintain her identity and her love of ballet by cultivating it in her daughter, Natalia. In this way Mariana manages, by means of art, to transcend the oppression of life, transmitting her dreams from one generation to another. Gabrielle recognizes that ballet has special importance for Mariana to be able to resist the oppressive power of her husband. "Ballet was the only space where marvelous things happened and I understood Mariana and Natalia's infinite sorrow when they were brutally torn from those lunar landscapes. . ." (280).[105] When Mariana and Natalia disappear mysteriously, we are given clues and speculations that they might have hidden in the theater. It seems that some theater people have helped them to escape. They vanish as if they had passed to another invisible dimension.

What relation does this other dimension of art have with the historical reality we live daily? Does it exist on a parallel but separate plane or is there some more direct contact between art and reality? Robert Weimann points out the "new and complex relationships between art and reality as well as between the individual and society."[106] Art is not only a product of our culture but also a "producer" of that culture. "By relating the activities of writing and those of reading to some comprehensive social context, we can view literature as both the (objective) product and the (subjective) 'producer' of a culture."[107] "Literature is in itself an act of history" says Richard Poirier, "and not a reflection of the history put together by historians; it can give us while we read a consciousness of life just as 'real' as any accredited to daily living."[108] Art has a social function which influences and is influenced by its aesthetic form. Weimann bases his theory of the (aesthetic) structure and the function of literature on a process which he calls *Aneignung*. This term is defined as the imaginative appropriation of the world and the nature of the human being in it.[109]

> By personalizing the social and by socializing the individual, art itself recreates the "I" in an ensemble that is larger than the self. The resulting imaginative experience of unity and contradiction is unique; precisely because its function is valuable, it cannot be replaced by another form of human activity. Thus, art was, and is, part of the more comprehensive dialectic by which the appropriation of objectivity and the realization of subjectivity are mutually intertwined. . . . Art . . . is both a force in history and a source of value that can survive the changing conditions it originally reflected.[110]

This process of appropriation is based on a dialectic between the significance of a work in its inception and the meaning it has for a reader. Both the creation and the reception of the work occur in complex socio-historical contexts, realities that must be considered for a complete interpretation of the work.[111] The literary work is also an historical document that can be studied as such. The Brazilian critic Luiz Costa Lima discusses the documental value of all writing. "There is . . . a documentary inevitability in everything that is touched by the human eye."[112] If we are not able to know the truth about Mariana, (even as historical Mariana), when we study the "document" we learn a lot about the times and society in which she lived. Even if it has to do with a totally invented world, we learn something about the world of the inventor and about our own reality while interpreting the work. At any rate, Mariana has left many tracks.

There are as many interpretations among Mariana's friends and enemies about her final fate as there are relationships with her. When she disappears, they try to imagine her situation. Augusto says that she has escaped to New York and is part of a plot to threaten his life and work (275–76). A friend thinks that he has seen Mariana begging at the doors of the Vienna Opera (282). Other friends who "know Mariana's secret" believe they see her dancing with the Bolshoi Ballet.

> Enchanted in our seats we would contemplate the beauty before us and we would look for our friends separated by magic. Who had

snatched from them that ephemeral and luminous destiny? No one!
Now that so many years have passed, I can confess that nobody
dragged them from the theater where they were hiding. The truth
and the only truth is that almost every night we would see them on
stage, hidden among the white figures of the dance chorus. At times
they would send us signals from the stage. (280)[113]

If Mariana is giving us signals from the stage (or from the
page), how should we interpret her gesture? Where is that theater
in which Mariana has hidden only to appear repeatedly in front
of her friends? Lima proposes the image of a *teatro mental* (mental
theater) as a metaphor for fictive discourse.

> a metaphor not merely approximate, since it has the advantage of not
> implying, as happens with the normal use of the term "fiction", a
> pure and drastic separation from the plane of reality. Instead of being
> nullified, the plane of reality works its way in and penetrates the fic-
> tional game, as a kind of desired echo of itself.[114]

This "mental theater" occurs in the imagination of each reader
and is re-created with each reading. The void behind the fiction
is like a mirror which reflects the image of the reader and the
reality outside which surrounds that reader. According to Martin again,

> in fiction, we must construct the schematic "reality" to which the words
> refer by imagining it, rather than filling in missing details by taking
> another look at the world or at other sources of information. Here
> the individuality of the reader comes into play, and the writer has
> provided for it in the gaps and blanks that exist in the text.[115]

Let's examine further this role of the reader in the production
of the work. The reader, like Mariana, is outside of the work but
at the same time forms part of its structure. First, the structure
of the work presupposes an implied reader, a passive presence
that listens to the three testimonies. As we have noted before,
there is no narrator or exterior frame to give unity to the three
parts except the presence of an implied reader who acts as a judge
or confessor. If Mariana is the thematic "absent center" of the
work, the reader is the structural one. In the theory of Wolfgang
Iser, the implied reader is part of the structure of any work of
fiction. The role of the reader is one of integrating the different
perspectives represented in the implied author, the characters,
and the plot. The narration (of any literary work) progresses like

a negation of partial or inadequate ways of understanding the world, leaving in its wake a variety of hypothetical perspectives that change according to the participation of the reader.[116]

Garro's novel, like any literary work, requires an active reader who in the process of reading brings the story to life. The work cannot "live" without this basic activity of reception. The active reader must also participate unconsciously in the "re-production" of the work with his or her personal and cultural interpretations. But this work of Garro's requires even more from the reader. In the text written on the pages there appear three testimonies as three independent stories which must be read linearly, one after the other. They cannot simply be added one to the other in a chronological chain of events. It is in the mind of the reader (the *teatro mental* that Lima suggests) where the linear progression of the pages of the text take on another dimension. The second story is superimposed on the first during the process of reading. The reader already has prejudices about the "case" and has to reinterpret the images and impressions of the first testimony according to the new perspectives of the second. Thus, in spite of the contradictions, the charcters become more fleshed out, more alive. They begin to escape from the confines of the page. The same thing happens with the third part. By the time we get to the third testimony, the work constructed in the mind of the reader almost slips away, as Mariana does, to another dimension.

In this way the active reader really does end up playing two roles. As the subject-agent he or she is the one who initiates the act of reading. The reader also participates as reader-protagonist of the work. Much like all the characters of *Testimonios sobre Mariana,* the reader is intensely affected by the question about Mariana's identity. This emotional experience is the motivating force of the story. In addition to the role of subject-agent of the work, the reader-protgonist suffers as an object "subject to" the same experience as the characters. In the style of a Kafka or Borges short story, the reader wanders helplessly through the labyrinthian world of Mariana. This reader-protagonist, like Mariana, has to find his or her own way out in order to solve the case. The motivation is the desire to know the truth and to find Mariana.

"Only reading loves the work, entertains with it a relationship of desire," says Roland Barthes. "To read is to desire the work, to want to be the work, to refuse to echo the work using any discourse other than that of the work."[117] The third testimony about Mariana is that of André, who devotes himself to his experience with her with the same kind of desire as the avid reader described by Barthes. Although André is never able to consummate his love for Mariana, he sees his life always tied to hers. "I was tied to her since that distant encounter in my cousin Bertrand's living room. I thought that logic wouldn't be enough to explain my mysterious ties to Mariana" (342).[118] André finds himself captivated by her and he can't help but love her. He tries to explain his experience, which turns out to be somewhat parallel to that of the reader of the book. "Mariana's triumph over me resided in her ambiguity and her capacity to sadden us and then disappear without a trace" (349).[119]

One night Mariana appears mysteriously in André's house, dressed all in white. She needs to know if he loves her, if she is truly loved. His affirmative response seems to transform her. Mariana takes refuge in André's love and he ends up identifying totally with her. "Now Mariana formed a part of me, we were cast of the same stone, of the same blood, and we were both part of the same picture" (339).[120] Later on André discovers that in realty Mariana had committed suicide by throwing herself out of a fourth-floor window several years before her visit to him. In the meantime she continued locked in a state of eternal repetition of her "sin." Only André's love can save her from "falling every night. . ." (353).[121]

André identifies so closely with Mariana that he doesn't realize that she already belongs to the past and will remain there forever. But on discovering the terrible truth of her life and death, André saves her from permanent isolation in the past. Mariana had told him once that "destruction is executed in secret. Everything terrible happens that way, in secret" (327).[122] The work of art has to confront that terrible secret truth, thus saving it (her) from the "daily bloody vertigo." (353).[123] The last time André sees Mariana, she tells him, "Since you love me and you don't want me to leave, I will always be with you" (341).[124] Like every reader who "loves" the text, André resuscitates Mariana and returns her to the flow of time. Marc Bloch said that "the past is, by definition, a datum which nothing in the future will change. But the knowledge of the past is something progressive which is constantly transforming and perfecting itself."[125] André realizes that, although Mariana is dead, the truth about her is yet to be born.

At that moment I knew that she would not come to find me, that I was the one that should find her. "And I will find her!" I promised myself, even though I might have to search for her in the labyrinth of time, in the cities of which only confusing traces remain or for

which men don't yet sense their future existence and through which
Mariana would pass followed by my footsteps. (342)[126]

Like André, we cannot change the past, but we can continue
searching for the truth about it in the labyrinth of time and in
the stories (histories) that we read and write.

4

José Emilio Pacheco: The Ethics of Writing

Years ago, in Leipzig, a woman read his palm and looking into
his eyes she declared:—You will die far away.[1]

José Emilio Pacheco has long been renowned as a poet, both in
Mexico and internationally. In recent years his short stories and
novels have also attracted attention and acclaim. His first novel,
Morirás lejos, was published in 1967, but only toward the end of
the 1970s did it begin to receive the attention it deserves. It is
an innovative and provocative work which examines the ethics of
writing while experimenting with the techniques of art and the
limits of the genre. It poses questions about the importance of
history for the present and the relationship of literature to our
understanding of the past and thus our responsibility to the
future.

The influence of Pacheco the poet can be seen clearly in the
composition of this novel. In the collage style that we have seen
in Poniatowska's *La noche de Tlatelolco, Morirás lejos* is composed of
fragments of texts, many of them of poetic nature. The poetic
tone and structure of the work reflect a tendency which Ann
Duncan identifies as one of the special characteristics of modern
experimental fiction, that is, "the erosion of the distinctions between prose and poetry, and the emergence of narratives created
through patterns of suggestion rather than by developing an ar-
gument—narratives that are self-sufficient works of art."[2]

There have been several important studies of *Morirás lejos* which
have been published recently. In 1979, Yvette Jiménez de Báez
and her collaborators published, as a result of the investigations
of a seminar on Mexican narrative, *Ficción e historia: la narrativa
de José Emilio Pacheco.*[3] This work presents a structuralist analysis
of *Morirás lejos* as well as many of Pacheco's short stories. It is a

careful work, of scientific method, which offers numerous interesting observations about many aspects of Pacheco's writing. They
open their discussion of *Morirás lejos* with the following comment:

> The treatment of the space and time which define the structure of this
> novel, can only be understood in its dynamism: *Morirás lejos* unfolds by
> means of a continual undoing and remaking, thereby making explicit
> its own process of production. In a sort of "model for assembly", the
> author opens the novel, through a limited series of materials, to the
> active participation of the reader.[4]

In spite of its utility as a reference book, above all for its socio-
critical perspective, this study suffers from a lack of coherence
which is tedious to read in its totality.

Another more recent study on Pacheco can be found in Duncan's inciteful book, *Voices, Visions and a New Reality: Mexican Fiction
Since 1970.*[5] She offers an excellent analysis of *Morirás lejos*, focusing on the moral aspect of the work. For Duncan, Pacheco is one
of the most outstanding writers in Mexico today and she considers
Morirás lejos to be his most important prose work.[6] In a summary
of the general merit of this experimental novel, Duncan comments:

> [*Morirás lejos*] is a text that explores the possibilities of literature, not
> just for their own sake, but in order to expose the ways in which
> narration distorts truth. So the book paradoxically undermines its
> own function and form, revealing as of secondary importance what
> at first seems to be its *raison d'être*. It is in this way more truly revolu-
> tionary than any recent techniques, widening their scope, redirecting
> the questions they raise, and thus combining the role of serious docu-
> mentary writing with that of art, whose form is its own justification.[7]

Carlos Fuentes comments, on the back cover of the third edition
(1980) of *Morirás lejos:* "Pacheco reverses the structures to the
world of change; here history was not: rather it is being, it is a
process incarnated in the personal and accidental speech of that
faceless narrator, whose discourse recovers the unchangeable syn-
chrony and converts it into diachronic plasticity, in an event of
words."[8] Let's enter now into that "history in process."

The story of the novel deals with an instant in the present, not
in motion but about to happen. We witness the gesture of an
anonymous figure who looks out between the Venetian blinds of
a window to observe an unknown man sitting on a bench in the
plaza reading a newspaper. We don't know the identity of the man

who is observing from the window (his name is M, an intentionally anonymous and dehumanized name, perhaps like Kafka's Joseph K) nor of the man being observed (called "Someone" by one of the narrators). We know very little about them, but it is enough for the conjecture of many, perhaps infinite possible versions of a story. As a possible narrator-implied author says, "There are only a very few authentic facts that can be useable to precipitate one among the thousand potential outcomes" (31).[9] But among the many seemingly unconnected images and speculations in the different hypothetical versions, there seem to resurface suggestions of M's past as a Nazi persecutor and his paranoia about being pursued by the man reading the newspaper. Alternating with these fragments of possible versions of a present about to happen, there are some sequences of documents that narrate events of the past; namely, the destruction of Jerusalem by the Romans and the extermination of the Jews in the Nazi concentration camps. The whole novel revolves around a paralyzed moment in a plaza in Mexico City. It is a moment just like any other, in which these two anonymous figures possibly exist or are going to exist, and we speculate on their relationship with the past; their past, our past, and the future which will soon become past. All of the possible actualizations of this instant are synchronized with past events by means of associations and coincidences of historical documents (some real and others simulated) as well as literary inventions. The fragmented narrative structure, which creates a counterpoint between the present and the past, between "historical" and "current" documents, between testimony and conjecture, gives the impression at first glance of a chaotic text. But little by little the logical order of the novel becomes clear.

The fragmented structure of this novel of diverse components reflects a postmodern vision of reality, and even of history. The traditional form of the novel no longer suffices to express the historical or aesthetic experience of contemporary writers. For these writers, history is not conceived of as a linear progression of events.[10] Writers like Pacheco have tried to free themselves from the limitations (philosophical, ideological, and graphic) of literary conventions, making use of varied forms and styles and of multiple narrative perspectives to create their writing.[11] There is no longer *one* story but many stories chosen from the infinite possible perspectives. Each story, whether real or invented, is constructed of the threads of many other stories.

For Pacheco, the artistic innovations do not exonerate the writer from a coherent moral position with regard to the complex reality in which we live. His interest in writing is not the result of a purely "narcissistic" attitude, that is, the fascination of the text for its own form and creation.[12] In Pacheco's writing it is more important to show how when we write we choose among the infinite possibilities of fiction certain structures and styles which influence our conception of reality. The fundamental theme of *Morirás lejos* is, according to John Brushwood,

> the invention of reality. It has to do with a narration which constantly confuses subject and object, so that one can't tell, for example, which of the characters is the pursued and which the pursuer. The (unstable) identity changes according to the powers of the imagination. Such invention occurs not only on the primary narrative level but also in the form of narration within the principal narration. It is important to clarify that the reading of this novel does not produce memories of characters but rather the possibilities of fiction.[13]

Pacheco recognizes the power and the dangers of communication itself, and therefore the responsibility of art. He doesn't offer us an already constructed image of reality. Rather he situates us as writers before the possible ingredients of such an image. From there we must experience, as reader-writers, the serious responsibility of the creative act. Duncan explains how Pacheco utilizes a collage of styles and narrative points of view to illustrate the ways in which we form opinions. She shows that the hypothetical conjectures about the identity of M are repeated later on in the text using the historical past tense, which, according to Duncan, relates them stylistically to the supposed documents of the novel, based on known events. Although there is no evidence offered to prove the suspicions created by this association, and the narration has exhorted us to question critically the truth of any statement, the case for the condemnation of M as an ex-Nazi is constructed little by little through suggestion and the skillful manipulation of language.[14]

> And yet, even while we admit that there are no real grounds for attributing a Nazi past to M, our irrational readiness to do so is considerable because we have been insidiously influenced both by the sheer repetition of an idea and by the novel's style, just as the crowds in the war were swayed by the oratory of their leaders.[15]

This very short novel (only 154 pages long)[16] takes on a whole ethics of writing as it imitates and furthers the literary innovations of its time. By means of poetic fragments and suggestive commentary, Pacheco presents the dilemmas which all writers must confront. Let's examine in detail a small poetic fragment found in the text of *Morirás lejos* which seems to embody a number of these dilemmas:

> but who is M
> who am I
> who is talking to me
> who is telling me this story
> to whom am I telling it
>
> (142)[17]

"but who is M?" The identity of M is a mystery that is central to the theme of this work, but for the moment we'll just discuss it in general terms. Writers must always decide what and about whom they are going to write. The identity of the characters is important and even more so the purpose they will serve in the story. In this aspect Pacheco, like other Mexican writers, is noted for the universal character of his work. In *Morirás lejos* there are no fixed characters nor a specific plot, only archetypal silhouettes in hypothetical relationships. Luis Leal writes in his essay on new Mexican novelists, "The new narrative is characterized more by the interest in universal themes and the treatment of issues unattached to Mexican social reality."[18] He cites Carlos Fuentes, who pointed to *Morirás lejos* as an example of the new cosmopolitanism in the Hispanic American novel.[19] This work associates in allegorical form universal questions about human life with the moral and social context of contemporary Mexico. It is a novel of synchronization between past and present, history and fiction, social responsibility and artistic experimentation. It was written *in* Mexico, but it is not limited to the national or contemporary. As Leal points out, "The fact that the action [in *Morirás lejos*] takes place in Mexico City in the minds of the characters interests us not so much because it reflects the national scene, but because, in the process, it relates the city with the international environment, in space and time."[20] As a result the identity of M (and perhaps that of Mexico) is defined not so much by his individuality as by being a member of the human race and a citizen of the world.

"Who am I?" Whose "I" is speaking here? The author's? The narrator's? The reader's? The terrible responsibility which the existentialists felt to define their identity weighs on the artist when creating his art. "Who am I?" is a question the artist must ask: "And what do I want to say? What are my moral responsibilities as a writer, a Mexican, or a human being? What does the (hi)story of others have to do with my reality?" These are questions found both implicitly and explicitly in Pacheco's text. The man on the bench is, in one of the possible versions of the story, a worker who is unemployed and looking for work in the newspaper ads. The reader (of the novel) looks along with this shadow of a character (the reader of the newspaper) for some identity among the fragments of information. Pacheco reveals in his work not only the process of writing but also that of reading. With the lack of characters, narrator, or fixed plot, the reader (one of the possible readers) finds him or herself without direction in a labyrinth of infinite possibilities. Thus it is possible that the reader will ask: "Who am I?" and "With whom can I identify in this book?" Besides being obligated to participate actively in the work, the reader has to consider some difficult moral questions and even examine his or her own conscience.

"Who is talking to me?" Who is going to inspire the writer? To what reality will he respond? And as an historian, the writer must select what history (about whom) to write, what voices will be allowed to speak. Pacheco carries on a dialogue with his own internal critics in the book and confronts objections such as, "This is no longer interesting—We have read it a million times," or "Why don't you write about the Indians of Mexico?" (59)[21] and many others which criticize the fact that this work does not deal with contemporary reality nor does it examine the history of Mexico. The author's answer seems to be that it doesn't matter if we write about historical or contemporary crimes, distant crimes, or ones close to home "because the hate is the same, the contempt is still there, the ambition is identical, the dream of planetary conquest continues without variation" (62).[22] At the same time he invites us to add other examples from our experience, suggesting names such as Da Nang and Quang Ngai (62).[23]

"Who is telling me this story?" Another problem for the writer has to do with the perspective and style of the narration. Who will narrate the story? And how will it be narrated? From what perspective, with what prejudices, what style? In *Morirás lejos* this question is presented directly in the text ("Who is telling us the story of the persecution of M?")(116),[24] as though expressing a probable complaint from a possible reader of the book. The identity of the narrator is so elusive that at times it seems that there are multiple narrators and at other times there appear to be none at all. Duncan elaborates on the situation.

Our attention is repeatedly drawn to the problem of discovering the narrator's identity, but we are invariably thwarted in this effort by the constant change in narrative voice. These are part of the many shifts of register in which Pacheco reminds his readers that there are countless ways in which the story could be told, as well as innumerable variations in the story itself, and that we should trust apparently direct statements no more than obviously enigmatic ones.[25]

And as Duncan shows throughout her whole discussion of Pacheco's work, this play with perspective and style is not only for the sake of artistic experimentation, but also in order to reveal the limitations and distortions of all communication, whether document or fiction.

"To whom am I telling it?" And finally, of interest is the identity of the reader of a text; not only an individual reader (who always participates in the interpretation of a story), but also the general audience. To whom is this work directed? With whom does the author identify? Is there a social message or is it only experimentation with technique and genre? We have already referred to the active participation that is required of any reader to be able to interpret this novel. According to Duncan again:

> *Morirás lejos* is an invitation to participate in an open-ended experiment. It is not, however, an experiment contained within the text; we are urged to complete the process initiated by the author . . . so that we may think anew about events that have a verifiable existence beyond the fiction. . . . This encouragement to seek a truth beyond the text is diametrically opposed to the moral vacuum so elaborately reflected in ludic literature.[26]

With this introduction to the problematics of writing, we have seen that the problems of artistic expression are for Pacheco inextricably associated with moral questions. Let's examine more carefully this relationship.

If we go to the heart of the problematics of writing presented in *Morirás lejos,* we are confronted with the limitations of language itself. An important symbolic myth in the history of languages is that of the Tower of Babel of the Old Testament. According to the biblical story, man wanted to construct a tower so high that it would reach Heaven. As a response to such a presumptuous aspiration, God punished him, dispersing people over all the land and making them speak in different tongues so that they would no longer be able to understand each other. The word lost its unique and privileged relationship with its referent. This myth is alluded to in *Morirás lejos:* "when they had the same words, before being scattered throughout the city and not understanding the familiar speech of others" (21).[27] The motif of the Tower of Babel (and of the tower in general) reappears throughout the novel. It might be a monument to a vision, a failed attempt to reach an impossible height.[28] A word is also only a symbol which, like the tower, points toward its original referent. And like a painting or any other inscription, a word is limited to approximations, suggestions, interpretations. As one of the novel's narrators muses, "Even though, shadows of things, echoes of deeds, words are illusions, attempts not to express but to suggest what happened in the [concentration] camps" (89).[29] The inert marks on the page which are the signs of writing cannot capture the fluid existence of life. But, on the other hand, there is no other option. We have to try to record and remember our experience so that it won't have to be repeated infinitely. Writing should be a testimony against forgetting, against the repetition of atrocities and injustices. The details are not important. The geographic, temporal, or social contexts may vary; there can be a thousand versions and conclusions to the story, but the important thing is the human testimony which must be given. As it is explained in one of the possible outcomes of *Morirás lejos,* "There is only the great crime—and everything else: paper feverishly stained so that all of that (if someone remembers it; if someone, besides those who lived it, remember it) won't be forgotten" (151).[30]

The function of writing is not just to record and remember an experience but also in a sense to re-produce it. Writing, like painting, also interprets and makes live again in the mind of the reader or viewer a moment of a past reality. From time to time in Pacheco's novel, an apparently all-seeing lens allows us to see with greater certainty the "authentic facts" of the story being narrated. We see that on the wall of M's apartment there hangs a reproduction of the painting, *The Tower of Babel,* by Pieter Bruegel. The painting is a reproduction of the myth of the Tower of Babel, first recorded in the biblical text. It is also a kind of memory of the historical moment in which Bruegel was painting. Although the cheap copy which hangs in M's room is only a re-reproduction, it does at any rate bring to life for M, the biblical myth and the historical time of Bruegel. The narrator of Pacheco's text suggests several interpretations and considerations with respect to the painting which are also associated with the life of M and with the focal moment of the story. "Perhaps it is an unconscious form of remembering the [concentration] camps. There were many languages spoken there and the majority of their inhabitants were in turn scattered over the Earth. Or perhaps it is a metaphor to signify that the Third Reich tried to erect on the whole planet the tower of a millenary empire" (113–14).[31] "It's similar to the ruins of the Reichstag but also to the cadaver of the Roman Coliseum. It is a spectacular warning about the impossibility of the empire, a sepulchral mound for all the tyrants of the world" (115).[32] And also:

> With all this, we must not forget another aspect: many of Bruegel's paintings are political painting: testimonies, protests against the Inquisition in Flanders. Or rather, much like what happens in M's life [they are], the paralysis of an imminent moment. The six or eight hundred figures [of the painting] can stay forever fixed and inert in their immobility—or they can begin to move at any moment. (115)[33]

In other words, every work has its history and its original context, but it also opens itself to infinite applications and meanings in a future moment about to become present. Writing, like painting, is a form of static preservation of a moment. The moment is preserved as part of the "past," frozen in the written words which "begin to move" in the present potentiality of each reading. That chain of images and reproductions, of associations and reminiscences which we have been contemplating, comes to rest finally in the letters on the page of Pacheco's text, which is paradoxically where they originated and also where they ultimately dissolve.

The tower and the well are some of the other few "authentic facts" of our imminent scene and its thousand versions. In that contemporary plaza in Mexico, "The tower of the well or the well in the form of a tower distantly evokes the image painted" [of the Tower of Babel](114)[34] along with all the other towers of the history of humanity. The tower with its phallic form of conquest covers a well, the counterpart of such monuments of power. In the well (which is, curiously, a feminine image; void, lack, wound) are found all of the sacrifices and victims of the ascent to power; the "horror which lies at the bottom of absolute power" (141).[35] And as an anonymous voice in the text perceives "The well which the tower covers must be very deep" (141).[36]

The tower in the plaza and the painting in M's room are objects which act as residual symbols of two series of reproductions, or remnants of a mythic repetition. Two myths, the Nordic myth of the Germanic epic poem and the biblical myth of the Tower of Babel, have influenced universal history as well as literature. The Nordic myth is based on the ancient Scandinavian and Germanic legends which gave form to the medieval epic of the *Nibelungenlied*.

Out of this tradition comes the German myth of the supremacy of the Aryan race. Yvette Jiménez de Báez, Dianna Morán and Edith Negrin indicate the relationship in history between Nazism and the German epic, the former which "functioned as one of the ideological reenforcements of Nazism in the Second World War."[37] Nazism would then be a type of reproduction of the Nordic myth in history as well as in Pacheco's work. In the "present" moment of the novel, in which M observes the man sitting on the bench, the reproduction of the Nordic myth arises from M's desire for the rebirth of Nazism. "Long years of confinement and anxiety because the Fourth Reich is still not setting fire to Europe and the wild geese fly at night, but they still are not enough, they lack the vigor of their heyday" (114).[38] So it is that M's desire, perhaps symbolized by the tower of the plaza in Mexico, is only a memory, a remote re-production of the myth.

We have seen earlier that the biblical myth also engenders a series of reproductions in history as well as in fiction. The myth of the Tower of Babel explains the origin of languages as a result of the failed attempt of men to reach Heaven. The painting by Bruegel is a reproduction of this myth which tries not only to represent the myth as it has come down to us through literary tradition, but also to capture the vision of the painter in the historical moment in which it was painted. It is an historical event in itself, an object of art produced by the painter Pieter Bruegel. In the text of *Morirás lejos*, it appears only as a cheap reproduction of the painting; that is to say, another re-reproduction, distanced from the "original" in time and space. But in the end, these two distant memories—M's desire and the cheap reproduction of the painting—come together on a plane even more remote from the origin of the myths: that is, in Pacheco's novel, in the materiality of a written text.

With this play of reproductions Pacheco's writing tries ironically to describe the indescribable, to say the unsayable. Even the most common and everyday experiences can be difficult to communicate in their specific individuality. But, for Pacheco, the atrocities that have been committed by human beings are veritably impossible to represent. Events like the Nazi persecution can be described with all the minute details, but you can never manage to capture the terrible experience of torture and suffering to which the Jewish people have been submitted. For this reason, Pacheco's text refers to "tortures that words cannot describe" (73) and "an anxiety which words will not be able to approximate" (86).[39] An authorial voice even invokes the participation of the reader in the impossible task of re-creating these horrifying scenes of persecution. "And add to these words of your own and others, others [words, stories] you have read, the photographs and documentaries you have seen. Try to reconstruct it all with your imagination and you will have an idea, barely approximate in its vagueness, of what all that was. It will be enough if the images torture you, if they don't ever leave you alone, and you feel horror, compassion, fear, shame" (152).[40] The description of the extermination of the Jews in the gas chambers reflects the limitations of language for communicating the horror. Here the text disintegrates with the violent shock of the act it describes. It is a language of loose fragments which float as if stunned or traumatized by trying to express the unthinkable.

> Then the confusion the shock the terror the search for air
> and the screams
>
> above all the screams
>
> the futile struggle to escape the places where the poisonous
> gas is spraying
>
> (85)[41]

At times, it is through an economy of words and graphic form that it manages to say the unsayable.

> Then Jurgen Stroop was able to inform Himmler:
> the
> ancient
>   Jewish
>   ghetto
>   of
>   Warsaw
>   ceased
>   to
>   exist
>
>   The
> number
>   of
>   Jews
>   executed
>   or
>   detained
>   climbs to 56,065.
>
> (64)[42]

In this example the words seem to wound the reader with their own physical forms. In the shape of daggers or streaks of lightning the words of power fall on their victims. It is almost as if these same simple words had caused the destruction to which they are referring, and they continue to injure whatever eye might read them. They remain on the page like an open wound or a reminder of the violent act and the instrument of aggression. In this way writing, or rather the graphics of writing, is able not only to represent an event, but also to give it life in the moment that a reader reads it.

The infinite possibilities of expression are limited not only by language in general, but by the particular systems of writing. Pacheco parodies this concept with his multiple versions which he names with different letters of the alphabet. He resorts to all the letters and when he gets to z he says: "End of the possible conjectures at this time: the hypotheses can go on forever. The alphabet doesn't go any farther. One could resort to compound letters, to pre-Phoenician signs or signs that preceded writing—similar to the inscriptions on the poplar tree or those which M traces with the nail of his left index finger on the plaster wall. . . ." And then the text makes fun of "the narrator" who "true to his monotonous ellipsis, to his way of passing the time and undoing the tension of an imminent moment, now proposes a system of related signs with the objective that *you* choose the one that you think is true" (66).[43]

The desire to search for a language to express another reality and create a new literature is an important characteristic of the literature of the "boom" and "postboom."[44] Pacheco gives us a parody of that tendency. Following the section we have just cited there appear other linguistic systems to name the many possibilities enumerated. The sequence is called "Totenbuch" (book of the dead) and it deals with the extermination of the Jews in Germany. The numbers of the possible versions of this sequence are written in German, reminiscent of the historical discourse presented about the Nazi era. There is also a sequence of numbers in Latin which corresponds to a scientific, biologic description of the possible sensations a human being might experience whose body had been frozen to wake up at some future time from a state of hibernation. This includes a discussion of the possible immortality of the human being; immortality "not in a figurative sense but in the physical sense which gives back its gravity to the word" (67).[45] More than mythical reproduction or a symbolic code, writing is the immortalization of a moment, a continuous process of awakening the past and preserving the present. The experiences, philosophies, and sensibilities of an era are "frozen" in writing, to awaken in a future context with new possibilities of meaning. The body (our hypothetical frozen human being) becomes a text for the future, and the written text becomes a body, an experimental time capsule which will outlive its author and original historical context.[46]

There are some images in *Morirás lejos* which seem to transcend the limitations of language and to maintain a more immediate contact with reality. Another of the few "authentic facts" that appear in the story about M is the smell of vinegar in the air, which is mentioned from the beginning of the book. ("Everything smells like vinegar")(5).[47] It is something which is presented not as one of the possible variations of actualization and association in the drama, but as something present and "real." The olfactory sense is fundamental to human existence and plays an important role in our memory. Although in the writing of the text we only have the words "smell of vinegar," merely linguistic signs for the olfactory experience, perhaps through the strong associations we have with that sense there remains a little of the original "essence" of the vinegar. It might be that vinegar is a symbol of the sourness of the empty and senseless life of a type like M. Or perhaps it represents the acerbic ambience that penetrates all who have been touched by violence, both victims and oppressors. "The smell of corruption tortured both besieged and besiegers" (27),[48] a voice tells us. In whatever form, the smell of vinegar is present in the work and functions as a sort of "real" referent which appears in (almost) all of the versions, a sharp reminder of the author's message. In only one of the textual fragments does this smell disappear. "But when the smell of vinegar disappears I lose the olfactory reference, my sense of composition and place is broken" (147).[49] On losing this anchor in reality, or at least in *a* reality, the words and their referential system begin to float aimlessly in a state of anarchy. "Because when the smell of vinegar disappears I lose the reference, I misplace my identity, I no longer know who I am among the characters I have presented underneath the poplar tree full of inscriptions. . ." (148).[50] The narrator, the fictitious author, the reader, we are all lost. But when we confront again the raw violence, a language in which signifier, signified, and referent are fused and confused, everything becomes clear for the narrator. In a scene in which the possible suicide of M is portrayed, the narrator orients himself again. "And everything comes back and is clarified; my sense of composition and place is restored, my momentary loss of identity, the meaning of my stay in the park, my doubt about who you were, with the descent of the smell of vinegar" (149).[51] The smell of vinegar with its symbolic value is always present in Pacheco's text. Through all the play of possibilities, the philosophical and artistic entanglement of the problematics of writing, this penetrating sensation communicates to us the bitter reality of a (hi)story we should not forget.

We have considered some problems and limitations of writing in general, whether it is historical or fictional narrative. Let's examine now the importance for Pacheco of the writing (and rewriting) of history and how this influences the creation of *Morirás lejos* and the story of M.

Part of the new consciousness of Latin America has been an obsession about the past, about origin and identity. The continent wants to define itself independently from European culture and the history of the Conquest. Traditional narrative tended to be linear, narrated by a single perspective. In history, the authoritative discourse of the historian dominated, and in fiction it was the presence of an author or a single narrative voice. In the literature of the sixties we see an attempt to found a new literature in order to rewrite the (hi)story of Latin America and redefine its identity. In *Morirás lejos,* as in many novels of the "postboom," this intention appears in the form of parody. It is not only a question of rewriting history, of breaking with the canonic model and replacing it with another for our times. In Pacheco's work, by shattering the model, we are left with a multiplication of texts and versions. When the original language is broken down in the myth of the Tower of Babel, the many languages and versions are spread over the land. The story becomes many stories with its subversions of the official (hi)story.

If history is the study of the past, it is in a sense a reading in reverse. We have to "read" from a present perspective the tracks which the passing of time has left for us. The more we progress in our task, the more we "regress" to the past. But history is also the past itself; the dynamic unfolding of events and relationships distanced from the present by the time that has transpired. And above all, history is the narration and interpretation of that past, not only in order to resuscitate it but also to understand better our present. The notion of a multifaceted and nonlinear history, however, causes problems for historiographical narration. The new narrative of Mexico, which we see exemplified in this work by Pacheco, makes use of recent literary innovations and creates new genres of writing. By means of the inventive freedom of fiction, Pacheco imitates in his narration the unfolding of history in reality. Through the accumulation of multiple testimonies, narrations, speculations, and possibilities,[52] he creates a representation of the past in a sense truer than the traditional narrations,[53] at the same time as he urges us to examine the present and our responsibility to the future. The literary technique of paralyzing a moment as if stopping the action of a film, gives us the advantage of being able to contemplate the present moment before it moves on to become past.

Historical events are repeated in time, with changes of details, and the possibilities of a moment about to happen are multiplied infinitely in space and then duplicated in different perspectives. For example, *Morirás lejos* multiplies diachronically the persecution of the Jews; first in the sequence called "Diáspora" with the history of the dispersion of the Jews and the destruction of Jerusalem by the Roman legions of Tito. Then, in the Spain of the "Reyes Católicos" and the Inquisition, the history of the persecution and expulsion of the Jews is repeated. In a possible version of the fictional story (possibly invented by the man sitting on the bench), a Jew flees from Salonica in Greece, just as many Sephardic Jews did in fifteenth-century Spain. In Germany during the Nazi era this story of dispersion and destruction is again repeated.

But it is not just a matter of a diachronic repetition of events. The possible versions of the same events are inexhaustible. There are as many different perspectives as there are narrators. And the narrations do not only serve to tell something unique. For example, a narrator of *Morirás lejos* comments on the intrinsic importance of narrations.

> The inoffensive and consoling utility of narrations: from the cavemen to the present, we all need them in some form. And M, as was said, would prefer to go on indefinitely playing with the possibilities of a very simple event: *A* is watching, sitting on the bench in a park, *B* observes from behind the blinds; he knows that from before Scheherazade fictions are a means of postponing the sentence of death. (42–43)[54]

Narration is a form of therapy or even exorcism.[55] It is a way to purge oneself of the shame and guilt of the past and the anxiety toward the future. All narration is a mixture of stories, of others' stories and one's own stories.[56] Individual history is a collage of the collective history of humanity, of specific events of the past, of individual experiences and perceptions, all integrated in a form appropriate to the personal moment. Consistent with this conception of narration and history, *Morirás lejos* is composed of a collage of fragments, some of diachronic progression and others of synchronic multiplication.

For example, some fragments narrate episodes of history.[57] In the sequence called "Diáspora" (dispersion) a Jew who functions as a witness or chronicler narrates the history of the sacking of Jerusalem. By means of a continuous attack, thousands of Jews are exterminated, and other thousands are dispersed throughout the land. The sequence titled "Grossaktion" (the Great Action) narrates the bombing of the Jewish ghetto of Warsaw by the Nazis. Jiménez de Báez, Morán and Negrin note the similarity of this battle with that of the Roman times in "Diáspora." "The development of this segment, as in Diáspora, follows the dynamic of the siege. It creates a functional and significant connection between the name Grossaktion, 'The Great Action' prepared by the Germans to destroy the ghetto and dominate the Jews, and the tactic of the siege to carry it out."[58] This segment not only repeats the history of the Jews in "Diáspora," but it does it incorporating the testimonies of several historical actors. It is a montage of historical documents narrated from differing perspectives.

The sequence of "Totenbuch" (Book of the Dead) has, as Jiménez de Báez, Morán, and Negrin note, an integrative function. "In it are gathered all the loose threads which identify M and Someone . . . [and] we follow the links between 'history' (past) and 'fiction' (present) about M which the text offers us."[59] Here the past and present of M are connected, as well as his internal (psychic) state and his external (physical) state and actions. M is seen as an observer but he is also being observed.

"Götterdämmerung" (The Twilight of the Gods) is rooted in the Germanic/Nordic myth of the Nibelungens. According to the myth, the good gods and the bad gods will fight and the whole universe will be destroyed (as in the biblical myth of Armageddon).[60] This section describes the downfall and death of Hitler and his dream of the Aryan superman. According to Jiménez de Báez, Morán, and Negrin, "From the mythic plane, . . . Hitler—already God, already historically absolute power—is the center of its development [of the section]."[61] Alternating with the segments of Hitler's final "story," we read fragments of the hypothetical thoughts of the mysterious M, who seems to identify with the Nazi vision. In this way the parallelism between Hitler's demise and M's destiny becomes obvious in the text. All of these sequences which narrate historical episodes alternate with the fragments of "Salónica" that represent perhaps a present moment in Mexico City with all its possible variations. The alternations and oppositions between past/present, history/fiction, and Europe/America, are confused in these segments. Even the name "Salónica" is not an expression which belongs only to the present. It alludes to the Salonica in Greece where the Jews of fifteenth-century Spain took refuge. In one of his possible identities, the man sitting on the bench is a playwright who writes a play called *Salónica* about the Spanish Inquisition and the expulsion of the Jews from Spain. Here, within the fictional frame of a drama written by an imagined hand (also within the fiction of Pacheco's novel), we find an historical account. The three Salónicas—the historical one in Greece, the one from the play, and the one from the sequence of fragments in a present moment in Mexico—are representative of the problematics of writing for Pacheco. This Salónica, which is now Mexico in Pacheco's fiction, is a repetition and an inversion of another time and another place. Writing is always a rewriting of history, while at the same time a writing conscious of itself.

In the last section, "Desenlace" (Conclusions), are presented the possible outcomes for the story of M. Jiménez de Báez, Morán, and Negrin discuss the importance of the opposition dominator/dominated which colors the whole work and the inversion of this which appears in the possible conclusions of *Morirás lejos*. M, once the pursuer, executioner, and torturer, becomes the pursued, the victim, and the tortured.[62] On crossing the ocean to the New World, the story has been inverted. In the present of the narration, it is the Nazi persecutor who is fleeing, instead of the persecuted Jew. And this time he is fleeing, not for the old Salonica of Greece (that is, fleeing from the present toward the classical world of Tradition) but rather for the new Salonica that is America. M is pursued by writers and writing, and also by the readers who won't let him rest in oblivion. And the writers and readers, by pursuing the crimes of the past, as accomplices and inheritors of that past, are pursued by their own consciences.

The problem of history leads, inevitably, to the question of identity, as we have seen in our discussion of *Testimonios sobre Mariana* by Elena Garro. Literature is not only a personal expression of the writer in his culture, but it also has a function at times prophetic. If we are able to understand who we are (an identity composed of the past) perhaps we will be able to see the direction of the future. And as a product of our experience, literature helps us to see who we are or might be. However, as we have seen in the discussion of the problematics of writing, the task for writers is not easy. They confront many dilemmas. What to write about? How to choose the theme? There is nothing "original" in literature, as Borges has said. One narrator of Pacheco's text answers the implied question about the origin of *Morirás lejos*. "All this, all this is an exercise so full of references to other books that to continue developing it is a waste of time" (38).[63] But the writing continues anyway because the time lost in this version can be recovered in another. Pacheco seems to affirm that one should write what one has to write. A writer has to exorcise the ghosts and demons of the past and write

> about a unique theme that concerns him and affects him as if he were guilty of having survived a distant war which nevertheless extended its terror through the black letters of the newspaper, photos, voices on the radio and above all cinematographic images seen with apparent impunity but whose violence left in us invisible signs, scars, stigmas. (58)[64]

The ghosts of the past appear in the advertisements of "El aviso oportuno" ("The Timely Alert") which the man sitting on the bench is reading; ads which sell the same insecticides that were used in the gas chambers to exterminate the Jews. "Farben of Mexico. Insecticides, rat poison, fumigants. German technology, immediate action." (7)[65] They are the traces of an inadvertent complicity. "The killings are repeated" (61).[66] The image of Nazism reverberates in the present-day Mexico in the allegorical form of the everyday war against the insects. But the real echo of Nazism reaches us from a more hidden place in society, in the secret racist desires of domination symbolized in the figure of M. Octavio Paz shows how any association with violence and persecution contaminates a whole society.

> Persecution begins against isolated groups—races, classes, dissidents, suspects—until it gradually reaches everyone. At first, a part of the population watches indifferently the extermination of other social groups or contributes to their persecution, as their internal hatred is stirred up. Everyone becomes an accomplice and the feeling of guilt extends to the whole society. Terror becomes generalized: there are no longer persecutors and persecuted. The persecutor then is very easily transformed into the persecuted.[67]

We cannot escape our guilt and responsibility; whether as M, persecuted by his paranoia, or "Someone," who is reading along with us "El aviso oportuno." Writing, for Pacheco, should be a "timely alert," that is, it should tell us what we need to know. And as is suggested by the name of the newspaper *(El universal)* which the man on the bench is reading, the alert is for all of us.

History is here and now and it is the (hi)story of M. But who is M? There are as many answers as there are versions of his story. "M among other things could be: evil, death, . . . murderer, macabre . . ." (131).[68] to name a few. M is many things, including "the letter which each of us carries imprinted on our hands" (131).[69] And like the woman who, after reading M's palm, says to him—"Morirás lejos" (you will die far away) (121), with these lines of his text Pacheco reads our palms as well.—You, reader, like M, could die far away. We are *all* M, possible ex-Nazis, or other accomplices in the atrocities of the world, or perhaps victims of those horrors. M is the world *[mundo]*, universal but also individual in an arbitrarily chosen moment "because what is narrated here is happening during several minutes on a Wednesday *[miércoles]*" (132).[70] M is also the emblem for Mexico, a possibility which does not appear among those enumerated in Pacheco's text. M is a character as well as a narrator; he narrates and is narrated; he observes and is observed. The look of the other defines us, said Sartre. And sometimes it is possible for that look to be, as for M, nothing more than a projection of our own paranoia, a phantom of our collective conscience.

The (hi)story of M is, then, the hi(story) of ourselves. The text offers us so few "authentic facts" that we are left with the infinite possibilities of speculation. As spectators of an allegorical and hypothetical drama, we find ourselves in a "specular" role where we see our own image projected onto the stage. And this image haunts us. Those who knew Mariana *(Testimonios sobre Mariana)* wanted to fix her identity with their own projections. But ironically, by being the object of the desires and designs of others, she also controlled them, and pursued them. In the same way, the author of a work by telling his story tries to define the other, the characters of his text. While he comments on reality and judges others, he knows that he will also be judged. By writing his work he reveals himself, he becomes an object of his own story,[71] the "author" that is imagined and "re-created" mentally by each reader of the work.[72] This fictitious author corresponds to the hypothetical reader ("Someone"?) which the writer imagines, and whom he addresses when creating the work. It is a process of mutual "re-creation" between supposedly opposing positions;

writers and readers, persecutors and persecuted, the American present and the European past.

There are so many narrative tricks in this novel that we never get to know the real M. It doesn't really matter, however, because this is "only literature." "Because everything in this story is unreal. Nothing happened as it is indicated. Events and places have been distorted by the attempt to touch the truth through a fiction, a lie. Everything is unreal, nothing happened as it is referred to here. But it was a feeble attempt to contribute so that the great crime will never be repeated" (152).[73] In the end, perhaps there is only one possible outcome of all those suggested in "Desenlace." "The sun doesn't go down. It insists on remaining (and it is already very late)" (152). "There are only the leaves glowing, permeated with acetic acid, and a spot of light shines deep down on the walls of the well" (153).[74] The moment moves on, still penetrated by the acid of reality. The man on the bench ("Someone"? the reader of this novel?) stops reading and goes away. But the writing has left for a moment a spot of light in the well. It has illuminated a shadow of our history, before yielding to the blank page of the future. And "the wind of the night whisks away 'El aviso oportuno', and the whole park vanishes under the mercurial lights which in this instant have just been turned on" (154).[75]

5

Federico Campbell: The Texture of History

He pretended he was classist so that they would believe that
he was in effect pretending to be classist in order to hide the
fact that down deep, underneath it all, he was viscerally and
inevitably classist.[1]

Federico Campbell, journalist, writer, and founder of the literary
press "La máquina de escribir" (The Typewriter) has been called
by Gustavo García "a 'rare bird' of the Mexican editorial environment . . . an attentive chronicler of literary and political happenings."[2] Until recently Campbell had published little in the literary
realm and his work had "passed almost unnoticed by the critics."[3]
In spite of the earlier scarcity of his production and the scant
attention he had attracted from the critics, his novel *Pretexta* is an
ingenious novel which should be included in the list of the most
important contemporary works of Mexican narrative.

Pretexta is a complex work, parodic on many levels and including strong social and political criticism. Although it is very
short (only 132 pages) and has the appearance of being unedited,
like a draft of a final text,[4] it in effect succeeds in creating a broad
vision of the literary and political world of the Mexican writer of
today.[5] His tone, alternating between bitter and playful, cynical
and passionate, colors a labyrinthian text in which authors and
characters become confused and history and fiction are skillfully interwoven.

In a sense this work is a testimony to an historical reality, the
same one as in Poniatowska's *La Noche de Tlatelolco*. It refers to
the era of the student movement of 1968 and the decade following. But instead of presenting that reality directly (in *Tlatelolco*
the events seem to narrate themselves), the historical references
in *Pretexta* are hidden among the fictitious layers of the text.
Everything is submerged in the subjectivity of the author (or

rather "the authors," who function on several levels of the work from Bruno and Ocaranza to Campbell himself), exemplifying, as in Pacheco's *Morirás lejos,* some of the ethical dilemmas that the contemporary writer faces. The universal philosophical and aesthetic questions of writing, seen in the historical context of the political repression and censorship of the press in Mexico, produce a moral crisis in the writer. The latter finds himself in a schizophrenic state in which on trying to write his story he runs into himself, not as author but as a mere character in another larger story, apparently controlled by a more powerful author. He discovers his own destiny as a servant of the State: *"criado"* in the double sense of the word, that is, educated to serve *(para servirle).*[6]

Pretexta is the story of the process of writing a story which is, in turn, a rewriting of history. Bruno Medina is a young journalist who has been contracted by the State to write a slanderous biography of the life of Professor Ocaranza, a former professor of his and a leader of the student movement of 1968, in order to dishonor and discredit him as a hero of the students and of others who might rebel against the repression of the government. He is supposed to go to the National Archive and, utilizing documents and historical data, "remake in another form the past of the former professor by means of the invention of tricks, falsification of data which in some way . . . partially overlapped with the real biography of the professor-journalist . . ." (10).[7] At the same time as we read the apocryphal biography being created about Ocaranza, we follow Bruno's experience as he works on it. We see how the latter becomes entangled in the story of the other, incorporating in his text facts and experiences from his own life.

But this is not the whole story. The more Bruno writes himself into the biography of Ocaranza, the more we know about him as a character and writer. Bruno is also the object of another investigation, since he is already entrapped in a great anonymous net of observation and counterobservation. Among the materials that are given to him in the archive for his task, Bruno finds a police report about his own activities and eventually decides to include it as well in his text. "His coherent attitude was to feign insanity and in all cases attribute the things written about him to the biographical past of Professor Ocaranza" (53).[8] We see Bruno editing his own life, observing himself while he writes his story. And beyond all this, at the same time another author is editing Bruno's story, perhaps projecting beyond that to Campbell's story as he writes *his* text.

In this way the work is structured like a "Chinese box," with stories inside of other stories, each one with its own author. The interior story is the one about Professor Ocaranza, who is the protagonist of the "biography" which Bruno is writing. Ocaranza is also a writer in his profession as journalist-editor and theater historian. In addition to being a literary character in the text that Bruno is composing, Ocaranza is, as Bruno confesses to the reader, also "in some autobiographical passages, the author of a good part of the document" (60).[9] In other words, in some parts of the work Bruno takes Ocaranza's own words, allowing him to be (without knowing it) the author of his own story. But Ocaranza, the "real" person, is also in part the author of Bruno's life, or at least an "authority" who influenced him greatly. In a sense he continues "writing" Bruno's fate, speaking to him internally as the voice of his own conscience.

On a second level we find instead of Bruno a postulated ficti- tious author, an anonymous presence which Bruno was supposed to create to give coherence to the work. "He had been contracted specifically for that reason: to provide uniformity of style, to be the emotion of a single man who would carry the narrative voice. That was what it was about, to construct an anonymous character who would give account of the events . . ." (14–15).[10] "He pre- tended that very probably the author of the document was an old man of very simple ideas about respectability and good manners" (127).[11] This mask permits Bruno a certain freedom to express without fear his own opinions. Behind the mask of the anonymous author Bruno is hiding, the "real" author of the document. This Bruno-writer, who like Ocaranza is a journalist and editor-histo- rian, ends up incorporating himself into his story about the other. He appears as a literary character in the story he is weaving and at the same time he is a "real" character in the police reports of those who watch over him while he fulfills his mission. In this way his literary role becomes confused with his "historical" role, which is also literary within another fictitious framework (that of Camp- bell's novel). For Bruno his own "real" actions are less important than the identity which he can assume as he carries them out. "He wasn't interested in writing but in obtaining the identity of writer, socially, or intimately anyway, in his own eyes" (11).[12]

There is a second fictitious author, an "absent presence" who as editor-historian gathers the fragments of diverse texts and com- poses the whole text which is read under the title of *Pretexta*. The omniscient perspective on Bruno, the testimonies of others, the texts which Bruno collects and the "biography" of Ocaranza are all part of the whole larger text, supposedly written by Federico

Campbell. At this level, Bruno and Ocaranza are mere characters subsumed in another story. Who is the author of this story? Bruno says to himself at one point, while thinking about his work, "It would be the perfect crime . . . there would be no author" (75).[13] The postulated presence, that feigned absence which has so "objectively" gathered all the fragments which compose the text, is another mask. And where, behind all this, is Campbell to be found?

The author of each story is also a character in another story. Like a Borges god who discovers that he has been dreamed up by another god who in turn was also dreamed up[14] . . . the writers of this work cannot escape their humble existence nor be outside the story. They don't fit neatly inside a fictional frame nor are they outside of it. The logical space inside a fictional frame spills over into another and thus the borders between "reality" and fiction are blurred. Wallace Martin refers to the image of a picture frame which Gregory Bateson and Jacques Derrida use to illustrate the problems of trying to distinguish between reality and fiction. The frame of the picture tells us that we should interpret all that is inside the frame in a different way than that which is outside it. But to establish this distinction, the frame has to be part of the picture at the same time as it is not part of the picture.[15] Where is the author or narrator of a work situated? Is he part of the work or outside of it? Is the act of representing (or narrating) part of that which is represented (or narrated) or outside of it? On one level, the writer as well as the reader has to live the experience of the text with his characters, limited by the temporality of the narration. He cannot reveal his omniscient and omnipotent perspective outside of the story without destroying the narration. According to Arthur C. Danto,

> "the logical structure of the narrative entails that the knowledge of the future is logically ruled out at the time it is future. . . . If the knowledge of the narrator were made available to the characters, the structure of narration would be destroyed. The knowledge available to him is *logically outside* the order of events he describes.[16]

But if the story that an author writes is in part the story of the writing of the text itself, the frame of the picture begins to blur and the picture becomes confused with the reality outside it.

All novels are composed of a network of narratives, according to Barbara Hardy. The interior narratives of a work often reflect metaphorically the meaning of the whole text. "A metaphor represents and realizes on its tiny scale, as the poem or play or novel of which it forms a part represents and realizes. Similarly, the narratives within narratives reflect the nature and structure of their totality. . . ."[17] Ann Duncan comments on this relationship in *Pretexta:* "The composition of the text mirrors the theory and eclectic method of Bruno, its writer-protagonist, who 'wrote down whatever came into his head, including, of course, the description of the very act of writing it'" (27).[18] In this way there is described within the work a circular relationship between the text as a whole and its internal narratives, as well as between the author and his characters. The stories of Bruno and Ocaranza reflect, we might suppose, Campbell's experience as a writer, while he at the same time imitates his writer-protagonists in the act of writing the novel.

"This voice, is it mine?—asks Bruno—Did I invent the signs which make up language? These code-books which are called dictionaries in all languages, do they belong to anyone in particular?" (74).[19] Bruno asks these questions following a discussion of plagiarism, in self-defense against the possible critique of his writing. But these questions have philosophical-linguistic as well as political resonance in the text. Does the writer have control over the language he uses? Moreover, should he assume responsibility for the meaning that a reader might derive from his work?

Linguistic signs, although stable in appearance, have a variable relationship with their referents. From the beginning of the book Campbell parodies the instability of language, which can be abused in the name of art or political repression. On the front cover of the book[20] there is a series of nine drawings, each of which has underneath it a label which does not correspond with the object. There is, for example, the image of a typewriter with the label "the pistol," or a mask which is called "the machine (typewriter)." At first, it seems a totally arbitrary confusion, but soon one begins to form new metaphorical associations. The typewriter could be "the pistol," that is, the weapon of the writer, his way of attacking and defending himself. "The only weapon he was carrying was his portable typewriter" (18).[21]—Bruno thinks to himself as he arrives in the city to carry out his mission. At the same time, the mask could be "the machine" (the metaphoric structure) which generates the book, the symbol of the "masked chronicler" (110) of the story. This symbolic and ultimately arbitrary function of language runs the risk of repressing or totally displacing the original meaning of the word. Even the simplest signs, words, or images, for example, can wear masks which hide a new meaning with a different referent, thereby distorting or

complicating the message which is communicated. Robert Weimann discusses the "changeable historical quality" of the relationships between the [linguistic] sign and its referent.

> The sign, as the materialized result of creative activity has more of
> an objective quality—the *reference*, resulting from both creative and
> receptive processes, involves a higher degree of subjectivity and
> change. . . . The sign is made to *refer* to an imaginary object, and it is
> the permanently renewed search for this *reference* that may be seen to
> reflect the never-ending need for interpretation and reinterpre-
> tation.[22]

These interpretations and verbal associations form part of the
constant process of signification (creating and communicating
meaning) within the social language of an era. The precise meaning of a word becomes clarified in the context in which it is used.[23]
"Each word tastes of the context and contexts in which it has lived
its socially charged life. . . ." says Mikhail Bakhtin.[24] But poetic
language, like political language, can be confined by a unitary and
closed system. Bakhtin explains:

> The language in a poetic work realizes itself as something about which
> there can be no doubt, something that cannot be disputed, something
> all encompassing. . . . The language of poetic genres, when they ap-
> proach their stylistic limit, often becomes authoritarian, dogmatic and
> conservative, sealing itself off from the influence of extraliterary so-
> cial dialects.[25]

If poetic language in its extreme forms can exclude social influences, becoming crystallized in the singular voice of the poet; then
political language can also isolate itself from social dialogue and
become a totalitarian language. Words become petrified until finally losing their meaning and they remain only as empty masks
of power. In his discussion on the era of the student movement
in Mexico, Octavio Paz criticizes the government for such an abuse
of language, referring to "the prison of words and concepts in
which the government has enclosed itself, all those formulas in
which nobody believes any more and which are condemned in
that grotesque expression with which the official family designates
the only political party: the Revolutionary Institution."[26] When
Bruno contemplates his surrender to total servitude of the State,
a series of pat phrases enter his mind, popular sayings which have
been converted into the empty rhetorical formulas of the official
state. Bruno (and Campbell?) mentally rebels.

Fed up. He was fed up. Not everything was black and white . . . not even gray. He was sick of let sleeping dogs lie, sick of don't confuse liberty with libertine, sick of criticism is fine but positive criticism, not negative, and what attracted him was the negative, the constructive. . . . But that was the language of the tribe. (59)[27]

Prose, and in particular the novel, says Bakhtin, works against this closed and impenetrable language. The form of the novel is by nature heterogeneous, and language opens up to the "dialogic play of verbal intentions" realized in the multiple voices and the social stratification which characterize this genre.[28] Novelists, like ventriloquists, speak indirectly through the mouths of others.[29] They don't try to silence the voices of others when they compose their texts, rather they take advantage of the social heteroglossia and "make use of words that are already populated with the social intentions of others and compel them to serve their own new intentions, to serve a second master."[30] Narrative, whether fiction, history, or political propaganda, is always a weaving together *(textura)* of words and intentions of others with the voice of the author.[31]

If we enter into an investigation of the title of the novel we can see more clearly the texture of languages, meanings, and stories that make up the text. "Ocaranza wanted us to establish with precision the etymology of *pretexta*," Bruno remembers of a university class that he had taken with the professor (33). The *pretexta*, "flowing toga which had underneath it a narrow strip of purple, worn by magistrates, consulates, praetors, censors, aldermen, and dictators in Roman times" (33–34)[32] was also a theater piece. We find on the first page of the book, as an epigraph to the novel, a definition of the word *pretexta* taken from the Encyclopedia Espasa Calpe, published in Madrid in 1922:

Pretexta: Latin tragedy whose characters dressed with the toga of this name and the subject matter was taken from the national history.[33]

But "rather than for being presented on a stage, these compositions were written to be read in public. . . . Their well-roundedness as a theater piece mattered little; their importance depended on parody, on fulfilling a role which these days would be that of the newspapers, with the purpose of dealing with an issue of more immediate local history" (34).[34] Within Campbell's *Pretexta* Bruno's pretexta unfolds, containing within it the professor's discourse on the historical pretexta, a discourse which ironically comments on the other "superpretextas" of which it forms a part. Much like the story that Bruno writes and even Campbell's novel, the pretexta was a spontaneous invention which not only narrated but also commented on its own process of creation. It presented the way of representing its subject as well as the subject itself.

It is interesting to investigate not only the cultural history of the "pretexta," but also the etymology of the word. The word itself is an interweaving of meanings which have evolved throughout history. The verb *praetexo* (Latin: to embroider) also had a figurative meaning: (to cloak, disguise, conceal; or to allege as a pretext). Bruno's task is that of "embroidering" or "adorning" other historical texts in order to create a new "credible" (hi)story, but at the same time to disguise the truth in accordance with certain political interests. Marc Bloch warns against such distortion of historical truth in the writing of history.

> There is a more insidious form of deception. In place of blunt, forthright . . . honest untruths, there are the sly alterations: interpolations in authentic charters or the embroidering of imaginary details upon the roughly trustworthy scheme of a narrative. Interpolations are generally founded on self-interest. Embroidery is frequently for the purpose of embellishment.[35]

This is Bruno's dilemma as writer-historian of the biography. The tensions between the political self-interest of the government and Bruno's dedication to art distort the story and make impossible "direct" writing or authentic representation of the truth.

If we continue with the linguistic deconstruction of the word *pretexta,* there comes to mind the metaphor of the text as a weaving or *textura.* The word *text* (Latin: past participle of the verb *texo;* to weave, construct, compose) takes on special significance if it is understood as a weaving still on the loom or in process, that is, a "pre-text." The loom has to be prepared first with the threads of the warp, which should be lined up in a set order to give structure or a base to the weaving (analogy to the facts and events of the story). Then the artist (or historian) weaves freely the threads of the woof (*trama* in Spanish, obvious analogy to the plot of a story). Thus the creation of the text results from this integration or interweaving, from the dialogue between the threads of the past and those of the present, the threads of "reality" and those of invention, the voices of others and one's own voice, the classic model and the parody of it.

Edward Hallett Carr defines history as "a continuous process of interaction between the historian and the facts, an unending dialogue between the present and the past."[36] Paul Hernadi adds that "historiography confronts an intricate fabric of interacting facts and texts, many of which are generated by each other. . . ."[37] We have already seen that the *praetexta* was a weaving *(textura);* not only a text but also a garment. In our novel the authors and characters continually change costumes, masks, and pretextas, thus "weaving" a complex net of stories and identities. Just as la Quebranta (female character in the novel, whom we will discuss later on) puts on her best dresses, one on top of the other (110), Bruno puts on his authorial masks. "I will call my self Lucius, Junius, Brutus, Brunus, Brunius . . . and my real name will be lost. I will have to recount all of this, I will be the masked chronicler" (110).[38]

The *"fábula praetexta"* was a "pre-text," a dramatic story not yet in its final form. *Pretexta* is also a "pre-text," the unedited draft of a novel. But at the same time it *is* a novel; the story of the process of writing, of weaving a (hi)story. We see the writer at work: the journalist collecting information, the novelist weaving his fictional world, the historian editing (and falsifying) history. Bruno feels that he is writing not to create the final product, but as a testimony to his own personal journey and a gesture of his inevitable servitude to the State. "He was supposed to proceed with the humility of the servant, with the dignity of the artist" (147).[39] And besides, "He knew that on the other hand no one would read the document, that in this country no one read anything and it didn't matter to anyone if you published or not,[40] that it was not something to worry about too much because in the end he wasn't writing directly for the press anyway. What he was putting on paper would stay there on the paper and could be changed or corrected or destroyed completely" (48).[41] Writing is a process of editing: the text is constructed from that which is selected and that which remains outside forms other possible texts. Professor Ocaranza had said that "in a sense one goes along editing one's life." (121)[42] Our experience is a continual process of selection, of daily choices. And as if he were conscious of his own literary existence, Ocaranza comments with an irony that seems to be aware of the game of all the masks of the novel. "We edit our conversation. On the other side of the line an editor more sagacious than we are comments suggestively, forming half-truths and half-lies and, like in photography, he leaves out of the picture what doesn't fit in the edition" (121).[43]

Bruno is obliged to turn in his manuscript to an anonymous

reader, another servant (*criado* in the double sense of the word) of the system who will serve as an editor of the manuscript. The reaction of this reader is included in the text, suggesting perhaps the comments of a reader or editor of Campbell's novel. The anonymous reader offers Bruno advice such as "Don't feel too guilty" and "Be careful with your manias" (90),[44] along with a lot of technical and stylistic criticism. He assures Bruno that, in spite of its faults, his work is worthwhile and he should continue. "As a reader of yours, outside the glass capsule in which you must be enclosed when you are writing, I can tell you that from the outside, the sobriety of what you have written seems to me sensational, very worthwhile, very effective . . ." (90). And he ends by encouraging him: "Carry on" (93).[45] Bruno continues with his text as does Campbell, and we readers keep reading.

Pretexta is finally, as Duncan notes, also a "pretext." "Obviously this story about Professor Ocaranza is only a pretext for Campbell to discuss, through Bruno's activities, the craft of fiction."[46] But it could also function in reverse. The discussion of the art of writing could be a pretext to allow Professor Ocaranza to speak, that is, to express a real protest about the impossibility of writing in a "country of servants" (59).[47] The same Bruno who at times gets lost in his literary art ["Bruno was capable of risking his life for a phrase, for a play on words" (60)[48]] also reveals another contradictory side. "There in his masked writing was the unguarded moment, the absolute lack of literary intentions, the crude and cynical and merciless reality of the urban, and by extention national, misery and corruption" (74).[49] The book has everything: confessions and alibis, revelation and repression, paranoia and parody. It is difficult to decide which are the masks and which is the real face of the author.

To begin his investigations, Bruno goes to the great repository of information, the National Archive. There is where history begins and ends. The data that Bruno is looking for can be found in the archive, already edited, classified, and controlled, and the very unwieldy file which he is preparing will end up being incorporated as yet another document in the archive. In order to search for the secret information he needs, Bruno has to go down to the basement of the building. It is a dark and damp place, "the center, the central nervous system of the workshop of libelous files"[50] which to Bruno seems like a mortuary. There is where the new secret histories are woven while the old ones decay. "Underground they contrived the false biographies, the apparently unofficial versions of recent events, of military or police actions unknown except by their perpetrators and victims" (46–47).[51] The atmosphere of the archive represented for Bruno a power impossible to resist or oppose.

> The galleries of power: the long offices all neatness and beauty, the heaven and hell to which everyone without exception aspired, suddenly took for Bruno the form of an institution in which obedience, silence, the restrained and quiet nullification of one's self constituted the qualities towards which one should aim one's efforts. His destiny was to smile at the others, bring them their food, listen to them and educate himself in the discipline of discretion. (47)[52]

The archive is the center of repression, not only because it controls the information but because it is the center of the creation of history.

> Only inside, within the institution, did history happen; there it was developed and directed. The outside, the real world, that of the streets happened out there. Here the inventoried, written word was the only thing that counted even though its association with things said and done might be prefabricated. The inventory, the archive: that was what counted. The rest, did not yet really exist. (58)[53]

The head of the archive is the supreme author of all of the manuscripts, the one who directs the flow of history. This invisible boss who "on the top floor dispatched [his orders] and only communicated by means of intermediary ushers" (47)[54] is obsessed by power, which for him

> was like heroin, it created in him a practically physical addiction and it carried him back to infancy. He would become the child king again who cries to satisfy his hunger, . . . the omnipotent baby whom no one can defy, much less Bruno. His declarations had a magic effect. It was enough for him to pronounce a phrase and reality would accommodate. (100)[55]

And from above, from that master who "should have been outside of the game,"[56] would come the sanction that converted stories into History, and crimes into Law.

What can the writer do in the face of such power, in "a country governed by gangsters" (68)? How can he write? Bruno realizes that if he wants to be a writer, he has to give himself over to the service of the State, to enroll in "a school of servants." If he loses his freedom on doing so, he also gains "a control over his words and the effects of his words on others" (73).[57] Bruno is convinced of the absolute power of the system. "They had everything, the means of production and communication, the monopoly of the machines and papers, the electronic and written means. Nothing would satiate them. Nothing would satisfy them enough. They wouldn't tolerate dissidence." (73) It is easier to obey, to join them, and work in peace. Bruno even admits "it was a pleasure to know how to obey" (58).[58] In order to be able to write, one must

> be institutional: believe in institutions, not in men. The relationship with authority, the boss, the living together with the other servants, would turn into a team of mules pulling carts trying to bite the carrot hanging on a string tied to a stick held by the boss from his place of command. (58)[59]

Octavio Paz said in 1959 that in Mexico the principal mission of the intellectual is "political action. The Mexican 'intelligencia' has not only served the country: it has defended it. It has been honorable and effective, but hasn't it stopped being 'intelligencia', that is, hasn't it given up being the critical conscience of its people?"[60] What has happened to writers, if they have renounced their consciences? Bruno identifies with Professor Ocaranza when the latter explains his own experience with journalism: "His concerns, his quixotic deliria, had no place in the world and so he opted to become marginalized so that, according to him, he wouldn't be swallowed up" (67).[61] Bruno feels marginalized (61), and his voice seems to become confused with Ocaranza's, whom he sees as "something of a byproduct of society, stripped of all possibility for criticism and reflection" (70). "It was a form of begging for us"—observes Ocaranza—"a dependency sought as a condition of survival" (71).[62]

For Bruno, his "definitive surrender" (58) is more of a relief than a tragedy. He feels seduced by the security and tranquility that is offered him in exchange for complete conformity. He becomes an "object," a small part of the whole machinery of the system. "He experienced his objectification with an illegitimate pleasure. It was much more bearable to fulfill the role of servant than to participate, easier to castrate oneself beforehand in a figurative sense. It was more practical and more passive than making decisions and assuming responsibilities" (59).[63] The final result of all this is the annihilation of the self. "The highest honor consisted in the destruction of his personal identity. He didn't want to be an individual. He had learned not only to not be himself, but to not be at all . . ." (59). "He was the invisible man . . . the passive object of history, the ghost writer, the masked chronicler . . ." (60).[64]

In the face of this situation of total surrender, of spiritual annihilation, Bruno thinks that "his only moral salvation was in pure and defiant cynicism" (74). "As for his possible accusors he would tell them to their faces . . . literature is shit, agreed, but I like shit. I am a true technician of shit; I feel at home in shit, so let me work in peace" (73).[65] And Bruno goes on writing the slanderous file; the biography of Ocaranza which is at the same time his own autobiography.

Georg Lukács maintained that the story narrated in a novel always assumes the exterior form of a biography of a problematic individual; the interior form is the search for self-recognition of that individual.[66] J. M. Bernstein adds that "if self-recognition is the *telos* of biographical form, then biographical form naturally evokes autobiographical form, the novelist's reflection on the story and discourse of his hero."[67] In *Pretexta* we see a complex relationship of biographies and autobiographies. While he worked on the false biography of Ocaranza, Bruno "couldn't resist the temptation of transposing certain moments of his own personal life" (28) into the gaps or holes in his text. His identification with Ocaranza is more than personal empathy or literary perspective. It is not only the product of their common experience as journalists. Bruno falsifies Ocaranza's biography with the fears, desires, and prejudices of his own life. Ocaranza (in the biography) is also Bruno: what he was afraid to be, what he would have liked to be, the incarnation of the internal struggle between his conscience and his paranoia. "And who was Ocaranza after all?" Bruno asks himself. "A tragic hero, misunderstood and weak, small, actually deserving of his own commiseration? That was a lie. That was the alibi: the libel of his own life" (58).[68]

When we study the human past, we inevitably study ourselves.[69] By writing the history of others, we write to a certain extent our own biography. The use of biography as an historical genre has been compared to the methods of psychoanalysis: According to Peter Loewenberg, "Biography, which studies the individual in depth and intensity, has been the classic forum where the blending of history and psychoanalysis, which is an individual clinical method par excellence, takes place."[70] History, like psychoanalysis, studies the past in order to explain the present. The former focuses on a collective past and the latter on the past of an individual. Given that such study can only be initiated from the present, it becomes a kind of reading in reverse. Historians and analysts have to "read" the data which they have about the past and reconstruct them in a narrative which explains an event, a relationship, or a "subject." Between the analyst and the subject there is a constant dialogue which functions as a basis for the selection and interpretation of data for the therapeutic narration. According to Loewenberg, this can cause distortion in the reception of the text.

> The observation, recording, and interpretation of historical phenomena are related and responsive to the historian's personal psychodynamics. The historian's personality accounts, not only for the historical material and themes selected, but also for the conscious and unconscious conceptual schemata imposed upon it. Distortion arises from the failure to account for the observer in each act of knowledge.[71]

In fiction, especially in the type of metafiction found in *Pretexta,* the "observer" is revealed as part of the game. The historical author also has a literary role. He is outside of the work at the same time as being part of it. As a writer, the author is also the protagonist of his own story and his consciousness is divided in a schizophrenic manner. Bernstein explains that this doubling of the author's subjectivity is representative of the dualism that invades subjectivity itself in the modern era. "The subject is now split or divided within itself. . . . This division within the self as manifested in the novel tells the story of how the self has become unnarratable, unable to tell its story and say who it is."[72] The writer plays the multiple role of observer and object observed, of analyst and subject analyzed. While working to uncover the truth and reconstruct history, he works as well to cover his own tracks, to disguise his own subjectivity. In the face of the "self-deceptions" of the writer,[73] the reader of a work has to assume the role of historian-analyst to try to reconstruct the true story and the subjectivity of the author.

In *Pretexta* Campbell clearly represents this schizophrenic state of the writer. While Bruno tries to compose the biography of Ocaranza, attributing to him all kinds of traumata and psychological unbalances, we see revealed in the text psychiatric reports on Bruno himself. With a careful reading we discover that many of the details which Bruno attributed to the story about the professor come from his own psychiatric history. He even says so at one point. "And as if the diagnostic baggage that he had at hand were not enough, Bruno reinforced this stretch of Ocaranza's life with a report that referred no more and no less than to Bruno Medina and not to any of the patients registered in the archive" (81).[74] Although Bruno is aware of what he is doing, at least in part, he is more worried about the dangers of his literary style. "The style, that was where the danger was" Bruno thinks to himself (85).[75] He feels a paranoic fear that they might be able to discover that he is the true author of the libelous document, behind his mask of anonymity. In his most insecure moments he feels that writing is a form of confession, in spite of all his efforts to hide his identity. "His fear was the possibility that one was editing one's own life by writing and, through writing in print, one might inadvertently be leaving behind a wake of 'linguistic footprints' . . ." (85).[76] Bruno feels persecuted by the problem of literary paternity and the ways of proving it. He studies feverishly the details of style, even to the point of worrying about the repetition of one word or another. He works to "cover up any leads for future investigators of the literary police" (75). "He would throw them off track, his possible pursuers, the exegetes, the library rats who would gnaw on the document with magnifying glass in hand" (45).[77]

The intense psychological relationship of Bruno with his writing is characteristic of the Latin American new narrative in general. As Noé Jitrik notes, there is an element

> which we might situate in the plane of the psychology of writing: It is what I call elsewhere "self-questioning", an attitude which makes all formalization consist above all of a questioning of the "writer" with respect to his own consistency, the referential value of his experiences and the homogeneity of his systems; the "writer" doesn't just glance critically at what surrounds him, projecting without knowing it his own previous mental structures . . . rather, when writing he realizes an operation of self-investigation which, and this is the important thing, is translated as an ensemble of visible, depictable forms, which in turn allows the circuit to be retraced and the process of its own genesis to be reconstructed.[78]

For Bruno this self-investigation reveals a division of his being. His identity seems to be an unstable balance between opposing forces. Both his personality and his writing, for example, struggle between his fascination for the past and the needs of the present, or between his subconscious desires and the obligatory repression of them. His interest in the past has always been very strong. "Nothing in the present stimulated him nor excited him like that apparently and falsely forgotten world no longer lived by anyone"

(20).[79] But when he was writing, when that real past became entangled with what he himself had constructed,

> it produced a sort of short circuit that put him in a neutralized position, . . . in a kind of coexistence with himself that was nothing but sterility, waste of time and of life, apathy, discouragement, difficulty in speaking or impossibility, indifference. His life split into two parts, the one that was here and now, and that one which pulled him back without knowing why. . . . (20)[80]

The imperatives of the here and now restrict somewhat Bruno's fascination for the past, as in Freudian terms the conscious represses the subconscious. In spite of that, incidents and emotions from his past as well as from his dreams invade Bruno's writing. Bruno writes as if he were talking in a psychotherapeutic session, writing down as if he were his own analyst "whatever idea passed through his head . . ." (27).[81] Thus the text represents not only Bruno's psychoanalytical history, but also the psychoanalysis of writing itself. The divisions between present and past, conscious and subconscious, repression and desire, are resolved by means of art. Norman Brown explains this integrative function of art according to Freudian theory:

> Art, like psychoanalysis itself, appears to be a way of making the unconscious conscious. . . . But while psychoanalysis tries to reach the unconscious by extending the conscious, art represents an irruption from the unconscious into the conscious. Art has to assert itself against the hostility of the reality-principle and of reason, which is enslaved to the reality-principle.[82]

The artist (writer) can resolve or at least express this divisive struggle within the self. By writing one can liberate that which is repressed while at the same time revealing the very process of repression.

Another division in Bruno responds to the tension between the internal and external authorities of his life; on one side his father and Professor Ocaranza, and on the other, the government. He suffers from a sense of guilt for having betrayed his father, whose words resound throughout the text as an echo of Bruno's conscience. "Many years ago his father had asked him never to work for the government . . ." (9). With these words the first line of Campbell's text begins. His father's words, which "began fading away in his memory almost an instant after he pronounced them, absurd, delirious, meaningless" (9)[83] for the boy and his childish fantasies, seem to speak again to the adult Bruno. From the perspective of many years later, his father's advice, already integrated into Bruno's own interior discourse, begins to gain importance.[84] In retrospect Bruno realizes the meaning of his "betrayal": "Many years earlier, the years which go from a useless maturity to an irrecuperable childhood . . ."(66)[85] he says contemplating the past in the light of the present. He was never able to identify with his father but he finds himself carrying on an internal dialogue with him as the voice of his own conscience. Bruno runs into himself "divided into two voices, . . . in stammering conversation . . . with the sad and desolate figure of his father.—Never become a policeman—he had told him" (10).[86] And by working in the archive on the slanderous file, Bruno does, in effect, work as a policeman for the government, thus violating the wishes of his father.

The anonymous editor of Bruno's work also refers to this betrayal. "I sense the whole thing rather as an involuntary dialogue of betrayal . . ." (89).[87] But it is not only his father that Bruno betrays. Another paternal figure for Bruno is Professor Ocaranza,[88] to whom he said once, "I will never work for the government" (102). While writing the libel of Ocaranza's life, he feels remorse and a sudden "memory of having forgotten his father, of having taken advantage of his mature and trusting innocence in order to derive from it the power which resides in confidence and which proceeds thus from all betrayals" (102).[89] Although his father has died, Bruno still carries with him "his father's remains," "his bones in a transparent plastic bag" (107).[90] The physical remains of his father, like his father's words, are not completely buried nor forgotten and they accompany Bruno as a symbol of his conscience.

The feeling of being a traitor which haunts Bruno is not only a result of having violated the words of his father and the professor. Bruno even betrays himself.

> He took material from his personal diaries, from his dreams, and he felt that he was plagiarizing himself. He felt that he was stealing his own ideas and phrases, that there was something illicit and unconfessable in the act of usurping from dreams realities which shouldn't even be named. And with that came the unconfusable feeling of the traitor who circled naked through the plaza. (102)[91]

In spite of these feelings of guilt and betrayal, Bruno surrenders his life to the State, sacrificing even the privacy of his unconscious. "To serve others was becoming a natural activity" (102)[92] for

Bruno and so in his moral struggle the external authority prevails. The law of the State is more powerful than the law of the father. Bruno recognizes the absolute supremacy of the former, which could be manipulated to justify any abuse of power.

> The law was conceived and made precisely to be used in favor of the interests of the State, but the law was the boundary, the point of reference, the line from here to there and there to here, the alibi of legality which conveniently served to orchestrate on all levels, to get around things. Everything but form. Everything but appearance; everything was sacrificeable. If the law required elements of trial or judgment, then those elements were provided. Form above all other things. Crimes were not even crimes if they were sanctioned by legality: the norm, the sacred order. (100)[93]

This external authority reaches the height of its power when it manages to penetrate the personal life of the individual, when it becomes internalized and confused with the conscience. Christopher Lasch comments on this process in the postmodern world. "The socialization of the young reproduced political domination at the level of personal experience. In our time, this invasion of private life by the forces of organized domination has become so pervasive that personal life has almost ceased to exist."[94] It is possibly to this internalization of the State which Bruno refers when he says "at times we all carry the police inside us" (102).[95]

The discussion of "authority" brings us back to the role of the author in the creation of the literary work. Who is the author of the text? Is it the person who has created the story or is it a presence created in and through that story? As a parody of this authorial duality, Campbell situates Bruno literally inside *and* outside of his own text.[96] The narrative voice changes perspective between first and third person, personal and impersonal narration, direct and indirect speech. As we witness the actions written on the page, we also witness the act of writing them. With all this play of perspectives, the coming and going between his interior and exterior voices, Bruno finally runs into himself. He narrates a dream of his which represents this state of division of the self in which the character lives. "Bruno takes me by the arm, we are both naked. I see the other Bruno take me fraternally by the arm and at the same time I feel myself taking Bruno by the arm and I see Bruno taking me by the arm" (112).[97] Ocaranza also talks about this experience of doubling in writing. "One can have a collision with oneself, you have in front of you the monstrosity of an invented activity, of a craft taken on without knowing when nor why" (122). The professor explains that this game "is not the ping pong of who was first the chicken or the egg. No. But it is the pleasurable adventure of the dreamed and the dreamer, the copulating with oneself . . ." (12).[98] When Bruno (in his dream) is on the point of killing the other Bruno with a scalpel and about to pierce his heart, the narrative voice says: "in this instant I wake up and I say, I say to *myself*, I say *to him:* You can have two bodies but not two hearts" (122).[99] In the same way, the writer can divide himself in two but not to the point of losing his common center (or heart) in the text. He has to wake up from the insanity of this doubling and self-reflection if he doesn't want to completely destroy his work.

These extremes of self-reflection and preoccupation with writing form part of the constant parody operating on many levels in *Pretexta*. As Duncan shows, "Not only does Bruno's role parody that of the journalist and fiction writer, but his mania for compiling material he then discards, cataloging, ceasing to observe life because he is living through archives and newspapers, parodies the laborious documentation of naturalist writers."[100] *Pretexta* is a complex work that requires the active participation of the reader. It exemplifies the ludic literature which "[centers] its structure on this absence of the author, which creates a dynamic relationship of reader and text."[101] But this work by Campbell is at the same time a *parody* of the contemporary genre of ludic literature, and as such it criticizes while it imitates the model.[102] While Campbell pretends to be absent from his text, he has Bruno, his author-protagonist also disappear. Anonymity is essential for Bruno, to give him freedom for writing and to protect him from criticism. By means of a constant parody of styles, Bruno tries to disguise himself and erase any traces of his identity. Duncan shows that this is also in itself a parody of Roland Barthes' theory of "the death" of the author in modern writing.[103] According to Barthes, the "Author-God" who in the past preceded the text and dictated a single message, has yielded to the modern writer who is born simultaneously with the text. The author is absent from the text on all levels and the unity of the latter is found not in its origin but in its destination, that is, in the reader.[104] *Pretexta* is as well, according to Duncan, a parody "of the Flaubertian ambition to be all-powerful, ubiquitous in his fiction, yet invisible; to destroy his identity so that his characters can speak for themselves."[105] Bruno describes himself as "an invisible creator, omnipotent, divine, situated everywhere and nowhere" (16).[106]

In spite of all his efforts to hide his identity as author of the text, Bruno always suffers the fear of being discovered.

> He believed, however, that all of that play of tricks, verbal turns, irreproachably invented references and extra effects, would have later on a boomerang effect against him. He would be identified: the collaborationist, the traitor, the mercenary pen, the ghost writer who threw the stone and hid his hand, the perfidious one. (51)[107]

Bruno has to ask for the help of a specialist in processing data to become conscious of "the key words that were peculiar to him and would most markedly define his style. . . . As in parody, he knew that the conscious peculiarities of a style could be imitated, but not the unconscious imprint which was precisely what would be investigated if a test of paternity were made against him" (86).[108]

Bruno's paranoia with regard to literary paternity points to a question central to literary theory: Is it possible when analyzing a text to "discover" or "reconstruct" the identity of the author? Luis Costa Lima addresses the problem in his discussion of the nature of fiction. Fiction is, for him, in one form or another a refraction of the "I" of the author. "Fiction . . . is a production directed by the (presumed) unity of the 'I'. A production which can always be examined in reverse, by a poet in reverse, that is, by a reader or analyst, who, depending on his or her talent, will soon be able to interpret that of which the refraction is a 'document.'"[109] What Bruno most fears is this psychoanalytical reconstruction of the author. He suspects that with each word he writes "there must be some kind of parallel interpretive method of Freudian deciphering of dreams: associations, symbolic realization of desires, creation of characters that are mere disguises of the dreamer himself, frustrated acts, significant omissions" (46).[110] His paranoia reaches such an extreme that he begins to study psychostylistics, psychographology, and psychostatistics, all methods of analysis which represent, in Campbell's text, a parody of literary deconstruction. In order to throw his pursuers off track (analysts, critics, and police), Bruno (and Campbell) puts on masks and lays traps.

Bruno not only hides behind the masks of writing in order to be an invisible and anonymous author, but also as a character he literally disappears from the text. A colleague of Bruno's narrates: "To try to track down the final fate of Bruno Medina is a useless objective. We all prefer to not know his whereabouts. Besides, he would always elude us . . . and in that same way he would disappear from the middle of things without explanation . . ." (16).[111] In this way Bruno the author also disappears, leaving in his place and without explanation police or medical reports as well as a mysterious "we" that appears from time to time in the narration.

This game of masks is not foreign to art. The purpose of art, according to Freud, is "the veiled presentation of deeper truth: hence it wears a mask, a disguise which confuses and fascinates our reason."[112] Fiction is a form of art which presents its truths veiled, under the mask of pretending. That is how Bruno understood the situation as he "worked through the means of representation, the path of pretending . . ." (54).[113] As he constructs his critique of some articles by Ocaranza (as part of the libel), Bruno seems to forget himself and drops the mask with which he has disguised himself. He can't seem to help but identify with the professor and he becomes impatient with the naive readers of Ocaranza's writing as well as his own.

> Didn't Ocaranza have a right to irony, as bitter as it might be? And if someone didn't understand his sarcasm it was his loss, poor soul: that someone, that imbecil who for the sake of the requirements of subsistence had to pretend to not be aware of the satirical character of a brazen and caustic discourse. [Is Bruno referring to himself here?] What was seriousness after all? That wasn't Professor Ocaranza's attitude. He would pretend that he was taking things seriously, feigning that he took them literally, but knowing, knowing very well that in that subtext, in that subdiscourse, in that statement behind what is said, he was literally shitting on what historiography and what diplomatic and academic decorum established as proper. Wasn't it sufficiently obvious? (128–29)[114]

But Bruno knows that he should be careful not to reveal his true identity or confess his true thoughts. He realizes "the dangers of his unrestrainable indiscretion." "He was his own worst enemy" (60).[115] He has to proceed with discipline in his writing "to moderate his voice, avoid excess, not commit any imprudences, even if he got the urge to wink at the reader . . ." (60).[116] Is this Campbell talking to us here? Is it perhaps Campbell himself who becomes impatient that we can't understand the game, and who asks us exasperated if it isn't sufficiently obvious what he is trying to say? . . .

"What does playing really consist of underneath?" Bruno asks himself. "What does seriousness mean?" (106).[117] Is the joke a mask for seriousness, or vice versa? Is there something serious behind the literary joke and what's more behind the parody of this joke? "A joke within a joke? Then, gentlemen, the thing is serious."[118] Bruno explains that "he pretended he was classist so they would believe that he was in effect pretending to be classist in order to hide the fact that down deep underneath it all, he was viscerally and inevitably classist" (129).[119] What is Campbell saying here? Can we say that fiction pretends to tell the truth so that we will believe that it is in effect pretending to tell the truth in order to hide the fact that down deep . . . it *really is* telling the truth?

Let's leave for a moment this discussion of fiction and return to a central theme of Campbell's work and of this study. How is history defined? Is it something which belongs to the past or does it begin in the archive with the data that survive from that past? Does it only become history when it forms part of a narration? If history is not what happened but what shall be remembered,[120] then it depends on the historian who writes it. For M. Oakeshott, "history is the historian's experience. It is 'made' by nobody save the historian: to write history is the only way of making it."[121] But it is not simply a question of recording what happened. Writing always "implies selection, organization, signification, or the creation of meaning."[122] Historians are not just scribes nor are they limited to being reporters or chroniclers of the past. These ideas point to a great debate in the field of historiography between the positivists and what are sometimes called "presentists" or "relativists." For the positivists "history is a ready (extant) structure of facts which it is only necessary to discover with the aid of documents, to collect and present in a raw form and from this history . . . will arise by itself."[123] In conflict with the positivists, the presentists believe that history is a creation of the present.

> History is comparatively projected into the past which should be understood in the sense that the interests and needs of the present-day condition both the historian's field of vision and his point of view: starting with what he considers to be an historical fact, including the interpretation and evaluation of these facts, up to the comprehension of the entire historical process.[124]

In *Pretexta* we see a parody of the philosophy and methods of positivism as well as an exaggerated representation of presentism. Bruno passes hour after hour in the archive, accumulating bits of information. There is all sorts of information in the stacks of the archive: "newspaper clippings, photographs, personal letters, notebooks full of notes, agendas, directories, birth certificates, credentials: the complete history of a character" (12).[125] He is given information that seems useless even to him; details that seem to satirize the scientific pretensions of the positivists. "The information kept coming in quantities that he didn't always need. Why find out the hour in precise minutes and seconds and fractions of a second? Why so much detail on the atmospheric pressure and humidity . . ." (43).[126] The function of so much information is to lend credibility to the story, situate the events in a likely setting. Bruno recognized that this was a method often used by the newspapers to throw up "a smokescreen: a lot of information (apparently diversified but basically identical) in order to not inform at all. It didn't have anything to do with clarifying but rather with muddying, not to make things visible but to hide them, not so they would see the forest but so the trees would keep them from scrutinizing it" (101).[127] But even though he recognizes the purpose of these techniques, Bruno nevertheless allows himself to be impressed by the accumulation of facts and details, enjoying more his role as antiquarian than as writer. "I find out things I don't need, he would say to himself, and at the same time I don't know anything about what is really happening. . . . But the novelty, the pleasure of communicating something that the others didn't know yet persisted in him like a vice preserved from adolescence" (43).[128]

This work of Campbell's seems to support, then, the presentists' theory, not as a prescription for history (what it should be), but as a description and a sharp criticism of what it is, at least in the context of contemporary Mexico. As a servant of the State, Bruno cannot simply collect data and permit the story "to arise by itself." When reconstructing history, he has to reform it and deform it pretending all the while an impartial objectivity. "He began to put together on the desk like pieces of a puzzle, the story and its different pieces . . . with the feigned objectivity or impartiality of the reporter" (52).[129] This feigned objectivity hides his acts of invention and distortion on reconstructing the events. Although his (hi)story is based on hundreds of true facts, it is in the relationships between the facts where the deceptions are woven. "There precisely, in those gaps, Bruno had the possibility to invent and more ground to enlarge on the actions and attribute them to one character or another" (39).[130] What's more, any approximation of objectivity would be a farce because all the available information, the "raw material" of history, is controlled by the State. "The uniformity of the information, the official bulletins, the nineteen daily newspapers that were handed him every day, not one of them was worth reading . . . a variety of newspapers that strictly speaking, looking closely, were the same but with a different title" (67).[131]

As Bruno resigns himself to his compromised and restricted position as a writer, he begins to enjoy the power that is left to him in certain aspects. He feels pleasure in his secret power as an anonymous writer. "To know that he was the true author of the glory or ruin of whoever fell into his hands, to feel himself the creator of the feigned chronicler who behind the pseudonym assumed a new existence . . . the intimate and solitary and obsessive gratification of the spy" (15).[132] Similar to M and the man reading on the bench in *Morirás lejos*, Bruno is the one who looks, the anonymous presence who defines our view: "the eye behind the binoculars or the telescopic gaze that penetrated the lighted windows of the buildings or approached the thighs of the couples reclined in the parks." "That's how he would proceed, like an untrappable and omnipresent force, with the sweet childish irresponsibility of one who knew himself to be invisible and evil, devastating, a devil, a God, a man of the State" (15).[133]

Bruno sees himself as a double spy. He occupies a position of power, but a dangerous, ironic power. The gun could backfire on him, and Bruno feels vulnerable from all sides. History is ironic and in the end it can't be controlled. Arthur Danto discusses the many philosophies that interpret history as irony, "where men not only make their history and in ways they never intended: but where what they bring about rather is *counter* to their intentions"[134] (as, for instance, revolutions turned into tyranny or totalitarian bureaucracy.) For Bruno, the great irony is that when he finally finds a way to write, to express himself, it turns out to be by means of the annihilation of his own being. The power and freedom which he had always coveted end up being another trap.

> Never in his youth had he imagined that around the corner, in one of those recesses of power, he, Bruno Medina . . . would run into doors open to uninhibited creation without secrets, without pitfalls, without obstacles to the imperturbably useless freedom which in the end could be found in the realm of the absolute: the libel of his own life. (131)[135]

"Writing is like prostitution" said Molière. "First you do it for yourself. Then you do it for some friends, and finally you do it for money." Bruno recognizes that he has arrived at such a state of degradation, that "he was doing it for money, that was clear" (14).[136] The prostitution of writing seems to be a symptom of the impotence of everyone in "a country of servants." "Everyone says yes. Like whores. And the incapacity to say *no*, the impotence, the serving so that the other can collect . . ." (59).[137] The muses have been degraded to the brothel. Clio, the classic muse of history and heroic poetry now serves the State. "Clio, learning an indiscriminate embrace over the course of her long life, is no longer an honest woman."[138]

The only female character in *Pretexta* is Lauca Wolpert García, also called "la Quebrantahuesos" (literally bone breaker) or "Quebrantacorazones" (heart breaker). Like some sort of muse, she seems to have an intimate relationship with both of the writers (Bruno and the professor) and with writing itself. She was a student of philosophy and attended Professor Ocaranza's classes in the same era as Bruno. She was also a political activist, Professor Ocaranza's lover, and a defender of his ideas. But the situation changes and she finds herself with Bruno, who, besides being her lover is also spying on her. Bruno is fascinated by Lauca ("la Quebranta") and the two occupy themselves with strange games. "I'd be standing up and she was on her head, I'd be holding her by the waist, I on my feet and she with her head down . . . and with a jump we would both flip, and with each turn I would land on my feet and la Quebranta upside down" (106).[139]

"La Quebrantahuesos" abandons the professor. If in other times she loved him and favored the resistence and political action of his life, now she lives with Bruno, the compromised writer of libel, and she enjoys herself playing with him. At night she is a rumba dancer in a cabaret, entertaining everyone with her suggestively erotic dance. For Bruno, this new relationship with la Quebranta is mysterious ["she was an intangible woman" (131)][140] and something about her disquiets him ["the fact that la Quebranta had her father in an urn in the dresser, perhaps." (107)][141] But in spite of his moments of uneasiness, Bruno prefers to forget those things and lead a life of fun with Lauca. "In that ludic way we would live at night, sleeping during the day."[142] Has writing been reduced, then, to a ludic exercise in the dark? Or is this inverted muse (standing on her head) just a disguise, a parody which hides a very serious message? Carlos Fuentes seems to answer this question.

Like Cervantes, we writers of today can only be such in an impure form, parodic, mythical and documentary at the same time, in which fiction, when re-presented, becomes the literary form closest to the truth because it is freed of the pretension of truth and the closest to reality because it undermines that reality with the illusory joke of a gentleman who says "believe me" and no one believes him; "don't believe me" and everyone believes him.[143]

The two carnavalesque faces of la Quebranta (the serious one and the ludic one) seem to reflect the two roles of the writer (perhaps represented in Professor Ocaranza and Bruno). Ocaranza is a quixotic man; impassioned and dedicated to action. He knows that "there was no remedy for things but at the same time one had to do something to change them. His bravery, his fortitude in opposing the system, his capacity for indignation . . . that was what kept him going and saved him from falling into the dung heap" (72–73).[144] Bruno is on the other side. He is a practical and cynical man who has resigned himself to serve the system. He works not to change things but to maintain them. "Bruno found himself on the side of the inquisitor, although furtively. From the other side of the events, and in another time, he would remake and organize history. Men live the events, he would say to himself, but I am the one who communicates them" (73).[145] But the game is more complicated than that. Bruno, who "wouldn't hurt anyone" (99), is not as submissive as he seems. He carries inside his "memory about to explode" and "words not spoken" (99)[146] which could break the barriers of repression in a future time. This hidden current has already irrupted in his dreams. "And it was there in his dreams where he saw himself invading the future, no, not the sinister future which he anticipated or foresaw for himself as justly deserved, no, but simply bursting into the center of the city and attracting everyone's attention" (99).[147] While la Quebranta "puts on her best dresses, one on top of the other" (110), Bruno dreams about putting on other clothes (identities, ideologies?) as well. He searches among the trash cans to put on "a pair of pants on top of the ones he was already wearing over his flannel pajamas, a checked jacket of Professor Ocaranza's, . . . a shirt on top of the rags that half covered him . . . and over his whole body he put Professor Ocaranza's great overcoat, long, black, down to the floor" (99).[148] Bruno retrieves from the garbage the clothes of others and he puts them on in the same way that he incorporates in his writing the texts of others. Is it possible that his dream reveals his true desire to wear the great black and solemn coat of the professor, that is, to assume his role as martyr?

Campbell's book ends with a scene that is both ludic and very serious. It seems to be a pessimistic conclusion. It is a carnavalesque vision in which a group of masked wrestlers, like those that fascinated Bruno all his life (symbol for writers?), and some rumba dancers (muses?) dance around Bruno while he says: "The professor, the professor is gone. He's gone. He's gone." "And then they all sang in a chorus, in a brawl, in a tangle, in a can-can: 'We-are-whores-we-are-whores from-the-Ber-ge-res-Fo-llies!'" (132).[149] If the professor is gone (and with him Bruno's conscience) and everyone has been sold to prostitution, it seems that all hope of redemption is lost. The professor, who had been a serious writer, dedicated to his ideals, is sacrificed to a marginal and impotent life. Bruno, who surrenders totally to the game (both political and literary), ends up losing his sanity. It is a pessimistic conclusion, but that is not the whole story. What is the final significance of Campbell's text?

Pretexta is not a closed work nor the final version of a story. It is only words on the page which can "be altered or corrected or totally destroyed" (48).[150] It is a "pre-text," not in the sense of being a draft for the final single text, but a story that will be rewritten and reinterpreted by other writers and readers. There will be other Ocaranzas and other Brunos, and probably even other Campbells who try to save them from martyrdom or insanity. And the story they will write is not only that of "how it was" but also of "how it is written." If we can reveal our subjectivity while trying to be objective, portray the writer weaving himself into the text, perhaps we will be able to transcend the dialectic of the positivists and presentists. In literature we can look for a balance between the deceit of realism with its illusory objectivity and the insanity of total relativism. Shoshana Felman discusses this need for balance in science, in words which seem pertinent here. "Science is the drive to *go beyond*. The scientist's commitment is at once to acknowledge myth and to attempt to *go beyond the myth*. . . . Only when the myth is not acknowledged, is *believed to be a science*, does the myth prevail at the expense of science."[151] By unmasking itself, narrative (including of course historiography) can at least recognize the myth and try to "go beyond" with its (hi)stories. *Pretexta* is a work which narrates several stories: the story of an historical era in Mexico and, more specifically, of the situation of the writer in that time. In this sense it narrates the history of writing. In addition, it is the story of the writing of that history of writing. "Where you got lost was the business about the pretexta," Professor Ocaranza had said to Bruno once (37).[152] This is where the readers could get lost as well if we try to compose mentally a final text or try to find some ultimate meaning for Campbell's work. With all its stories and masks, *Pretexta* pretends to be a text so that we will think that in effect it is pretending to be a text. In reality it *is* a text, that is, a weaving *(textura)* of all that.

6

Conclusion: The End of the Story?

To write in Latin America is to bet on freedom, to tell oneself
intimately in the act of writing that it is urgent to keep alive
the culture of the past because without it we will not have a
true present nor an intelligible future. . . .[1]

Latin American narrative was founded with the "invention" of
America[2] on the part of the first European discoverers and
chroniclers. This early literature about an America dreamed up
from the outside was gradually replaced by a narrative that revealed new American identities. The novelists of the 1960s pro-
posed a "reinvention" of America and the foundation in her
literature of an identity defined from within and in her own voice.[3]
The modern age of discovery no longer deals with a foreign land
and all its marvels but with America and its own New World,
its culture and history. Modern writers continue to invent and
discover new adventures through language. Included in these ven-
tures is an exploring of the past in search of revised interpretations of the surrounding reality. By discovering the secrets of the
past we can understand better the mysteries of the present. And
it is important not only to try to see the past with more clarity
but also to examine our own perspective on that past. How do we
interpret the past and how do we define ourselves as we write
our histories?

Friedrich Nietszche maintained that only through art can we
transcend our existence to be able to see ourselves better:

but not any "realistic" art, not an art that is merely imitative of nature. . . . What is needed is an art that is aware of its metaphysical
purpose . . . art provides the only transcendence that man can hope
for, and it provides this not only by creating the dream but by dis-
solving the pseudo reality of the dream that has atrophied.[4]

If the writing of history recovers or re-creates the past for us, then that conscious art of which Nietzsche spoke can give us a double view of the process. While we read the history that is being narrated, we can at the same time see the position from which we are writing. When we rewrite history we re-form our vision of present reality. We can't change the past, only our conception of it. From this "conception" (creation) is born a new identity which will in turn reinterpret the past. Octavio Paz refers to the "invisible history" that we live every day. This history is a kind of a document which becomes only partially "visible" in writing, as the theme of the (hi)stories we narrate.

> The history we live is a writing; in the writing of visible history we should read the metamorphoses and the changes of the invisible history. That reading is a deciphering, the translation of a translation: we will never read the original. Each version is provisional: the text changes endlessly (although perhaps it always says the same thing) and hence from time to time some versions are discarded in favor of others which, in turn, had been discarded earlier. Each translation is a creation: a new text. . . .[5]

This creative and re-creative process of writing (both in historiography and literature) can lead to confusion about the line between history and fiction. But this does not mean that the distinction between them disappears, as Louis Minc notes. "If the distinction were to disappear, fiction and history would both collapse back into myth and be indistinguisable from it as from each other."[6] Although the separation between history and fiction has never been as clear as was thought, in the new narrative of Mexico we see a conscious *rapprochement* between them that coincides with a bilateral tendency to move away from myth. In the field of history there has been a rejection of the official and totalizing version of the past thereby encouraging a resulting critique of the present. Yvette Jiménez de Báez explains in the following manner:

> It is evident . . . that by questioning the socio-historical context of the present, one questions as well the mythified vision of history. . . . At the base of all this critical process there is a decisive questioning of institutionalized history, which encompasses the economic, political and ideological level with clear predominance on the last two."[7]

The demythification of history allows multiple versions and perspectives to arise, subject always to scrutiny and rewriting. In fact, it seems that the more information there is available, the more difficult it becomes to produce a uniform explanation. Hayden White notes that

> each new historical work only adds to the number of possible texts that have to be interpreted if a full and accurate picture of a given historical milieu is to be faithfully drawn. The relationship between the past to be analyzed and historical works produced by analysis of the documents is paradoxical; the more we know about the past, the more difficult it is to generalize about it.[8]

Similarly, in the field of fiction, writers resort to multiple perspectives in search of a broader and more flexible vision of reality. This literary fiction is a fiction that recognizes itself as such and thus avoids, according to Frank Kermode, the degeneration into myth. Kermode relates the theory of literary fiction to one of fictions in general.

> Fictions can degenerate into myths whenever they are not consciously held to be fictive. . . . Myth operates within the diagrams of ritual, which presupposes total and adequate explanations of things as they are and were; it is a sequence of radically unchangeable gestures. Fictions are for finding things out, and they change as the needs of sense-making change. Myths are the agents of stability, fictions the agents of change.[9]

This writing of multiple versions and variable perspectives cannot have a "closed" form or ending. It is always open to new interpretations and readings. The urgency which Fuentes mentions of keeping alive the culture of the past does not lead to the attempt to write the final history or explain definitively the meaning of the past. On the contrary, to keep alive the culture of the past we need a continual process of revision of history and reformation of our conceptions about the form it should take. And through this process of revision we can create as well a "vision" for the future, in the sense which Paz suggests of "transfiguring the nightmare into vision."[10]

Art that questions and transgresses the traditional limits of the historical or literary canon can be called "subversive." It is, as Kermode has said, an agent of change.[11] And so it is that the apparent lack of "final" form in the four works we have examined is not only a function of artistic experimentation. These texts with their multiple versions (collected, invented, speculated, or unedited) embody an inquiry into the meaning of writing itself, thus undermining and exposing to light the sacred precepts of literary and historiographic tradition. These "sub-versions" reveal part of the "invisible" history—the counterparts of the historical and creative processes that are generally hidden "behind-the-scenes." We listen to the marginalized and forgotten voices that were excluded from the official history (Poniatowska); we search for the truth of a story that has been repressed among a labyrinth of fictions (Garro); we consider the infinite possibilities and moral ramifications of writing history or fiction (Pacheco); and finally we see the underside of the text, the process of its formation and the interior struggle of the writer (Campbell).

On reading *La noche de Tlatelolco* we "uncover" the testimonies and versions of hundreds of people about what happened at Tlatelolco. We discover that under the uniform surface of the official story there are many other stories which, when brought out into the light, begin to undermine the very foundations of the myth that the government has maintained. The many voices or "sub-versions" of history that result from this excavation form an alternative vision of the past and its meaning for the present moment. This work of "testimonies of oral history" is not a fragmented text, but rather a mosaic constructed of many pieces, a chorus of voices which by singing together as a whole does not lose its underlying plurality.

Testimonios sobre Mariana is also a work constructed of "sub-versions." There is no dominant version for the three fictitious testimonies of the story beyond what each reader of the work imagines or projects onto it. In the partial stories of the three narrators we can search for the tracks left by a woman who has disappeared. It is up to the reader to reconstruct by means of these "documents" a past which has gone by forever and an identity for one who cannot speak for herself. We see how writing gives a voice to those who have been silenced ("I forbid you to speak" Augusto had said to Mariana) and rescues their stories from a secret oblivion. It becomes clear also how much our identity, both individual and collective, is a narrative composed of many different stories.

Morirás lejos is a play of possibilities. On examining a paralyzed (fictitious) moment, there are spun many possible (sub)versions of the story and of history. Not only are the possible combinations to create a fiction theoretically infinite, but there are also many historical perspectives on what happened or will happen in reality. When we read Pacheco's work we confront with the writer the ethical and artistic dilemmas of writing. While we play with speculations and hypothetical versions of the story, we are urged not to forget the real cases of oppression and horror in the world and the human testimony of those who have been sacrificed to the power of others. Under each tower there is a well, a hidden, sub-version of the celebrated history which must be told.

In *Pretexta,* by revealing the reverse side of the cloth (text), we see a whole tangle of knots and threads of the weaving. This "sub-version," that is, the unedited story of the writing of the work, includes a lot of material that would be cut out of a final version. We also read the story behind the writing, the portrait of the writer in the midst of his creative act. Through a form of self-psychoanalysis the text reveals its own subconscious level. At the same time this work represents a parody of the excesses of literary analysis as well as a sharp criticism of the role that the Mexican State has played in the substitution of history by an official "fro-zen" historiography. From the basement of the archive and the subconscious of the writer the texts are insidiously or uncon-sciously fabricated; the libels and fictions which condemn others while exposing the intimate face of the author himself.

The literary experiments of Poniatowska, Garro, Pacheco, and Campbell reflect an interest in probing the depths of the meaning of history and writing. The overlooked and omitted versions need to be included in our texts, the histories of marginalized people, the forgotten events or repressed thoughts of a culture. Even the apparently mundane mechanisms of writing take on importance in the formation of contemporary narrative. And the more elabo-rately hidden they are below the surface of the text, the richer the sub-(hi)story to be revealed. The repression of one story only imprints another one in reverse relief.

The task of the contemporary writer, as has been suggested to us by four Mexican masters, is a continual process of unraveling our human history and reweaving it. Like the historian, archae-ologist, detective, or psychologist, writers and readers must look for these hidden stories and continue rewriting and rereading history. Our cultural identity is a narrative in continual re-forma-tion. It is a complex story that depends on an understanding of the past and an ending open to the future. From the rubble of the Tower of Babel we have to construct a narrative that gives meaning to our existence. That is the purpose of writing and the "end" of the story. The end of one story is the beginning of an-other. And the past extends each moment toward the future—a future that we can understand only when it becomes part of one of our stories.

Notes

Chapter 1. Introduction: The Beginning of the Story

1. Djelal Kadir, "Historia y novela: tramatización de la palabra," in *Historia y ficción en la narrativa hispanoamericana,* ed. Roberto González Echevarría (Yale University Colloquium: Monte Avila, 1984), 299. "El escritor hispanoamericano reconoce que su reto más perspicaz está en la institución de la historia y que el rival más perspicaz de la invención poética en Hispanoamérica es la invención histórica." All translations are my own unless otherwise stated.

2. Angel Rosenblat, "La primera visión de América," in *La primera visión de América y otros estudios* (Caracas: Ministerio de Educación, 1965), 45. "Así, los nombres de las cosas y de los lugares y la visión misma del conquistador de América representan una proyección de la mentalidad europea. Los descubridores y pobladores hicieron entrar la realidad americana en los moldes de las palabras, los nombres y las creencias de Europa. Es decir, la acomodaron a su propia arquitectura mental. Sobre el mundo americano proyectaron no sólo la realidad tangible de su mundo europeo, sino también su tradición literaria, mitológica y religiosa."

3. Manual Duŕan, "Notas sobre la imaginación histórica y la narrativa hispanoamericana," in *Historia y ficción,* 289. "Todo el esfuerzo de conquistadores, cronistas, historiadores era encontrar a la verdadera Dulcinea, desencantar la campesina—inventar una América digna de ser comparada con las hermosas descripciones del mundo clásico y del mundo original."

4. Tzvetan Todorov, *The Conquest of America,* trans. Richard Howard (New York: Harper and Row, 1985), 15.

5. Roberto González Echevarría, "Humanismo, retórica y las crónicas de la conquista," in *Historia y ficción,* 155.

6. Ibid., 157. ". . . que daba un lugar prominente al valor estético de la historia . . . de organizar los hechos de modo coherente y armonioso. . . ."

7. Ibid., 160. ". . . él firmamente daba cuenta de su persona y de los hechos pertinentes al caso—el contacto de un yo con la realidad circundante."

8. Ibid., 162. ". . . de ahí su valor antropológico e histórico en el sentido moderno de la palabra. Pero de ahí también su valor literario posible, también en un sentido moderno."

9. Ibid., 162.

10. Enrique Pupo Walker, "Primeras imágenes de América: notas para una lectura más fiel de nuestra historia," in *Historia y ficción,* 89.

11. That is, writing functioned to preserve and explain the indigenous culture in the face of the European invasion while also appealing to the sense of justice of the new rulers.

12. Of course there are other texts that do not enter into the *mestizaje* of the new tradition. The silenced voice of the conquered is lost in oblivion and remains asleep, to appear much later, like a recessive gene, on the literary and historical

scene. The "discovery," for example, of another version of the conquest in the *nahuatl* texts (*Visión de los vencidos. relaciones indígenas de la conquista*, trans. Angel María Garibay K. Universidad National Autónoma de México, Biblioteca del Estudiante Universitario, 1972) offers a text that has not been integrated into the literary canon and is subversive of the traditional history.

13. El Inca Garcilaso de la Vega, *La Florida* (Mexico: Fondo de Cultura Económica, 1956), 5. ". . .viéndome obligado de ambas naciones, porque soy hijo de un español y de una india. . . ."

14. Hugo Rodríguez Vecchini, "Don Quijote y 'La Florida' del Inca," in *Historia y ficción*, 106, 109. "The historian was supposed to separate himself from the poet and from literature, the latter being identified more and more with 'the lie', that is, invention and falsity." ["El historiador debía separarse del poeta y de la literatura, ésta que se identificaba cada vez más con la mentira, o sea, invención y falsedad."]

15. Ibid., 105. "1) la irrupción del "yo" testimonial 2) la elusividad del autor implicado en un proceso de autoreferencialidad 3) la apertura de un espacio en que la escritura dramatiza su propia realización"

16. Vega, *La Florida* (Proemia al lector), 6, 8, 322. "Y esto baste para que se crea que no escribimos ficciones. . . ." "Sin la autoridad de mi autor, tengo la contestación de otros dos soldados, testigos de vista. . . ." "Porque la verdad de la historia nos obliga a que digamos las hazañas, así hechas por indios como las que hicieron los españoles. . . ."

17. Ibid., 295. "Volviendo a Juan Ortiz, que lo dejamos en gran peligro de ser muerto. . . ." and "Volviendo a nuestra historia un poco atrás de donde estábamos. . . ."

18. Mary Ellen Kiddle, "The Non-Fiction Novel or 'Novela Testimonial' in Contemporary Mexican Literature," Ph.D., diss., Brown University, 1984, 74.

19. Ibid., 76.

20. Ibid., 80.

21. It is important to note here that the so-called novels of the revolution were written during a period of new direction in the historiographic tradition of Mexico. These works came out during a time of intellectual rejuvenation and national self-examination in Mexico. The historians began to look with a critical eye at the myths of the Revolution and to worry more about the cultural identity and destiny of Mexico. See Charles A. Hale, "The Liberal Impulse: Daniel Cosío Villegas and the *Historia moderna de México*," *Hispanic American Historical Review* 54, no. 3 (August 1974): 479–98, and also by the same author, "The History of Ideas: Substantive and Methodological Aspects of the Thought of Leopoldo Zea," *Journal of Latin American Studies* 3 (1971): 59–70. The ideas mentioned here are from "Liberal Impulse," 480–81.

22. Ibid., 94.

23. Ibid., 201.

24. Edward Hallett Carr, *What Is History?* (London: MacMillan, 1961), 129.

25. Emir Rodríguez Monegal, *El boom de la novela latinoamericana* (Caracas: Editorial Tiempo Nuevo, 1972), 14, defines the phenomenon of the boom in its economic, cultural, and ideological aspects as well as the purely literary. The boom is a result of a new generation of readers. "After World War II, a new generation of readers appears in Latin America and determines (by its numbers, by its orientation, by its dynamism) the first *boom* of the Hispanic American novel." ["A partir de la segunda guerra mundial, una nueva generación de lect-

ores aparece en América Latina y determina (por su número, por su orientación, por su dinamismo) el primer *boom* de la novela hispanoamericana."]

26. Margo Glantz, "Estudio preliminar," Introduction to *Onda y escritura en México: jóvenes de 20 a 33*, ed. Glantz (Mexico: Siglo 21, 1971), 33. ". . . sólo una dimensión del hombre, sino el hombre como un ser verbal, como una dimensión del lenguaje."

27. Carlos Fuentes, *La nueva novela hispanoamericana* (Mexico: Joaquín Mortiz, 1969), 26. "Pues el sentido final de la prosa de Borges—sin la cual no habría, simplemente, moderna novela hispanoamericana—es atestiguar, primero, que Latinoamérica carece de lenguaje y, por ende, que debe construirla." Although it is clear that Borges's prose had a tremendous impact on the new hispanoamerican literature, one could argue that his influence was more Europeanizing and universalizing that anything else. Still, one must recognize that Borges opened new roads in the creation of a new Latin American literature that would attract international attention.

28. Octavio Paz, "Literatura de fundación," Introduction to *Puertas al Campo* (Mexico: Universidad Nacional Autonoma de México, 1966), 13. ". . . inventar nuestra propia realidad." "Nuestra literatura es la respuesta de la realidad real de los Americanos a la realidad utópica de América. Antes de tener existencia histórica propia, empezamos por ser una idea europea . . . Nuestro nombre nos condenaba a ser el proyecto histórico de una conciencia ajena: la europea."

29. Ibid., 19. ". . . nuestra propia realidad." "La literatura hispanoamericana es regreso y búsqueda de una tradición. Al buscarla, la inventa. Pero invención y descubrimiento no son los términos que convienen a sus creaciones más puras. Voluntad de encarnación, literatura de fundación."

30. Ibid., 31. "Inventar un lenguaje es decir todo lo que la historia ha callado. . . ." "Nuestro lenguaje ha sido el producto de una conquista y de una colonización ininterrumpidas; conquista y colonización cuyo lenguaje revelaba un orden jerárquico y opresor." "La nueva novela hispanoamericana se presenta como una nueva fundación del lenguaje contra los prolongamientos calcificados de nuestra falsa y feudal fundación de origen y su lenguaje igualmente falso y anacrónico."

31. Julio Ortega, "*Cien años de soledad*," in *La contemplación y la fiesta—notas sobre la novela latinoamericana actual* (Caracas: Monte Avila, 1969), 118. ". . . sueño de restablecer una realidad original. . . ."

32. Echevarría, "*Cien años de soledad:* The Novel as Myth and Archive," *Modern Language Notes* 99, no. 2 (March 1984): 358–80.

33. Ibid., 373.

34. Ibid., 378.

35. Fuentes, *La nueva novela hispanoamericana*, 35.

36. Ibid., 9. ". . . en nuestra parte del mundo [donde] . . . nos sobran cosas que decir." "Hay mucho que decir . . . y no hay otra manera de decirlo que ésta, paradójica y frágil entre todas, de escribir libros para quienes, mayoritariamente, no saben leer y de proponer palabras e ideas en sociedades en las que a veces no es posible distinguir los gritos de la oratoria y los de la tortura."

37. Ibid., 12. ". . . la obligación de asumir la función crítica, informativa, esclarecedora, función de perspectiva y también de inmediatez, de debate, de defensa y voz para quienes padecen injusticia y silencio . . . y ser, también, legislador, periodista, filósofo, padre confesor, líder obrero, redentor de indios, cirujano social y abanderado de causas más o menos perdidas."

38. This metadiscourse and self-reflectiveness of writing, although consid-

ered special characteristics of the new narrative, are not unique to contemporary writing. We see them already established in the *Quijote* and even in *La Florida* of the sixteenth century. See Vecchini, "Don Quijote y 'La Florida' del Inca," in *Historia y ficción,* 105–48.

39. John Brushwood, *La novela mexicana 1967–1982* (Mexico: Grijalbo, 1984), 105. "El enfoque sobre el acto de narrar destaca el aspecto creativo de la tarea literaria. Cuando esto ocurre en una sociedad que, desafortunadamente, reprime la inclinación creativa del ser humano, se provoca una apertura o posiblemente una ruptura en la experiencia convencional. En este sentido la metaficción se aprecia como otra faceta del cambio social. . . ."

40. Adriana Méndez Rodenas "¿Texto, *Pretexta* o Pre-texto?: historia y parodia en la narrativa mexicana contemporánea," in *La historia en la literatura iberoamericana: memorias del XXVI Congreso del Instituto Internacional de Literatura Iberoamericana,* ed. Raquel Chang-Rodríguez and Gabriella de Beer (Hanover, N.H.: Ediciones del Norte, 1989), 379. ". . . subvierten el modelo de novela establecida por los grandes narradores del período anterior."

41. Ibid., 1–2. "Si García Márquez funda el prototipo de novela épico-mitica en *Cien años de soledad,* enmarcando la narración de la historia en la leyenda y el mito, los nuevos narradores de los años setenta rechazan el impulso totalizador de abarcar la historia entera de nuestro continente en una magna empresa narrativa. Todo lo contrario, la narrativa del 'post-boom' se empeña en crear una novela fragmentada, o un fragmento de novela, en el intento de desvirtuar la herencia del 'boom,' o sea, el postulado de que la ficción mediatice—directa o indirectamente—la historia."

42. Echevarría, *"Biografía de un cimarrón* and the Novel of the Cuban Revolution," *Novel* 13, no. 3 (Spring 1980): 252.

43. Hayden White, *Metahistory: The Historical Imagination in 19th-Century Europe* (Baltimore: The Johns Hopkins University Press, 1973), ix.

44. Erich Kahler, *The Meaning of History* (New York: Braziller, 1964), 22.

45. Paul Ricoeur, *Time and Narrative,* trans. Kathleen McLaughlin and David Pellauer (Chicago & London: University of Chicago Press, 1983), 99.

46. Paul Hernadi, "Clio's Cousins: Historiography as Translation, Fiction, and Criticism," *New Literary History* 7, no. 2 (Winter 1976): 247.

47. Ibid., 247.

48. Ibid., 248.

49. Ibid., 250–51.

50. White, *Metahistory,* ix–x.

51. Ibid., xi–xii.

52. Lionel Gossman, "History and Literature," in *The Writing of History: Literary Form and Historical Understanding,* ed. Robert H. Canary and Henry Kosicki (Madison: University of Wisconsin Press, 1978), 3.

53. Djelal Kadir, "Historia y novela," in *Historia y ficción,* 297. "La literatura tiene sus orígenes en el lenguaje y las posibilidades del lenguaje, es decir, en las constelaciones de nuestra palabra secundaria. . . . La historia y lo histórico se originan en los hechos—hechos que dependen del lenguaje y de las posibilidades de él para su concreción. . . . Para nuestra civilización y su dependencia de la palabra escrita, literatura e historia conjugan y conjuegan en el ámbito de la escritura. La novela utiliza el hecho histórico y la historia la tramatización lingüística."

54. Wallace Martin, *Recent Theories of Narrative* (Ithaca, N.Y.: Cornell University Press, 1986), 71.

55. Hernadi, "Clio's Cousins," 250.
56. David William Foster, *Alternate Voices in the Contemporary Latin American Narrative* (Columbia: University of Missouri Press, 1985), 147–48.
57. J. Hillis Miller, "Narrative and History," *English Literary History* 41 (1974): 455.
58. Glantz, "Estudio preliminar," Introduction to *Onda y escritura.*
59. Ibid., 29. "Hablar de 'escritura' puede significar muchas cosas o quizá sea sólo una escapatoria bizantina."
60. Ibid., 30. ". . . actitud explícita, tendencias cuyo punto de convergencia sería la preocupación escencial por el lenguaje y por la estructura."
61. Roland Barthes, *Writing Degree Zero,* trans. Jonathan Cape, Ltd. (Boston: Beacon, 1967).
62. Gustavo Sainz, in Glantz, *Onda y escritura,* 30. "Las novelas son ahora problemas. . . ."
63. Ibid., 30.
64. Ibid., 30. "La preocupación de 'escribir bien' tan propia de Martín Luís Guzmán o Salvador Novo tiene ahora una oposición: la de aquellos que no creen más en los ceremoniales literarios. Si escribir es entrar en un *templum* que nos impone . . . una religión implícita, . . . escribir es, también, querer destruir el templo incluso antes de edificarlo; es por lo menos, antes de franquear el umbral, interrogarse sobre las servidumbres de semejante lugar, sobre el pecado original que constituirá la decisión de encerrarse en él."
65. Ibid., 30.
66. Miguel Barnet, "La novela testimonio: socio-literatura," in *La Fuente Viva* (Havana: Editorial Letras Cubanas, 1983).
67. Brushwood, *La novela mexicana,* 17, 58. Brushwood defines metafiction as "the observation, on the part of the author, of his own creative act. . . . la observación, por parte del autor, de su propio acto creativo." Tlatelolco refers to the culminating tragedy of the student movement of 1968 in which hundreds of people were killed. Also included in this reference is the literary and political impact that this event had on subsequent years.
68. Brushwood, "Períodos literarios en el México del siglo XX: la transformación de la realidad," in *La crítica de la novela mexicana contemporánea,* ed. Aurora M. Ocampo (Mexico: Universidad Nacional Autonoma de México, 1981), 169.
69. Claude Fell, "Destrucción y poesía en la novela latinoamericana contemporánea," in *III Congreso Latinoamericano de Escritores* (Caracas: Ediciones del Congreso de la República, 1971), 208, in Brushwood, "Períodos literarios," 169. ". . . la fascinación de la creación creándose."
70. Rodenas "¿Texto, *Pretexta,* o Pre-texto?" 2–3. "Hacer literatura en México significa heredar una gran tradición nacional de novela histórica—la canonizada 'novela de la Revolución mexicana'. Y también requiere asimilar la reescritura de esta tradición emprendida por Carlos Fuentes en *La muerte de Artemio Cruz* (1962), míticamente depurada en *Pedro Páramo* (1955) de Rulfo."
71. From a short story by Jorge Luís Borges, "Pierre Menard, autor del Quijote," in *Ficciones* (Buenos Aires: Emecé Editores, 1956), 45–57.
72. Borges plays with this idea when he makes Pierre Menard's text *literally identical* to the section of the *Quijote.* Nevertheless, the fictitious author of Borges's story says with characteristic irony that "the second one [the translation] is almost infinitely richer" ["el segundo es casi infinitamente más rico"]. Ibid., 54.

73. Ibid., 56. ". . . del anacronismo deliberado y de las atribuciones erróneas."

74. Barnet, "La novela testimonio," 30, suggests that the aim of the testimonial novel is to portray the "esencia real" of a society or historical era.

75. Brushwood, *La novela mexicana*, 59. ". . . uno de los experimentos más interesantes en la narrativa mexicana."

76. Ann Duncan, *Voices, Visions and a New Reality: Mexican Fiction Since 1970* (Pittsburgh: University of Pittsburgh Press, 1986), 62.

77. Rodenas "¿Texto, *Pretexta* o Pre-texto?" 3. ". . . la alternativa quizás más radical: la fragmentación del formato narrativo al descomponerse la historiografía tradicional en una serie de textos carentes de legitimidad. Herederos de Salvador Elizondo, este grupo de escritores someten la obsesión por la escritura al cuestionamiento de la versión oficial (PRI-ista) del México moderno."

78. Carlos Monsiváis, *Días de guardar* (Mexico: ERA, 1970), 17. "A partir de 1968 los caminos posibles parecen ser la asimilación sin condiciones al régimen o la marginalización con sus consecuencias previsibles."

Chapter 2. Elena Poniatowska: Testimonial Tapestries

1. Elena Poniatowska, *La noche de Tlatelolco*, 43rd ed. (Mexico: ERA, 1984). The words cited in the epigraph are from page 164 of this edition. All parenthetical references in this chapter are from this edition. All translations are my own unless otherwise stated.

2. In a conversation with Beth Miller that appeared in *26 autores del México actual* (Mexico: Costa-Amic, 1978), 304, Poniatowska was asked: "Do you consider yourself a journalist?" She answered, "Yes, totally. But I'm trying to take the step from journalism to literature which is the most frightening step one can take, isn't it?" ["¿Tú te consideras periodista?" "Sí, totalmente. Pero trato de dar el paso del periodismo a la literatura que es el paso más aterrador que pueda darse, ¿no?"]

3. Isabel Fraire, "Testimonial Literature: A New Window on Reality," *The American Book Review* (September-October 1983), 6, says of *La noche de Tlatelolco* that "it was an instantaneous success and it is still being reprinted."

4. Fraire, "Testimonial Literature," 5, refers to a brutal realism in Latin American literature "which revels in calling a spade a spade and focuses on the more violent and distressing aspects of life."

5. Miguel Barnet, "La novela testimonio: socio-literatura," in *La Fuente Viva* (Havana: Editorial Letras Cubanas, 1983), was the one who initiated the new interest in this genre. Barnet states that the original inspiration for his works and the idea of the people "without history" ["sin historia"] came from Ricardo Pozas Arciniega, *Juan Pérez Jolote, biografía de un tzotzil* (Mexico: Fondo de Cultura Económica, 1959).

6. Laura Rice-Sayre, "Witnessing History: Diplomacy vs. Testimony," in *Testimonio y literatura*, ed. René Jara y Hernán Vidal (Edina, Minn.: The Society for the Study of Contemporary Hispanic and Lusophone Revolutionary Literatures, 1986), 52. "If we assume that literature is an ideological form because it gives imaginary representations of real social relations, we recognize that testimony lies somewhere between 'literature' in its more traditional forms and real social relations."

7. Victor Casaus, "Defensa del testimonio," in *Testimonio y literatura*, 327.

"Quizá la mayor riqueza actual y perspectiva de este género se exprese precisamente en la dificultad que encontramos para definirlo, para clasificarlo. Esta resistencia del género seguramente proviene de su juventud, pero también, creemos, de su enriquecedora flexibilidad para tomar rasgos de otros modos de narrar y de expresar la realidad tan (aparentemente) disímiles entre sí como la narrativa, la gráfica, el cine o el periodismo . . . (para producir) una forma nueva de expresión."

8. Mikhail Bakhtin, *The Dialogic Imagination* (Austin: University of Texas Press, 1981), 301.

9. Rice-Sayre, "Witnessing History," 51.

10. Jorge Narvaez, "El testimonio 1972–1982. Transformaciones en el sistema literario," in *Testimonio y literatura*, 236. ". . . el surgimiento de un nuevo agente democratizado en el escenario de la comunicación social, y en el proceso de producción de sentido histórico."

11. Barnet, "La novela testimonio, 12–42.

12. Ibid., 23. ". . . tomando los hechos que más han afectado la sensibilidad de un pueblo y describiéndolos por boca de uno de sus protagonistas más idóneos."

13. Ibid., 27. ". . . quitándole al hecho histórico la máscara con que ha sido cubierto por la visión prejuiciada y clasista." In another article, "Testimonio y comunicación: una vía hacia la identidad," *Testimonio y literatura*, 303–13 [originally published in *La fuente viva*, 43–60] Barnet develops this idea further.

14. Renato Prada Oropeza, "De lo testimonial al testimonio: notas para un deslinde del discurso-testimonio," in *Testimonio y literatura*, 13, 19.

15. Ariel Dorfman, "Código político y código literario: el género testimonio en Chile hoy," in *Testimonio y literatura*, 177–79. The words that Dorfman uses are *acusar, recordar,* and *animar.*

16. Nubya Casas, "Novela testimonio: historia y literatura," Ph.D. diss., New York University, 1981, 31.

17. Rice-Sayre, "Witnessing History," 51.

18. Ambrosio Fornet, "Mnemosina pide la palabra," in *Testimonio y literatura*, 345, refers to this new perspective of the testimony. "Before the tribunals of History, Mnemosina asks to speak in the name of the popular classes. The testimony is her megaphone." ["Ante los tribunales de la Historia, Mnemosina pide la palabra en nombre de la clases populares. El testimonio es su megáfono."]

19. Casaus, "El testimonio: recuento y perspectivas del género en nuestro país," in *Testimonio y literatura*, 334. "In the unfolding of the testimony one feels clearly the respiration of history." ["En el desarrollo del testimonio se siente de manera clara la respiración de la historia."]

20. Barbara Foley, *Telling the Truth: The Theory and Practice of Documentary Fiction* (Ithaca, N.Y.: Cornell University Press, 1986), 26.

21. Barnet, "La novela testimonio," 23. ". . . un protagonista representativo, un actor legítimo. . . ."

22. Domitila Barrios de Chungara with Moema Viezzer, *Si me permiten hablar . . . Testimonio de Domitila una mujer de las minas de Bolivia* (Mexico: Siglo 21, 1977), 13. "La historia que voy a relatar, no quiero que en ningún momento que la interpreten solamente como un problema personal. Porque pienso que mi vida está relacionada con mi pueblo. Lo que me pasó mí, les puede haber pasado a cientos de personas en mi país."

23. Some well-known examples of this type of collective character are Barnet's Esteban Montejo, *Biografía de un cimarrón* (Havana: Academia de Ciencias,

1966) and Poniatowska's Jesusa Palancares, *Hasta no verte Jesús mío* (Mexico: Era, 1969).

24. Rice-Sayer, "Witnessing History," 68, comments that "What *testimonio* does for contemporary history is break through the barrier of anonymity."

25. Paz, *Posdata* (Mexico: Siglo 21, 1970), 21, cites Prague, Chicago, Paris, Tokyo, Belgrad, Rome, Mexico City, Santiago . . . as places of commotion and demonstrations that year.

26. Ibid., 39.

27. Luis Leal, "Tlatelolco, Tlatelolco," *Denver Quarterly* 14, no. 1 (1979): 3–13.

28. Paz, *Posdata*, 32. "Como una suerte de reconocimiento internacional a su transformación en un país moderno o semimoderno, México solicitó y obtuvo que su capital fuese la sede de los Juegos Olímpicos en 1968."

29. Ibid., 33–34. "El movimiento estudiantil se inició como una querella callejera entre bandas rivales de adolescentes. La brutalidad policíaca unió a los muchachos. Después, a medida que aumentaban los rigores de la represión y crecía la hostilidad de la prensa, la radio y la televisión, en su casi totalidad entregadas al gobierno, el movimiento se robusteció, se extendió y adquirió conciencia de sí. En el transcurso de unas cuantas semanas apareció claramente que los estudiantes, sin habérselo propuesto expresamente, eran los voceros del pueblo."

30. Ibid., 34.

31. Ibid., 38.

32. Ibid., 34. "En el momento en que los recurrentes, concluido el mitin, se disponían a abandonar el lugar, la Plaza fue cercada por el ejército y comenzó la matanza."

33. Some estimates exceed 300. For example Paz, *Posdata*, 38, cites the number given by the English newspaper *The Guardian*, 325 dead; Leal, "Tlatelolco, Tlatelolco," refers to more than 300 dead; Alan Riding, *Distant Neighbors* (New York: Knopf, 1985), 60, mentions between 200 and 300; and Fraire, "Testimonial Literature," 6, cites between 400 and 500 dead. Fuentes, "La disyuntiva mexicana," in *Tiempo mexicano* (Mexico: Joaquín Mortiz, 1972), 153, cites the testimony of a friend of his. "A doctor friend of mine calculated that there were 500 cadavers in the morgue where he went to look for his son." ["Un médico amigo mío calculó que había quinientos cadáveres en la morgue donde fue a buscar a su hijo."]

34. Paz, *Posdata*, 38. "The 2nd of October of 1968 ended the student movement. It also ended an era in the history of Mexico." ["el 2 de octubre de 1968 terminó el movimiento estudiantil. También terminó una época de la historia de México."] Leal, "Tlatelolco, Tlatelolco," 4. "The event, like the one in 1910, changed the course of Mexico's political, social and intellectual life." Fuentes, "La disyuntiva mexicana," 147. "The events of 1968 signified for Mexico a crisis of growth, transformation and of consciousness only comparable to those which the history manuals and public monuments consecrate as definitive stages of our national existence: Independence, Reform and Revolution." ["Los sucesos de 1968 significaron para México una crisis de crecimiento, de transformación y de conciencia sólo comparable a las que los manuales de historia y los monumentos públicos consagran como etapas definitivas de nuestra existencia nacional: Independencia, Reforma y Revolución."]

35. Leal, "Tlatelolco, Tlatelolco," 4.

36. Ibid., 13.

37. John S. Brushwood, *La novela mexicana (1967–1982)* (Mexico: Grijalbo, 1984), 18. "En otras palabras, lo sucedido de Tlatelolco engendra, por el solo hecho de ser evocado, un complejo de reacciones que bien pueden alterar el efecto de cualquier otro acontecimiento."

38. Leal, "Tlatelolco, Tlatelolco," 11.

39. Included in the Appendix of this book is a partial list of such works.

40. To date there have been forty-three editions printed.

41. "Son muchos. Vienen a pie, vienen riendo. Bajaron por Melchor Ocampo, la Reforma, Juárez, Cinco de Mayo, muchachos y muchachas estudiantes que van del brazo en la manifestación con la misma alegría con que hace apenas unos días iban a la feria. . . ."

42. ". . . jóvenes despreocupados que no saben que mañana, dentro de dos días, dentro de cuatro estarán allí hinchándose bajo la lluvia, después de una feria en donde el centro del tiro al blanco lo serán ellos. . . ."

43. ". . . los veo nublados pero sí oigo sus voces, oigo sus pasos, pas, pas, pas, paaaaas, paaaaas, como en la manifestación del silencio, toda la vida oiré esos pasos que avanzan. . . ."

44. *La feria* by Juan José Arreola (Mexico: Joaquín Mortiz, 1963), although fictional, is composed of the same technique of a collage of voices. This form brings to mind as well the "polyphony" of Bakhtin, *Dialogic Imagination*, 315, 320, who has shown that the foundation of style in the novel is the diversity of discourse and the stratification of language. The social heteroglossia of an epoch is re-created artistically in the many and diverse voices which form the discourse in the novel. This includes the incorporation of other genres of all types. The difference in this work by Poniatowska is that the diverse fragments do not appear incorporated into the primary discourse of one narrator or implied author, but rather separately and independent of any apparent structure.

45. Bakhtin, *Dialogic Imagination*, 48–49.

46. Michel Foucault, "What Is an Author?" in *Textual Strategies: Perspectives in Post Structuralist Criticism* (Ithaca, N.Y.: Cornell University Press, 1979), 159.

47. "La oscuridad engendra la violencia / y la violencia pide oscuridad / para cuajar el crimen. / Por eso el dos de octubre aguardó hasta la noche / para que nadie viera la mano que empuñaba / el arma, sino sólo su efecto de relámpago."

48. "En su mayoría estos testimonios fueron recogidos en octubre y en noviembre de 1968. Los estudiantes presos dieron los suyos en el curso de los dos años siguientes. Este relato les pertenece. Está hecho con sus palabras, sus luchas, sus errores, su dolor y su asombro."

49. "Aquí está el eco del grito de los que murieron y el grito de los que quedaron. Aquí está su indignación y su protesta. Es el grito mudo que se atoró en miles de gargantas, en miles de ojos desorbitados por el espanto el 2 de octubre de 1968, en la noche de Tlatelolco."

50. ". . . basada en los hechos a que se refieren los estudiantes en sus testimonios de historia oral."

51. David William Foster, "Latin American Documentary Narrative," *PMLA* 99, no. 1 (1984): 45. "The ironic framing—the foregone conclusion as the point of departure for the chain of events represented—the authorial intervention in organizing the material gathered, the eloquent juxtaposition of oral texts with various other sources, the interplay between personal commentaries and impersonal, antiphonic choruses like the banners and posters are conscious artistic decisions that lend *Noche* its special narrative and novelistic texture."

52. "La noche triste de Tlatelolco—a pesar de todas sus voces y testimonios—

sigue siendo incomprehensible. ¿Por qué? Tlatelolco es incoherente, contradictorio. Pero la muerte no lo es." "Ninguna crónica nos da una visión de conjunto."

53. The testimonial novel, as Barnet reiterates, should communicate the collective human experience, the essence of the reality of an epoch. (Barnet, "La novela-testimonio," 23.)

54. This reflects again Bakhtin's concept of heteroglossia, *Dialogic Imagination*, 326. Bakhtin refers to the "fundamental, socio-linguistic speech diversity and multi-languagedness" of the novel.

55. Foster, "Latin American Documentary Narrative," 45.

56. Lionel Gossman, "History and Literature," in *The Writing of History*, ed. Robert H. Canary and Henry Kozicki (Madison: University of Wisconsin Press, 1978), 31.

57. Hayden White, *Metahistory: The Historical Imagination in 19th Century Europe* (Baltimore: The Johns Hopkins University Press, 1973), 7.

58. Gossman, "History and Literature," 7.

59. The historical novel is also composed of historical facts in a fictive structure. But, unlike the documentary novel which maintains a direct contact with reality, the historical novel creates a fictional realm in which representative characters move. "The sense of the real is replaced by realism." Foley, *Telling the Truth*, 142, 143–84.

60. Ibid., 268.

61. But including, of course, alterations by the author.

62. Foley, *Telling the Truth*, 25, addresses this problem: "The documentary novel constitutes a distinct fictional kind. It locates itself near the border between factual discourse and fictive discourse, but it does not propose an eradication of that border. Rather, it purports to represent reality by means of agreed-upon conventions of fictionality, while grafting onto its fictive pact some kind of additional claim to empirical validation."

63. Gossman, "History and Literature," 20.

64. Roberto González Echevarría, "*Biografía de un cimarrón* and the Novel of the Cuban Revolution," *Novel* 13, no. 3 (Spring 1980): 249–263, 255.

65. The historical school of positivism believed that the work of the historian was only to show *wie es eigentlich gewesen* (how it really was) and not to interpret or teach. Adam Schaff, *History and Truth* (Oxford: Pergamon Press, 1976), 77.

66. See, for example, John Hellmann, *Fables of Fact: The New Journalism as New Fiction* (Urbana: University of Illinois Press, 1981); Ronald Weber, *The Literature of Fact: Literary Nonfiction in American Writing* (Athens: Ohio University Press, 1980); John Hollowell, *Fact and Fiction: The New Journalism and the Nonfiction Novel* (Chapel Hill: University of North Carolina Press, 1977).

67. Hellmann, *Fables of Fact*, 3.

68. Ibid., 24.

69. Norman Mailer, *Advertisements for Myself* (New York: Putnam, 1959), 199, in Hellmann, *Fables of Fact*, 35.

70. Although "the incident" was mentioned the following day in all the daily newspapers, they were quite reserved and timid accounts. Paz recounts with indignation: "How many died? In Mexico not a single newspaper has dared to publish the figures" (Paz, *Posdata*, 38). ["¿Cuántos murieron? En México ningún periódico se ha atrevido a publicar las cifras."]

71. "Tlatelolco, Campo de Batalla. / Durante Varias Horas Terroristas y Solda- / dos Sostuvieron Rudo Combate. / 29 Muertos y más de 80 Heridos en Am- / bos Bandos; 1 000 Detenidos."

72. "Manos Extrañas se Empeñan en Despresti- / giar a México. / El Objetivo: Frustrar los XIX Juegos. / Francotiradores abrieron fuego contra la / Tropa en Tlatelolco. / Heridos un General y 11 Militares; 2 Sol / dados y más de 20 civiles muertos en la peor refriega."

73. Bakhtin, *Dialogic Imagination,* chap. 4, utilizes the term *hybridization* to refer to the combination of two styles, classes, or systems of language in a person's (character's) speech. Here we are referring to a hybridization of genre.

74. I have invented a term in Spanish that is itself a hybrid of the words *periodismo* (journalism) and *poesía* (poetry).

75. Literally "aide-de-camp" but in this case probably a kind of usher or monitor for a meeting.

76. "La Cruz Roja reportó tener 46 heridos, casi todos de bala y algunos de ellos muy graves. Informó además, que cuatro personas que fueron lesionadas murieron en el hospital. No han sido identificados."

77. This line has more poetic imagery in Spanish: "La mujer lloraba a sollazos como pedradas."

78. "Bajo las pancartas, las mantas ensopadas por la lluvia, había dos cadáveres. . . ."

79. "Nunca hemos llorado tanto en esos días, sí, nosotras las mujeres. Como si quisiéramos lavar a fuerza de lágrimas todas las imágenes, todos los muros, todas las aristas, todas las bancas de piedra manchadas de sangre de Tlatelolco, todas las huellas de los cuerpos desangrándose en los rincones. . . . Pero es mentira que las imágenes se lavan a fuerza de lágrimas. Allí siguen en la memoria."

80. "Una mujer descalza / cubierta la cabeza con un rebozo negro / espera que le entreguen a su muerto. / 22 años, Politécnico: / un hoyo rojo en el costado / hecho por la M-1 / reglamentaria."

81. "Se llevaron los muertos quién sabe a dónde. / Llenaron de estudiantes las cárceles de la ciudad." "Detrás de la iglesia de Santiago Tlatelolco / treinta años de paz más otros / treinta años de paz, más todo el acero y el cemento empleado para las fiestas del fantasmagórico país, más todos los discursos / salieron por boca de las ametralladoras."

82. "Los empleados / Municipales lavan la sangre / en la Plaza de los Sacrificios."

83. "Y es que en América / está ya en flor la gente nueva / que pide peso a la prosa / y condición al verso / y quiere trabajo y realidad / en la política / y en la literatura."

84. *Visión de los vencidos. Relaciones indígenas de la conquista,* trans. from *nahua* texts by Angel María Garibay K. (Mexico: Universidad Nacional Autonoma de México, Biblioteca del Estudiante Universitario, 1972).

85. Paz, *Posdata,* 40. "Fue una repetición instintiva que asumió la forma de un ritual de expiación; las correspondencias con el pasado mexicano, especialmente con el mundo azteca, son fascinantes, sobrecogedoras y repelentes. La matanza de Tlatelolco nos revela que un pasado que creíamos enterrado está vivo e irrumpe entre nosotros."

86. Michael Stanford, *The Nature of Historical Knowledge* (New York: Basil Blackwell, 1987), 1, defines *res gestae* as "history-as-events" and *historia res gestarum* as "history-as-story."

87. White demonstrates this in *Metahistory* as does Gossman in "History and Literature."

88. See, for example, White, *Metahistory;* Leo Braudy, *Narrative Form in History and Fiction* (Princeton: Princeton University Press, 1970); González Echev-

arría, ed., *Historia y ficción en la narrativa hispanoamericana* (Coloquio de Yale, Monte Avila, 1984); Robert H. Canary and Henry Kozicki, eds., *The Writing of History: Literary Form and Historical Understanding* (Madison: University of Wisconsin Press, 1978).

89. Gossman, "History and Literature," 24.

90. Paul de Man, "Literary History and Literary Modernity," in *Blindness & Insight: Essays in the Rhetoric of Contemporary Criticism,* 152.

91. For example, the traditional omniscient narrator creates the illusion of objectivity but lacks the authenticity of direct experience. The personal narrator (first person), on the other hand, creates the illusion of authenticity but his credibility suffers from a perspective that is too subjective.

92. Luis Spota, *La Plaza* (Mexico: Joaquín Mortiz, 1972).

93. Leal, "Tlatelolco, Tlatelolco," 12.

94. Ronald Christ, "The Author as Editor," *Review of the Center for Inter-American Relations,* no. 15 (1975): 78.

95. Foster, "Latin American Documentary Narrative," 46.

96. A term that comes from Coleridge, developed by T. S. Eliot. It means to allow oneself to enter into the drama, to accept the dramatic conventions of the theater as if they were real.

97. Ibid., 46.

98. Jean Franco, "The Critique of the Pyramid and Mexican Narrative after 1968," in *Latin American Fiction Today, A Symposium,* ed. Rose S. Minc (Takoma Park, Md./Montclair, N.J.: Hispamérica/Montclair State College, 1979), 49–60, 51. That official silence weighed heavily in the days and months after Tlatelolco. There was almost no official reaction or explanation and after one day, there was silence in the newspapers as well.

99. Octavio Paz maintains that in the case of the student movement and the tragedy of Tlatelolco it is not the historically marginalized classes who are demonstrating. "It is clear that we are not seeing an intensifying of class struggle but rather a revolt of those sectors which, in a permanent or temporary way, the technological society has placed on the margins. The students belong to the second of these categories" (Paz, *Posdata,* 22). ["Es claro que no estamos ante un recrudecimiento de la lucha de clases sino ante una revuelta de esos sectores que, de un modo permanente o transitorio, la sociedad tecnológica ha colocado al margen. Los estudiantes pertenecen a la segunda de estas categorías."]

100. "Esto viene a cuento porque creo que los jóvenes campesinos, los obreros y los estudiantes tienen pocas perspectivas dignas de vida, porque las fuentes de trabajo se crean en beneficio de intereses particulares y no de la colectividad. Se nos dice continuamente: 'Ustedes son el futuro del país.' Pero se nos niega sistemáticamente cualquier oportunidad de actuar y participar en las decisiones políticas del presente. . . . Nosotros queremos y PODEMOS participar ahora, no cuando tengamos sesenta años. . . ."

101. "Yo ya no creo en las palabras. . . ." "Ha llegado el día en que nuestro silencio será más elocuente que las palabras que ayer callaron las bayonetas."

102. ". . . sólo se oían los pasos. . . . Pasos, pasos sobre el asfalto, pasos, el ruido de muchos pies que marchan, el ruido de miles de pies que avanzan. El silencio era más impresionante que la multitud. Parecía que íbamos pisoteando toda la verborrea de los políticos, todos sus discursos, siempre los mismos, toda la demagogia, la retórica, el montonal de palabras que los hechos jamás respaldan, el chorro de mentiras; las íbamos barriendo bajo nuestros pies. . . ."

103. ". . . diálogo, diálogo, diálogo. . . ." "Hace cincuenta años que el gobierno

monologa con el gobierno. . . ." "El gobierno cree que en México sólo existe una opinión pública: la que lo aplaude, la que lo lambisconea. . . ." "Pero existe otra: la que critica, la que no cree en nada de lo que dice. . . ."

104. Franco, "Critique of the Pyramid," 49.

105. Fuentes, *Tiempo Mexicano*, 151. "¿Y podía responder con inteligencia y generosidad un sistema adormecido por treinta años de autoelogio, monolitismo, monólogo consigo mismo y remachados mitos de autoengaño: unidad nacional, equilibrio político, milagro económico?"

106. This reflects the central idea of Bakhtin's work *(Dialogic Imagination),* in which the novel is composed of many discourses in constant dialogue on many levels.

107. Herbert Lindenberger, *Historical Drama: The Relationship of Literature and Reality* (Chicago: University of Chicago Press, 1975), 107.

108. Friedrich Schiller, "Über die tragische Kunst," 165, in *Historical Drama,* 70.

109. Lindenberger, *Historical Drama,* 70.

110. "—Te traje fabada. . . .—Ay abuela, estoy malo del estómago! (Entra Gilberto Guevara con una gorra de lana que según Luis y Raúl y Saúl el Chale, no se quita jamás. La abuela le tiende los brazos.)—¡Mi Guevara! Lo abraza un largo rato. Es la clásica abuelita de los cuentos para niños; gordita, dulce, el pelo blanco, una bolita de ternura. —(Decías que estás malo del estómago Raúl? . . ."

111. "¡Alto! ¡Alto el fuego! ¡Alto!" (Voces en la multitud) "¡No puedo! ¡No soporto más!" (Voz de mujer) "¡No salgas! ¡No te mueves!" (Voz de hombre) "¡Cérquenlos! ¡Ahí! ¡Ahí! ¡Cérquenlos, cérquenlos les digo!" (Una voz) "¡Estoy herido! ¡Llamen a un médico. Estoy! . . ." (Una voz)

112. "Me voy a morir. Me duele. Estoy seguro de que me voy a morir. . . . Aquí estoy en Tlatelolco, hoy 2 de octubre, tengo veinticuatro años. Me está saliendo mucha sangre. . . . ¡Cómo corren todos! Y yo que no puedo ni jalar esta pierna hacia mí. No veo ni un maldito camillero, no se oye nada con estas ametralladoras. Si me muero me dedicará la mitad de su columna, a lo mejor toda la columna. . . . ¿Quién le pasará mis datos?"

113. "Un estudiante de 19 años de edad -Luis González Sánchez—perdió la vida a manos de un policía, el 17 de noviembre de 1968, por el delito de ser sorprendido pintando propaganda del Movimiento en una pared, cerca del Periférico."

114. "El día 8 de diciembre que llevamos a enterrar a Jan. . . ."

115. "Las escenas de dramatismo son inenarrables."

116. We will see such paralysis and traumatization of language in the face of horror in *Morirás lejos* by José Emilio Pacheco, discussed in Chapter 4.

117. It is interesting to note that many of the fragments of this work are excerpts chosen from other texts: from poems, articles, plays, etc. In the end, it is a text made of other texts, written by multiple authors.

118. See, for example, *Los días y los años* by Luis González del Alba (Mexico: ERA, 1971); *Con él, conmigo y con nosotros tres* by María Luisa Mendoza (Mexico: Joaquín Mortiz, 1971); and *El otoño de revolución (octubre)* by Sócrates Campos Lemus (Mexico: Costa-Amic, 1973).

119. Christ, "Author as Editor," 78.

120. For example, there are ten people who "speak" more than five times according to the way in which Poniatowska divides up the testimonies. Some speak more than fifteen times and one even more than twenty times in the text.

121. Christ, "Author as Editor," 78. "From these solos, some of which come

from voices repeated in varying frequences, 'characters' begin to emerge, so that we read the book, sewing widely separated passages together, fabricating personalities out of verbal remnants."

122. Included in this note are all of the fragments of Diana's testimony. "Perdimos de vista a Reyes y oí un grito de mi hermano: '¡No me sueltes!' Nos agarramos de la mano fuertemente. . . ." "Si me hubiera dado cuenta de que Julio ya estaba muriéndose. . . ." "Hermanito, ¿qué tienes? Hermanito, contéstame. . . ." "¡Una camilla, por favor!" "Las personas que estaban tiradas en la Plaza; los vivos y los muertos se entremezclaban. . . ." "Hermanito ¿por qué no me contestas?" "Julio tenía 15 años, estudiaba en la vocacional número 1 que está cerca de la Unidad Tlatelolco. Era la segunda vez que asistía a un mitín político." "Mi padre murió poco tiempo después de que murió Julio. Como resultado del choque tuvo un ataque al corazón. Era su hijo único, el menor. Repetía muchas veces: 'Pero ¿por qué mi hijo? . . .' Mi madre sigue viviendo, quién sabe cómo."

123. Miguel Barnet, "The Documentary Novel," *Cuban Studies/Estudios Cubanos* 11, no. 1 (January 1981): 23, and in footnote 8, p. 32, refers to the technique of the Japanese film *Rashomon* (1950), directed by Akira Kurosawa, in which the same story is narrated from different points of view.

124. Fragments of the testimony of Margarita Nolasca appear on pp. 171, 172–73, 175, 221–22, 235, 244, 248, 269, and 272.

125. "Abrí la puerta de la casa. —¿Y Carlitos? —No ha llegado. No sabemos nada. —Entonces comenzó la peor noche de mi vida." "Empezamos a tocar de puerta en puerta: . . . Yo gritaba 'Carlos, Carlitos, Carlitos, ¿dónde estás?'"

126. ". . . y Margarita, ya fuera de sí, iba puerta por puerta gritando: '¡Carlitos, soy yo! ¡Abreme!' Era Kafkiano."

127. ". . . una madre . . . una madre gritando: '¡Carlitos!' por pasillos y escaleras, sollozando en busca de us hijo y preguntando por él."

128. "Siento que después de esa fecha no soy el mismo de antes: no podría ser."

129. "Me pareció increíble cómo todo volvía a la vida normal. Era como si lo de Tlatelolco no hubiera existido." "Al salir de Tlatelolco, todo era de una normalidad horrible, insultante. No era posible que todo siguiera en calma."

130. Paz, Introduction to the English translation of *La noche de Tlatelolco, Massacre in Mexico,* trans. Helen R. Lane (New York: Viking, 1975), viii.

131. González Echevarría, "*Biografía de un cimarrón,*" 251, discusses the idea of conversion, which he defines as the desire to declare the beginning of a new era and the coming of a new human existence.

132. "Por lo menos, esto sirve para crear conciencia, una conciencia nacional."

133. These words of Poniatowska's were taken from an interview with Margarita García Flores of *Revista de la UNAM* 30, no. 7 (marzo, 1976), 27. They also appear in an interview with Miller in *26 autores del México actual,* 314–15.

134. "En agosto de 1968 empezaron a contarme algunas cosas de las manifestaciones, a las cuales no iba porque acababa de tener a Felipito. El tres de octubre vinieron a mi casa tres mujeres: María Alicia Martíez Medrano, Margarita Nolasco y Mercedes Oliver. Llorando me contaron lo sucedido, lo que habían presenciado en Tlatelolco. Pensé que estaban histéricas, exaltadas. ¡Claro, lo que había salido en los periódicos era en sí lo suficientemente aterrador! Me contaron de pilas de cadáveres tirados en la plaza; cómo habían corrido para salir de allí. . . . Enloquecida de horror, a la mañana siguiente fui a Tlatelolco y todavía estaban en las puertas de los elevadores, en las paredes, las huellas de las

ametralladoras, las huellas de los balazas, incluso la sangre en el piso. Todavía estaba el ejército. No había agua en los edificios y muchas de las familias habían abandonado sus casas. Me pareció terrible. Empecé a recoger los testimonios de los muchachos que querían hablar, cambiándoles sus nombres. Después, cuando salió el libro, muchos estudiantes me dijeron 'yo tengo cosas más terribles que relatarle que las que usted escribió.' Eso siempre sucede, al principio nadie quiere hablar, despuès todos quieren hacerlo."

135. Paz, Introduction to *Massacre in Mexico,* vii–viii.

136. Ibid., vii.

137. Fuentes, *Tiempo mexicano* (Mexico: Joaquín Mortiz, 1972), 149. Fuentes creates this image to describe the relationship between the social and cultural base of Mexico and the political and economic structures, the latter which he portrays as pyramids (as did Paz in *Posdata*), and the former as a river: ". . . A river, a current which corrodes the pyramids, pounding against them and trying to convert stone into water." [". . . un río, un flujo que corroe a las pirámides, embate contra ellas e intenta convertir la piedra en agua."]

138. Oscar Handlin, *Truth in History* (Cambridge: Harvard University Press, 1979), 405.

139. A soldier says this to the journalist José Antonio del Campo, from *El Día.* This fragment appears on pp. 172, 198, and 273. They are the last words of the narrative part of the book.

140. To repeat Poniatowska's words, p. 170.

Chapter 3. Elena Garro: The Inversions of Fiction

1. Elena Garro, *Testimonios sobre Mariana* (Mexico: Editorial Grijalbo, 1981), 164. All references are to this edition. "La gente cree con más facilidad una mentira que una verdad." All translations are my own unless otherwise stated.

2. John Brushwood, *Mexico in Its Novel* (Austin: University of Texas Press, 1966), 52–53 in Beth Miller and Alfonso González, *26 autoras del México actual* (Mexico: Costa-Amic, 1978), 203.

3. See the note about the Japanese film of this name in the preceding chapter.

4. "La primera vez que la vi fue en una fotografía que nos mostró Pepe a su regreso de Paris. . . . Estaba recargada sobre el tronco de un árbol en un bosque brumoso."

5. "Mariana empezó en ese bosque ligeramente borrado por la bruma. . . ."

6. "No hablo en orden. . ." "¿Cuál es el orden con Mariana?"

7. "No sabía nada de ella, era la viajera imprevista, la desconocida sin pasado y sin futuro. . . . Tenía algo artificial, era como si no existiera de una manera perdurable. . . ."

8. "Está atrapada, no se salvará nunca. . . . Tomo riesgos inútiles ayudándola."

9. "Mi trabajo me obligaba a traicionar a mi amiga. La palabra traición es injusta, ya que sacrificarme por ella hubiera sido inútil. Mariana era una desclasada, se sabía colocada en una situación límite que fatalmente la empujaría a tomar soluciones también límites. Yo no podía salvarla."

10. "Romualdo me llevó a la casa de Mariana. A priori, el personaje me resultaba antipático." "De pronto apareció Mariana. No era la mujer fatal que

había imaginado. Llevaba el cabello rubio suelto sobre los hombros, usaba pantalones y calzaba unas viejas zapatillas de ballet."

11. . . . "gígolo sudamericano. . . ." ". . . un joven rubio de aspecto atlético y sonrisa infantil [who] poseía un poder venenoso de seducción."

12. "Una joven fumaba sentada en un canapé de terciopelo de color tabaco. Calzaba mocasines y me miraba con ojos desparpajados."

13. "Mariana no es lo que tú piensas. . ."

14. "A veces creo que Mariana sólo fue un sueño que soñamos entre todos."

15. It's not exactly clear what really happens to Mariana, but if she isn't murdered, she is at least destroyed. The ambiguity of the crime at the level of the plot contributes to the general air of mystery and to the freedom of interpretation of the work.

16. ". . . imagen transfigurada por la ausencia. . . ."

17. ". . . no sabes nada, nada."

18. "Si Mariana desaparecía de mi vida se convertiría en una Mariana imaginada . . . sólo quedaría su substancia como una sombra melancólica de color ocre." "Podemos reflejar nuestra vida, dibujándola en hojas de papel y nunca será nuestra vida verdadera. El papel no recoge el tono de voz, la ligereza de unos pasos, la intensidad de un dolor o el golpe definitivo de una puerta al cerrarse. . . ."

19. ". . . también yo pensaba que la vida sólo era un juego literario."

20. ". . . fábulas que inventa ella. . ."

21. ". . . su marido había cerrado el capítulo de nuestro amor."

22. This summary of the Hegelian dilemma is derived from Genevieve Lloyd's "Masters, Slaves and Others," *Radical Philosophy* 34 (Summer 1983): 2–8.

23. "¡Voy a domar a Mariana!"

24. ". . . para destruir a alguien primero hay que destruir su imagen" and that "Eso lo ignoraba la pequeña Mariana, que segura de sus pasos se movía como en un escenario, sin saber que alguien había cambiado las luces de los reflectores, para proyectar sobre su figura clara, una luz negra que la desfiguraba. . . ."

25. Ibid., 2–8.

26. Simone de Beauvoir, *The Second Sex*, trans. H. M. Parshley, cited in *Masters, Slaves and Others*, 6–8.

27. "Me siento mirada."

28. "La vida de mi amiga no era su propia vida, estaba determinada por personajes que se acercaban a ella, dejaban su huella y desaparecían."

29. "La mujer objeto nos aprisiona, nos obliga a llevar una vida artificial. Yo, por mi parte, viviría en una buhardilla entregado al amor y a mis estudios, pero no puedo. Mariana y la niña me encadenan al dinero, a lo cotidiano y a la vida artificial."

30. "La toma de conciencia de Sartre es la explicación filosófica de la voluntad de poder adquisitivo en el burgués."

31. "Libro ambiguo. Se diría que justifica el crimen." "¡Te prohibo que hables!"

32. Oliver Sacks, Professor of the Neurological Clinic of Albert Einstein College of Medicine, in his book, *The Man Who Mistook His Wife for a Hat and Other Clinical Tales* (New York: Harper & Row, 1987), 110–11.

33. Ibid., 110.

34. "Era un presente intenso." "Me pareció que tenía una capacidad magnífica de olvido. . . ."

35. "Me pareció verla reflejada en un espejo hecho astillas y que también ella contemplaba su imagen mutilada y multiplicada."

36. "Cada vez que intentaba acercármele algo imprevisto la convertía en intocable e invisible. . . ."

37. ". . . La encontré al pie del muro blanco leyendo también un libro en blanco. Supe que allí estaba escrito nuestro destino y que en sus hojas no existía ninguna palabra."

38. Méndez Rodenas, "Tiempo femenino, tiempo ficticio: 'Los recuerdos del porvenir', de Elena Garro" in *Revista Iberoamericana,* nos. 132–33 (July–December 1985), 848. Rodenas cites Garro's novel, *La casa junto al río* (Mexico: Editorial Grijalbo, 1982), 7. "In the novels and short stories by Elena Garro, feminine time is a 'manifest destiny', where the past determines the future, a 'circular time identical to itself, like a mirror reflecting another mirror that repeats us.'" ["En las novelas y cuentos de Elena Garro, el tiempo femenino es un 'destino manifiesto', donde el pasado determina el futuro, un 'tiempo circular e idéntico a sí mismo, como un espejo reflejando a otro espejo que nos repite.'"]

39. "El pasado está escrito en el tiempo y sólo es la imagen del futuro. . . ."

40. ". . . a un lado estaba el pasado, en el otro el futuro, exactamente igual al pasado, como un simple reflejo del primero. . . ." Méndez Rodenas notes that in *Los recuerdos del porvenir,* the first of Garro's novels, (Mexico: Joaquín Mortiz, 1977), the generals' lovers are confronted with a "circular future." It is a destiny enclosed in a "time of repetition, a feminine future without change," ibid., 849.

41. Ibid., 848. ". . . mujeres olvidadas que representan la herencia sin salida, el destino trágico y repetitivo de la mujer."

42. "Se romperán todos los espejos en el instante en que usted abandone la ciudad. . . ."

43. "La veía en sueños, en las calles, y en verano se aparecía mar adentro. Por la noche me llamaba y mis amigos se convirtieron en formas incoherentes. Durante mis sueños, Mariana se me aparecía bajo el agua mirándome con los ojos muy abiertos, yo estaba sobre ella y despertaba sudando. Le contaba mis noches visitadas por ella y se convirtió en mi conciencia lejana. . . ." ". . . busqué su imagen en los espejos y la encontré quieta, en el fondo de lagos desde los que me enviaba signos."

44. "Me había equivocado en el amor de Mariana. Los sentimientos eran fugaces e ilusorios, como los fuegos de artificio. Después, quedaba la noche solitaria y yo había entrado en una dimensión oscura. Al llegar al hotel no me reconocí en los espejos."

45. Anthony Wilden, *Speech and Language in Psychoanalysis: Jacques Lacan,* trans. with notes (Baltimore: The Johns Hopkins University Press, 1981), 160.

46. Anika Lemaire, *Jacques Lacan,* trans. David Macey (London: Henley; Boston: Routledge & Kegan Paul, 1977), 178.

47. Wilden, *Speech and Language,* 165.

48. Ibid., 173.

49. Ibid., 165–66.

50. Glantz, "Estudio preliminar," Introduction to *Onda y escritura en México: jóvenes de 20 a 33,* ed. Margo Glantz (Mexico: Siglo 21, 1971).

51. Octavio Paz, *El laberinto de la soledad* (Mexico: Fondo de Cultura Económica, 1967), 10, in *Onda y escritura,* 8. ". . . no puede olvidarse de sí mismo pues apenas lo consigue deja de serlo."

52. Glantz, *Onda y escritura,* 8. "Esta trágica paradoja hace que el joven sea en esa etapa de su vida un Narciso detenido en el acto de contemplarse, un

Narciso incapaz de reconocer su rostro, porque el espejo que lo refleja se fragmenta antes de que su imagen se clarifique, antes de que logre perfilar sus facciones. La rebeldía es el espejo roto antes de que se cumpla la develación."

53. ". . . un grave error histórico. Vivía en una dimensión imaginaria, se negaba a ver la realidad y ahora huía como una colegiala en vez de afrontar los hechos."

54. "No dudes de que aparezca suicidada un día. Está a un paso de la esquizofrenia y ha cerrado los canales de comunicación con el mundo exterior." "Mariana era incapaz de exteriorizarse, siempre hablaba de cosas ajenas a ella misma."

55. ". . . para siempre en el interior de aquel espejo."

56. ". . . a pesar del frío que corría por la casa. . . ."

57. The name "Augusto," which as an adjective means "inspires fearful admiration," symbolizes extreme power, like that of the first emperor of Rome, Augustus Caesar.

58. "Nadie podía confiar en ella y resultaba terrible para la persona que la amara. Tuve la impresión de que existían dos Marianas, una dulce y otra perversa."

59. "Esa noche, contemplando a la madre y a la hija, tuve la extraña sensación de que las dos eran la misma y que una de ellas había inventado a la 'otra' para hacernos creer que gozaba de alguna compañía."

60. "Fue diez años después de mi primer encuentro con ella, cuando vi a ella y a su doble en la terraza del Hotel Carlton en Cannes." "Tuve la impresión de que Mariana se había desdoblado en su hija y de que eran la misma persona."

61. "Muchas veces tuve la extraña impresión de ver superpuesto sobre el rostro rubio de Mariana el rostro rubio del sudamericano. Imaginé que el pensamiento de mi amiga proyectaba aquel rostro lejano sobre el suyo para hacerla olvidar lo que la rodeaba."

62. "No existe un caso singular o una persona única. Los hechos y las personas se repiten en otros hechos y otras personas exactamente iguales, una se salva y la otra se pierde. Dios nos crea, nos echa a andar en circunstancias iguales, uno se desvía y se pierde, el otro sigue las huellas dejadas por su ángel y se salva."

63. "La mano que borró la imagen de Mariana guardada en la memoria de sus amigos como una imagen reflejada en el agua, fue la mano de Augusto su marido, que implacable revolvió el agua, desfiguró su rostro, su figura, hasta volverla grotesca y distorsionada. Al final, cuando las aguas se aquietaron, de Mariana no quedó ¡nada! Cambiar la memoria para destruir una imagen es tarea más ardua que destruir a una persona."

64. "Algún día sabremos la verdad. . . ." "Lo miré escéptico, la verdad tiene tantas caras como la mentira."

65. Marc Bloch, *The Historian's Craft,* trans. Peter Putnam (New York: Vintage Books, 1953).

66. Ibid., 49.

67. Ibid., 101.

68. Ibid.

69. Paz, *El laberinto de la soledad,* 65. ". . . teñidos de humanidad, esto es, de problematicidad."

70. Henri Marrou, *The Meaning of History,* trans. Robert J. Olson (Baltimore: Helicon, 1966), 152, cited in Paul Ricoeur, *Time and Narrative,* trans. Kathleen McLaughlin and David Pellauer (Chicago: University of Chicago Press, 1984), 98.

71. Bloch, *Historian's Craft*, 110.
72. Ibid., 55.
73. Oscar Handlin, *Truth in History* (Cambridge: Harvard University Press, 1979), 405.
74. Erich Kahler, *The Meaning of History* (New York: Braziller, 1964), 17.
75. Ibid., 220.
76. Louis Mink, "Narrative Form as a Cognitive Instrument," in *The Writing of History*, ed. Robert H. Canary and Henry Kosicki (Madison: University of Wisconsin Press, 1978), 143.
77. Ibid., 145.
78. Gossman, "History and Literature," 29.
79. Mink, "Narrative Form," 147.
80. Ibid., 143. Mink maintains that, although we might have rejected the idea of a universal *historiography* (it would be impossible to write), we still presuppose the concept of a universal *history* in the form of a cumulative chronicle that ideally would be able to relate "what really happened."
81. Ibid., 143.
82. To the image of the chain as a metaphor for the Universal History (the Ideal Chronicle) one could add another more complicated image of a net of chains as found in *El mundo alucinante* by Reinaldo Arenas (Mexico: Editorial Diógenes, 1978), 147–53. In this parodic section a past event is narrated, that of the binding in chains of Fray Servando, imitating in the description of the process the construction of the text itself. Here the story in its function of defining and preserving an historical moment (embodied in the friar), reveals its own narrative complexity as a net of linked and overlapping relationships (chains).
83. "Entonces, ¿la verdad no importa frente a la ley?" "Mariana, la ley es la verdad."
84. Wallace Martin, *Recent Theories of Narrative* (Ithaca, N.Y.: Cornell University Press, 1986), 119–20.
85. "Las Marianas diminutas de las fotos se habían convertido en seres reales y algunas me miraban con tristeza, mientras otras me obsequiaban sonrisas alegres y relampagueantes. Yo pasaba largos ratos descifrándolas. . . ."
86. "El tiempo lo borra todo."
87. I am referring to the famous verses: "Nuestras vidas son los ríos / que van a dar en la mar / que es el morir": by Jorge Manrique, "Coplas por la muerte de su padre" (CXCIII). "El se va. . . ." "Siempre se va. . . ."
88. "Si tú te vas, yo me muero. . . ."
89. Barbara Herrnstein Smith, *On the Margins of Discourse: The Relation of Literature to Language* (Chicago: University of Chicago Press, 1979), 12, cited in *Recent Theories of Narrative*, 183.
90. Martin, *Recent Theories of Narrative*, 183. Martin cites Jonathon Culler, "Problems in the Theory of Fiction," *Diacritics* 14, no. 1 (1984):2–11 and Chris Hutchinson, "The Act of Narration: A Critical Survey of Some Speech-Act Theories of Narrative Discourse," *Journal of Literary Semantics*, 13 (1984):3–35.
91. "Me convertí en una asidua al salón de Mariana, en donde se fabricaban teorías literarias, filosóficas, sexuales y sociológicas. Augusto escogía a su mujer para ilustrar los temas. En presencia de la muchacha se discutía su educación, sus tendencias autodestructivas, su frigidez sexual, su lesbianismo latente, etc. . . ."
92. "Recordé que la naturaleza imita al arte y decidí darle un final feliz, que cambiaría su destino." "Me encerré a escribir, mi personaje era complejo, su vida era un inexplicable laberinto, pero yo la conduciría através de aquellos vericuetos

tenebrosos a una salida inesperadamente luminosa. Era lo menos que podía hacer por la pobre Mariana."

93. ". . . era un nombre inpronunciable. Unicamente Barnaby se atrevió nombrarla por su nombre y publicó su libro titulado *Mariana*. La novela fue un éxito entre sus amigos, aunque la heroina no era nada grata."

94. Roberto González Echevarría, "*Biografía de un cimarron*, and the Novel of the Cuban Revolution," *Novel* 13, no. 3 (Spring 1980):250.

95. John Searle, "The Logical Status of Fictional Discourse," in *Expression and Meaning: Studies in the Theory of Speech Acts* (Cambridge: Cambridge University Press, 1979), 58–75 in *Recent Theories of Narrative*, 186.

96. Martin, *Recent Theories of Narrative*, 186.

97. "La gente cree con más facilidad una mentira que una verdad. Si ahora le mintiera me creería."

98. "Ocultaba una verdad que quizá ni ante ella misma quería confesar."

99. "Allí en el cementerio, frente a la tumba abandonada de Mariana y Natalia, supe que la verdad siempre es terrible y que el conocerla nos aniquila."

100. Frank Kermode, *The Sense of an Ending: Studies in the Theory of Fiction* (New York: Oxford University Press, 1967), 55.

101. Jean-Paul Sartre, *Nausea* (New York: New Directions, 1964) in *Sense of an Ending*, 35.

102. Kermode, *Sense of an Ending*, 145, citing Sartre.

103. Robert Alter, *Partial Magic: The Novel as a Self-Conscious Genre* (Berkeley: University of California Press, 1975), 144, in his discussion of Joyce.

104. ". . . Un conjunto, una obra mágica, una pieza maestra."

105. "El ballet era el único espacio en donde sucedía lo maravilloso y comprendí la infinita desdicha de Mariana y de Natalia, arrancadas brutalmente de aquellos paisajes lunares. . . ."

106. Robert Weimann, *Structure and Society in Literary History: Studies in the History and Theory of Historical Criticism* (Baltimore: The Johns Hopkins University Press, 1984), 3.

107. Ibid., 7.

198. Richard Poirier, *The Performing Self* (New York: Oxford University Press, 1971), 28.

109. Weimann, *Structure and Society*, 9.

110. Ibid., 11.

111. Weimann emphasizes that in order to relate the social function of literature and the structure of its artifice, one must understand some complementary relationships. For example: the relationship between its literary origin *(Entstehungsgeschichte)* and the aesthetics of representation or structure *(Darstellungsästhetik)*, on the one hand, and the impact of the work *(Wirkungsgeschichte)* and the aesthetics of its reception *(Rezeptionsästhetik)*, on the other hand (ibid., 12–13).

112. Luiz Costa Lima, "Documento e ficcão," in *Testimonio y literatura*, 23. "Há . . . uma inevitabilidade documental em tudo que é tocado pelo olhar humano."

113. "Hechizados en nuestras butacas contemplábamos a la belleza que nos visitaba y buscábamos a nuestras amigas separadas de la magia. (Quién les había arrebatado aquel destino efímero y luminoso/ ¡Nadie! Ahora que han pasado tantos años, puedo confesar que nadie las arrancó del teatro en donde se escondieron, pues la verdad y única verdad es que casi todas las noches las veíamos en escena, confundidas entre las figuras blancas de los coros de baile. A veces nos hacían alguna seña desde el escenario."

114. Ibid., 24. "Metáfora não meramente aproximativa, porquanto tem a van-

tagem de não implicar, como sucede com o uso normal do termo 'ficção', um puro e drástico corte com o plano da realidade. Em vez de anulado, o plano da realidade se insinua e penetra no jogo ficcional, como desdobramento desejado."

115. Martin, *Recent Theories of Narrative*, 162.

116. Wolfgang Iser, *The Act of Reading: A Theory of Aesthetic Response* (Baltimore: The Johns Hopkins University Press, 1978). This summary was taken from *Recent Theories of Narrative*, 161–62.

117. Roland Barthes, *Criticism and Truth*, trans. Katrine Pilcher Keuneman (London: Athlone Press, 1987), 93.

118. "Estaba unida a ella desde antes de aquel lejano encuentro en el salón de mi primo Bertrand. Pensé que no bastaba la lógica para entender mi misteriosa liga con Mariana."

119. "El triunfo de Mariana sobre mí residía en su ambigüedad y en su capacidad para entristecerme y luego desaparecer sin dejar huella."

120. "Ahora Mariana formaba parte de mí mismo, estábamos hechos de la misma piedra, de la misma sangre y ambos éramos el mismo paisaje."

121. ". . . caer todas las noches. . . ."

122. ". . . la destrucción se ejecuta en secreto. Todo lo terrible sucede así, en secreto."

123. ". . . cotidiano vértigo sanguinolento."

124. ". . . como me amas y no quieres que me vaya estaré siempre junto a ti."

125. Bloch, *Historian's Craft*, 58.

126. ". . . en ese momento supe que no vendría a buscarme, debía ser yo el que debía encontrarla. '¡Y la hallaré!' me prometía a mí mismo, aunque tuviera que buscarla en el laberinto del tiempo, en las ciudades de las que sólo quedan huellas confusas o en las que los hombres todavía no presienten su futura existencia y por las cuales Mariana debería transitar seguida de mis pasos."

Chapter 4. José Emilio Pacheco: The Ethics of Writing

1. José Emilio Pacheco, *Morirás lejos* (Barcelona: Montesinos Editor, 1980), 121. All subsequent references are to this edition. All translations are my own unless otherwise stated. ("Años atrás, en Leizig, una mujer leyó las líneas de su mano y mirando a sus ojos sentenció:—Morirás lejos.")

2. Ann Duncan, *Voices, Visions and a New Reality: Mexican Fiction Since 1970* (Pittsburgh: University of Pittsburgh Press, 1986), 6.

3. Yvette Jiménez de Báez, Diana Morán, and Edith Negrin, *Ficción e historia: la narrativa de José Emilio Pacheco* (Mexico: El Colegio de México, 1979).

4. Ibid., 175. "El tratamiento del espacio y el tiempo que definen la estructura de esta novela, sólo puede entenderse en su dinamismo: *Morirás lejos* se desarrolla mediante un continuo deshacerse y rehacerse, explicitando su propio proceso de producción. En una especie de 'modelo para armar', el autor a partir de una serie limitada de materiales, abre la novela a la participación activa del lector."

5. See n. 2.

6. Ibid., 35–36, 39.

7. Ibid., 40.

8. Carlos Fuentes, on the cover of the edition cited in n. 1. "Pacheco revierte las estructuras al mundo del cambio; aquí, la historia no fue: está siendo, es un proceso encarnado en el habla personal, accidental, de ese narrador sin rostro,

cuyo discurso recoge la inmutable sincronía y la convierte en plasticidad diacrónica, en evento de la palabra."

9. "Sólo hay escasos datos auténticos que pueden ser utilizables a fin de precipitar uno entre los mil virutales desenlaces."

10. It is important to recognize here that modern social history has rejected the traditional approach of history with its emphasis on events and official institutions, to focus more on the individual and collective experiences of a society. This more recent "history from below" tries to construct its narrative, that is, reconstruct history, from the fragments of other texts.

11. Like the writing *(écriture)* of Roland Barthes (*Writing Degree Zero*, trans. Annette Lavers and Colin Smith [New York: Hill and Wang, 1968]), this new narrative rejects the formal style of traditional literature in which language is used to adorn an already existing reality. In these works language is the central forum of reality and literature is reduced to a problematic of language.

12. In this respect, Pacheco's works differ from the works of Salvador Elizondo, for example, at the extreme end of the trend which Margo Glantz has defined as *escritura* in *Onda y escritura en México: jovenes de 20 a 33* (Mexico: Siglo 21, 1971).

13. John Brushwood, *La novela mexicana 1967–1982* (Mexico: Grijalbo, 1984), 61. ". . . la invención de la realidad. Se trata de una narración que confunde sujeto y objeto constantemente, de manera que no se sabe por ejemplo, cuál de los personajes es el perseguido o cuál el perseguidor. La identidad (inestable) cambia según el poder de la imaginación. Tal invención ocurre no solamente en el primer nivel narrativo sino también en forma de narración dentro de la narración principal. Conviene aclarar que la lectura de esta novela no produce recuerdos de personajes sino de las posibilidades de la ficción."

14. Duncan, *Voices, Visions and a New Reality*, 59.

15. Ibid., 59.

16. The third edition (1980) consists of 154 pages. As Duncan mentions, Pachecho extended the original version of 1967, which was even shorter. (See Duncan, 39–40.)

17. ". . . pero quién es eme / quién soy yo / quién me habla / quién me cuenta esta historia / a quién la cuento."

18. Luis Leal, "Nuevos novelistas mexicanos," in *La crítica de la novela mexicana contemporánea* (Mexico: Universidad Nacional Autónoma de México, 1981), 218. "La nueva narrativa se caracteriza, mejor, por el interés en los temas universales y el tratamiento de asuntos despegados de la realidad social mexicana."

19. Ibid., 217.

20. Ibid., 218. "Que la acción transcurra en la ciudad de México en la mente de los personajes nos interesa no tanto porque refleja la nota nacional, sino porque, en el proceso, relaciona la ciudad con el ambiente internacional, en el espacio y el tiempo."

21. "Esto ya no interesa—Lo hemos leído un millón de veces" "¿Por qué no escribe sobre los indios de México?"

22. ". . . porque el odio es igual, el desprecio es el mismo, la ambición es idéntica, el sueño de conquista planetaria sigue invariable. . . ."

23. Remember that this novel was published in 1967, in the middle of the Vietnam era, one year before Tlatelolco. Brushwood, *La novela mexicana*, 60–61, notes the importance of *Morirás lejos* as a foreshadowing of Tlatelolco.

24. "¿Quién nos cuenta la historia del acoso de eme?"

25. Duncan, *Voices, Visions and a New Reality*, 49.

26. Ibid., 40.

27. ". . . cuando tenían unas mismas palabras, antes de ser esparcidos por la ciudad y no entender el habla familiar de los otros."

28. For example, as Báez et. al., *Ficción e historia*, 192–3, show, the tower is a symbol of the Third Reich: "The narrator mentions it [the tower] in relation to the intentions of its builders ('the tower of a millenary empire') in the same way as [he mentions] the image of the Reichstag at the moment of its defeat (1945)" ["El narrador la menciona lo mismo en relación a las intenciones de sus constructores ('la torre de un imperio milenario') que a la imagen del Reichstag en el momento de la derrota (1945).").

29. ". . . aunque, sombras de las cosas, ecos de los hechos, las palabras son ilusiones, intentos no de expresar sino de sugerir lo que pasó en los campos."

30. "Sólo existe el gran crimen—y todo lo demás: papel febrilmente manchado para que todo aquello (si alguien lo recuerda; si alguien, aparte de quienes lo vivieron, lo recuerda) no se olvide."

31. "Tal vez sea una forma inconsciente de recordar los campos. En ellos se hablaron todas las lenguas y sus habitantes mayoritarios fueron a su vez esparcidos sobre la Tierra. O quizá una metáfora para significar que el Tercer Reich pretendió erigir en todo el planeta la torre de un imperio milenario."

32. "Se parece a las ruinas del Reichstag pero también al cadáver del Coliseo Romano. Es una aparatosa advertencia sobre la imposibilidad del imperio, un túmulo sepulcral para todos los tiranos del mundo."

33. "Con todo, no hay que olvidarse de otro aspecto: muchos cuadros de Bruegel son pintura política: testimonios, protestas, contra la Inquisición en Flandes. O bien, a semejanza de lo que ocurre en la vida de eme, está paralizada una inminencia. Las seiscientas u ochocientas figuras pueden permanecer para siempre fijas e inertes en su inmovilidad—o pueden echarse a andar en cualquier momento."

34. "La torre del pozo o el pozo en forma de torre evoca lejanamente la imagen pintada. . . ."

35. ". . . horror que yace al fondo del poder absoluto." Octavio Paz, *El laberinto de la soledad* (Mexico: Fondo de Cultura Económica, 1959), 70, bases his famous discussion of "La Chingada" on such a sexual image. "In summary, 'chingar' is to do violence to another. It is a masculine verb, active cruel: it pierces, wounds, rends, stains. . . . 'La chingada', the female, pure passivity, defenseless to the outside. The relationship between the two is violent, determined by the cynical power of the first and the impotence of the other." ["En suma, chingar es hacer violencia sobre otro. Es un verbo masculino, activo, cruel: pica, hiere, desgarra, mancha. . . . La relación entre ambos es violenta, determinada por el poder cínico del primero y la impotencia de la otra."]

36. "El pozo al que cubre la torre ha de ser profundísimo."

37. Báez et. al., *Ficción e historia*, 194. "Funcionó como uno de los refuerzos ideológicos del nazismo en la Segunda Guerra Mundial."

38. Ibid., 195. (Quote from text:) "Largos años de encierro y angustia porque el Cuarto Reich aún no incendia a Europa y las ocas salvajes vuelan en la noche, pero aún no son bastantes, carecen del vigor de su bella época."

39. ". . . torturas que no pueden describir las palabras . . ." ". . . una angustia de que las palabras no podrán dar idea. . . ."

40. "Y añade a estas palabras propias y ajenas las otras que leíste, las fotografías y los documentales que has visto. Trata de reconstruirlo todo con la imaginación y tendrás una idea, apenas aproximada en su vaguedad, de lo que fue

todo aquello. Basta para que las imágenes te torturen, no te dejen jamás, y sientas horror, compasión, miedo, vergüenza."

41. "Entonces la confusión el azoro el terror la búsqueda / de aire y los gritos / sobre todo los gritos / la inútil pugna por alejarse de los sitios en que brota / gas venenoso."

42. "Entonces Jurgen Stroop pudo informar a Himmler:
el / antiguo / barrio / judío / de / Varsovia / dejó / de / /existir
El / número / de / judíos / ejecutados / o / detenidos / asciende at 56 065."

43. "Terminación de las conjeturas posibles en este momento: las hipótesis pueden no tener fin. El alfabeto no da para más. Podría recurrirse a letras compuestas, a signos prefénicos or anteriores a la escritura—semejantes a las inscripciones en el chopo o las que traza eme con la uña del índice izquierdo en la pared de yeso. . . ." "Fiel a sus monótonas elipsis, a su forma de pasar el tiempo y deshacer la tensión de una inminencia, propone ahora un sistema de posibilidades afines con objeto de que *tú* escojas la que creas verdadera."

44. See the Introduction to this book and works such as Emir Rodríguez Monegal, *El boom de la novela latinoamericana* (Caracas: Editorial Tiempo Nuevo, 1972), or Fuentes, *La nueva novela hispanoamericana* (Mexico: Joaquín Mortiz, 1969).

45. ". . . no en el sentido figurado sino en el sentido físico que devuelve su gravedad a la palabra."

46. Severo Sarduy plays with the idea of the text as a body. Writing, then, becomes an erotic act of repetition which results in the fixing or rhetorical bondage of an experience. See, for example, Severo Sarduy, *Escrito sobre un cuerpo; ensayos de crítica* (Buenos Aires: Editorial Sudamericana, 1969) for Sarduy's theory on this.

47. "Todo huele a vinagre. . . ."

48. ". . . el olor de la corrupción torturaba a sitiados y sitiadores. . . ."

49. "Pero al desaparecer el olor a vinagre pierdo la referencia olfativa, se rompe mi composición de lugar."

50. "Porque al desaparecer el olor a vinagre pierdo la referencia, extravío mi identidad, ignoro quién soy entre todos los personajes que he representado bajo el chopo ahito de inscripciones. . . ."

51. "Y todo vuelve, se clarifica, se rehace—mi composición de lugar, mi pérdida de identidad momentánea, el sentido de mi estancia en el parque, mi duda acerca de quién eras, con el descenso del olor a vinagre."

52. In this sense Pacheco anticipates with his technique Poniatowska's *La noche de Tlatelolco* with its cinematographic style of montage.

53. Traditional historiography generally created the illusion that there was a single history, which unfolded directly and linearly.

54. "La inofensiva y consoladora utilidad de las narraciones: desde el habitante de las cavernas hasta el último todos necesitamos en alguna forma de ellas. Y eme, como se dijo, preferiría continuar indefinidamente jugando con las posibilidades de un hecho muy simple: *A* vigila sentado en la banca de un parque, *B* lo observa tras las persianas; pues sabe que desde antes de Scherezada las ficciones son un medio de postergar la sentencia de muerte."

55. *Fantasmas aztecas* by Gustavo Sainz (Mexico: Editorial Grijalbo, 1979) tells the history of its own writing as an exercise of exorcising the phantoms of the past.

56. Mikhail Bakhtin studies the importance of the words and stories of others in a person's own discourse. "One's own discourse is gradually and slowly wrought out of others' words that have been acknowledged and assimilated,

and the boundaries between the two are at first scarcely perceptible." *Dialogic Imagination* (Austin: University of Texas Press, 1981), 345, n. 31.

57. For a good summary of the sequences of these historical fragments, see Jiménez de Báez et al., *Ficción e historia*, 233–43, to whom I am deeply indebted.

58. Ibid., 235. "El desarrollo de este segmento, como en Diáspora, sigue la dinámica del cerco. Media una conexión funcional y significativa entre el nombre de Grossaktion, "la gran acción" preparada por los alemanes para destruir el gueto y dominar a los judíos, y la táctica del cerco para lograrlo."

59. Ibid., 236. "En él se unen todos los hilos sueltos identificadores de eme y Alguien . . . (y) seguimos las marcas vinculadoras de 'la historia' (pasado) y 'la ficción (presente) de eme que el texto proporciona."

60. The myth of the Nibelungens is defined in the Encyclopedia *Duden* in the following manner: "Downfall of the gods and the world before the beginning of a new world age:—The dawn of civilization" ["Untergang von Göttern und Welt vor Anbruch eines neuen Weltzeitalters: –Das Abendrot der Zivilisation"].

61. Jiménez de Báez, et al., *Ficción e historia*, 210. "Desde el plano mítico, . . . Hitler -ya Dios, ya históricamente poder absoluto-es el centro de su desarrollo."

62. Ibid., 243.

63. "Todo esto, todo esto es un ejercicio tan lleno de referencias a otros libros que seguir su desarrollo es tiempo perdido."

64. ". . . sobre un tema único que le atañe y le afecta como si fuera culpable de haber sobrevivido a una guerra lejana que sin embargo extendía su pavor a través de letras negreantes en el periódico, fotos, voces en la radio y sobre todo imágenes cinematográficas miradas con aparente impunidad pero cuya violencia dejó en nosotros invisibles señales, holladuras, estigmas."

65. "Farben de México. Insecticidas, raticidas, fumigantes. Técnica alemana, acción inmediata."

66. "Las matanzas se repiten."

67. Paz, *El laberinto de la soledad*, 62. "La persecución comienza contra grupos aislados—razas, clases, disidentes, sospechosos—hasta que gradualmente alcanza a todos. Al iniciarse, una parte del pueblo contempla con indiferencia al exterminio de otros grupos sociales o contribuye a su persecución, pues se exasperan los odios internos. Todos se vuelven cómplices y el sentimiento de culpa se extiende a toda la sociedad. El terror se generaliza: ya no hay sino persecutores y perseguidos. El persecutor, por otra parte se transforma muy facilmente en perseguido."

68. These are all words which in Spanish or French begin with *m*. "Eme entre otras cosas puede ser: mal, muerte, . . . meurtrier, macabre. . . ."

69. ". . . la letra que cada uno lleva impresa en las manos. . . ."

70. ". . . porque cuanto aquí se narra sucede en algunos minutos de un miércoles."

71. See the next chapter about *Pretexta* by Federico Campbell (Mexico: Fondo de Cultura Económica, 1979), where the author literally becomes the protagonist of his own work.

72. Murray M. Schwartz, "Critic, Define Thyself," in *Psychoanalysis and the Question of the Text*, ed. Geoffrey H. Hartman (Baltimore & London: The Johns Hopkins University Press, 1978), 10, discusses the process on the part of the reader and critic of trying to "find" the author or the speaker of a text. "The author I seek is actually always a fiction I re-create through his fictions. . . . The collective activity of criticism [reading] can be seen as an interminable 'authorization' of authors."

73. "Porque todo es irreal en este cuento. Nada sucedió como se indica. Hechos y sitios se deformaron por el empeño de tocar la verdad mediante una ficción, una mentira. Todo irreal, nada sucedió como aquí se refiere. Pero fue un pobre intento de contribuir a que el gran crimen nunca se repita."

74. "El sol no se va. Insiste en permanecer (y ya es muy tarde) . . ." ". . . Sólo brillan las hojas trasminadas de ácido acético y una mancha de luz se hunde en las paredes del pozo."

75. ". . . el viento de la noche deshoja, arrastra 'El aviso oportuno', y el parque entero se desvanece bajo las luces mercuriales que en este instante acaban de encenderse."

Chapter 5. Federico Campbell: The Texture of History

1. Federico Campbell, *Pretexta* (Mexico: Fondo de Cultura Económica, 1979), 129. All the parenthetical references from this chapter refer to this edition.

2. Gustavo García, "Federico Campbell: Literatura y poder, una conversación con Gustavo García," *Revista de la Universidad de México* 34, no. 8 (April 1980):14.

3. Adriana Méndez Rodenas, "Texto, *Pretexta* or Pre-texto?" historia y parodia en la narrativa mexicana contemporánea," *Actas del XXV Congreso del Instituto Internacional de Literatura Iberoamericana*, 4. This—"in spite of Campbell's having written one of the texts which question most acutely the traditional concepts of history and fiction" ("había pasado casi desapercibido por la crítica . . . a pesar de haber escrito Campbell uno de los textos que más agudamente cuestionan los conceptos tradicionales de la historia y la ficción.") In the last few years Campbell has published several new works: *La memoria de Sciascia* (essay), *Tijuanenses* (a collection of short stories and a short novel), *Navajoa* (a short autobiographical narrative), and *Territorios sentimentales* (short stories).

4. The first edition appeared in 1977 in the literary press "La máquina de escribir" (The Typewriter), founded by Campbell himself. There he printed his first pages of *Pretexta* (some 47 pages), a fragment of a novel so that, in the author's words, "I would be obliged to continue writing it" ["Obligarme a seguir escribiéndola"]. From a personal correspondence with the author in December of 1988.

5. According to García, "Federico Campbell," 14, *Pretexta* is "one of the most serious reflections on journalism and writing as instruments of power" ["una de las reflexiones más serias sobre el periodismo y la escritura como instrumentos del poder"].

6. In Spanish *criado* is a noun meaning "servant" but it can also be seen as a past participle of the verb *criar* (to raise, educate). The expression *para servirle* is commonly said in Mexico, particularly in relationships with customers, to show deference and eagerness to serve; an equivalent of "At your service."

7. ". . . rehacer de otra manera el pasado del viejo periodista mediante la invención de artimañas, la falsificación de datos que de algún modo . . . se imbricaban parcialmente en la biografía real del profesor periodista. . . ."

8. "Su actitud coherente era fingir demencia y en todo caso atribuir lo escrito sobre él al pasado biográfico del profesor Ocaranza."

9. ". . . en algunos tramos autobiográficos, el autor de buena parte del mamotreto."

10. "Por eso específicamente había sido contratado: uniformar el estilo, ser la emoción de un único hombre que llevara la voz narradora. De eso se trataba, de construir al personaje anónimo que daba cuenta de los sucesos. . . ."

11. ". . . fingía que muy probablemente la autor del mamotreto era un anciano de ideas muy elementales sobre la respetabilidad y las buenas costumbres."

12. "No le interesaba escribir sino conseguir la identidad de escritor, socialmente, o íntimamente por lo pronto, ante sí mismo."

13. "Sería el crimen perfecto . . . no habría autor."

14. As, for example, in the famous story by Borges, "Las Ruinas circulares," in *Ficciones* (Buenos Aires: Emecé Editores, 1965), 59–66.

15. Wallace Martin, *Recent Theories of Narrative,* (Ithaca and London: Cornell University Press, 1986), 187.

16. Arthur C. Danto, *Narration and Knowledge* (New York: Columbia University Press, 1985), 353, 356.

17. Barbara Hardy, *Tellers and Listeners* (London: Athlone Press, 1975), 3.

18. Duncan, *Voices, Visions and a New Reality,* 207.

19. "Esta voz, es mía? . . . Inventé yo los signos que componen el idioma? Estos códigos que se llaman diccionarios en todas las lenguas son de alguien en particular?"

20. The 1979 edition. A later edition (1988) has a different cover.

21. "El arma única que llevaba era su máquina de escribir portátil." Rodenas, "Texto, *Pretexta* o Pre-texto?" n. 8, points out that this must be a veiled reference to the first edition of the novel by the marginal press, "La máquina de escribir" which Campbell founded.

22. Robert Weimann, *Structure and Society in Literary History. Studies in the History and Theory of Historical Criticism* (Baltimore: The Johns Hopkins University Press, 1984), 185–86.

23. Bakhtin, *Dialogic Imagination,* 259ff.

24. Ibid., 293.

25. Ibid., 286, 287.

26. Paz, *Posdata,* 36. ". . . la cárcel de palabras y conceptos en que el gobierno se ha encerrado, todas esas fórmulas en las que ya nadie cree y que se condenan en esa grotesca expresión con que la familia oficial designa al partido único: el Instituto Revolucionario."

27. "Harto. Estaba harto. No todo era blanco y negro . . . ni siquiera gris. Harto del no hay que hacer leña del árbol caído, harto del no hay que confundir la libertad con el libertinaje, harto del está muy bien la crítica pero la crítica positiva, no negativa, y a él la que le atraía era la negativa, la constructiva. . . . Pero ése era el lenguaje de la tribu."

28. Bakhtin, *Dialogic Imagination,* 277.

29. Ibid., 299.

30. Ibid., 299–300.

31. Ibid., 293. "The word in language is always half someone else's."

32. "Ocaranza quería que estableciéramos con precisión la etimología de *pretexta . . .*" ". . . rozagante toga que llevaba por abajo una tira de púrpura y que vestían magistrados, cónsules, pretores, censores, ediles, y dictadores en la escena romana. . . ."

33. This epigraph is found on page 8 of the first reprinting of *Pretexta* in 1984. It does not appear in the 1979 version. "*Pretexta:* Tragedia latina cuyos personajes vestían con la toga de este nombre y el asunto estaba sacado de la historia nacional."

34. ". . . más que para ser representadas en un escenario estas composiciones se escribían para leerse ante el público. . . . Poco importaba su redondez como pieza de teatro; su importancia estribaba en la parodia, en el cumplimiento de una función que ahora sería como la de los periódiocos a fin de dirimir un asunto de la historia local más imediata."

35. Marc Bloch, *The Historian's Craft*, trans. Peter Putnam (New York: Vintage Books, 1953), 97.

36. Edward Carr, *What Is History?* (London: MacMillan & Co., 1961), 24.

37. Paul Hernadi, "Clio's Cousins:Historiography as Translation, Fiction, and Criticism," *New Literary History* 7, no. 2 (Winter 1976):254.

38. ". . . me llamaré Lucius, Junius, Brutus, Brunus, Brunius . . . y se extraviará mi verdadero nombre. Habré de contar todo esto, seré el cronista enmascarado."

39. "Debía proceder con la humildad del criado, con la dignidad del artista."

40. Kiddle, "The Non-Fiction Novel or 'Novela Testimonial' in Contemporary Mexican Literature," Ph.D. diss., Brown University, 1984, 157, discusses the phenomenon of the strong self-censorship on the part of the television and writing industries. According to her (and her extensive investigation), there is more freedom to do political criticism in books than in the newspapers or television. Luis González de Alba (in an interview with her) attributes this to the fact that the government realizes that in Mexico there are relatively few people who read books in comparison with the number who read newspapers or the large population who watch television.

41. "Sabía que por otra parte que nadie leería el mamotreto, que en el país nadie leía nada ni a nadie le importaba que se publicara o no, que no era cosa de angustiarse demasiado porque en última instancia no estaba escribiendo directamente para la imprenta. Lo que ponía en el papel en el papel se quedaba y podía enmendarse y corregirse o destruirse en su totalidad."

42. ". . . en cierto modo uno va editando la vida . . ."

43. "Editamos nuestra conversación. Al otro lado de la línea un editor más sagaz que nosotros comenta a medias, conforma verdades y mentiras a medias y, como en la fotografía, deja fuera de encuadre lo que no encaja en la edición."

44. "No tenga usted demasiados sentimientos de culpa. . . ." "Cuidado con las manías. . . ."

45. "Yo, como lector suyo, exterior a la cápsula de cristal en la que debe estar metido al escribir, le puedo decir que desde afuera a mí la sobriedad de lo que lleva escrito me parece sensacional, valiosísima, muy efectiva. . . ." "Siga adelante."

46. Duncan, *Voices, Visions, and a New Reality*, 208.

47. ". . . país de criados . . ."

48. "Bruno era capaz de arriesgar la vida por una frase, por un juego de palabras. . . ."

49. "Allí en su escritura enmascarada estaba el desparpajo, la absoluta falta de intenciones literarias, la verdad cruda y cínica y despiadada de la miseria y la corrupción urbanas y, por extensión nacionales."

50. ". . . el centro, el sistema nervioso central del taller de mamotretos. . . ."

51. "Bajo tierra se fraguaban las falsas biografías, las versiones aparentemente extraoficiales de hechos recientes, de acciones militares o policíacas no conocidas salvo por sus actores y víctimas."

52. "Las galerías del poder: las largas oficinas toda pulcritud, el cielo y el infierno a los que todos sin excepción aspiraban, tomaron de pronto para Bruno

la forma de un instituto en el que la obediencia, el silencio, la contenida y callada anulación de sí mismo constituían las cualidades a las cuales debía apuntar sus esfuerzos. Su destino era sonreír a los otros, ponerles la comidilla en la mesa, escucharlos y educarse en la disciplina de la discreción."

53. "Sólo en su interior, en intramuros, corría la historia, se desarrollaba y dirigía. El exterior, el mundo real, el de la calle, sucedía allá afuera. Aquí, la palabra inventariada, escrita, era lo único que contaba aunque su asociación con hechos o dichos fuera prefabricada. El inventario, el archivo: eso era lo que contaba. Lo demás, todavía no cobraba existencia."

54. "... en la planta alta despachaba y sólo se comunicaba por medio de interpósitos ujieres. ..."

55. "... era como la heroina, le causaba una adicción prácticamente física y lo retrotraía a la infancia. Volvía a ser el niño rey que llora para saciar su hambre, ... el bebé omnipotente a quien nadie podía desafiar, mucho menos Bruno. Sus declaraciones tenían un efecto de magia. Bastaba que pronunciara una frase para que la realidad se acomodara."

56. "... debía estar fuera del juego. ..."

57. "... un país gobernado por gangsters. ..." "... una escuela de criados. ..." "... un control sobre sus palabras y los efectos de sus palabras en los demás."

58. "Ellos lo tenían todo, los medios de producción y de comunicación, el monopolio de las máquinas y del papel, los medios electrónicos ye escritos. Nada los saciaba. Nada los satisfacía suficientemente. No toleraban la disidencia." "Era un placer saber obedecer."

59. "... ser institucional: creer en las instituciones, no en los hombres. La relación con la autoridad, el patrón, la convivencia con los otros criados, se volvía allí una carrera de mulas que jalaban carretas tratando de morder la zanahoria colgada de un hilo amarrado a una vara sostenida por el jefe desde el puesto de mando."

60. Paz, *El laberinto de la soledad*, 142. "... la acción política. La 'inteligencia' mexicana no sólo ha servido al país: lo ha defendido. Ha sido honrada y eficaz, pero ¿no ha dejado de ser 'inteligencia', es decir, no ha renunciado a ser la conciencia crítica de su pueblo?"

61. "Sus inquietudes, sus delirios quijotescos, no tenían cabida en el mundo y optó entonces por irse marginando para, según él, no ser tragado."

62. "... algo así como un subproducto de la sociedad despojado de toda posibilidad de crítica y de reflexión." "Era una forma de mendicidad la nuestra. ..." "... una dependencia buscada como condición de sobrevivencia."

63. "Experimentaba su cosificación como un placer ilegítimo. Era mucho más soportable cumplir con el papel de criado que participar, más fácil castrarse de antemano en un sentido figurado. Era más práctico y más pasivo que tomar decisiones y asumir responsabilidades."

64. "El más alto honor consistía en la destrucción de su identidad personal. No quería ser un individuo. Había aprendido no sólo a no ser él mismo, sino a no ser del todo. ..." "Era el hombre invisible ... el objeto pasivo de la historia, el redactor fantasma, el cronista enmascarado. ..."

65. "... su única salvación moral era el cinismo limpio y desafiante." "A sus posibles acusadores les diría en su cara ... la literatura es mierda, de acuerdo, pero a mí la mierda me gusta. Yo soy un verdadero técnico de la mierda; en la mierda me encuentro a mis anchas, déjenme entonces trabajar en paz."

66. Georg Lukács in J. M. Bernstein, *The Philosophy of the Novel: Lukács, Marx-*

ism and the Dialectics of Form (Minneapolis: University of Minnesota Press, 1984), xxi.

67. Bernstein, *Philosophy of the Novel*, 150.

68. "¿Y quién era a fin de cuentas Ocaranza? . . . Un héroe trágico incomprendido y débil, pequeño, realmente digno de su propia conmiseración? Mentira. Esa era la coartada: el libelo de su propia vida."

69. Peter Loewenberg, *Decoding the Past: The Psychohistorical Approach* (New York: Knopf, 1983), 8.

70. Ibid., 29.

71. Ibid., 12.

72. Bernstein, *Philosophy of the Novel*, xxii.

73. Jürgen Habermas, *Knowledge and Human Interests* (Boston: Beacon, 1971), 218, discusses the hermeneutics of the psychoanalytical theories of Freud, who tries to interpret the texts in which the author deceives himself; the analysis of the text ends up being the psychoanalysis of the author himself.

74. "Y como si el bagaje de diagnósticos que tenía a la mano fuera insuficiente, Bruno armó este tramo de la vida de Ocaranza con un informe que se refería nada más ni nada menos que a Bruno Medina y no a ninguno de los pacientes registrados en el archivo."

75. "El estilo, ése era el peligro. . . ."

76. "Su temor era la posibilidad de que uno fuera editando su propia vida si escribía y, mediante la escritura impresa, pudiera inadvertidamente ir dejando al paso una estela de 'huellas digitales lingüísticas'. . . ."

77. ". . . cubrir todo resquicio a futuros investigadores de la policía literaria." "Despistaría a sus posibles perseguidores, a los exégetas, a las ratas de biblioteca que roerían el mamotreto con lupa en mano."

78. ". . . que podríamos situar en el plano de la psicología de la escritura: es lo que en otra parte llamo el 'autocuestionamiento', actitud que hace que toda formalización consista ante todo en una interrogación del 'escritor' respecto de su propia consistencia, del valor referencial de sus experiencias y de la homogeneidad de sus sistemas; no arroja ya el 'escritor' una mirada crítica sobre lo que lo rodea proyectando sin saberlo sus propias estructuras mentales previas . . . sino que al escribir realiza una operación de autoinvestigación que, y eso es lo importante, se traduce por un conjunto de formas visibles, captables, que permiten a su turno rehacer el cirucito y recomponer el proceso de su génesis."

79. "Nada en el presente lo estimulaba, lo exitaba tanto como aquel mundo aparente y falsamente olvidado y ya no vivido por nadie."

80. ". . . se producía una especie de cortocircuito que lo colocaba en una posición neutralizada, . . . en una suerte de coexistencia consigo mismo que no era sino esterilidad, desperdicio del tiempo y de la vida, apatía, desaliento, dificultad para hablar o imposibilidad, indiferencia. Se dividió en dos partes su vida, la que estaba aquí y ahora, y aquella que lo retrotraía sin saber por qué. . . ."

81. ". . . cuanta idea le pasaba por la cabeza. . . ."

82. Norman Brown, *Life Against Death: The Psychoanalytical Meaning of History* (Middletown, Conn.: Wesleyan University Press, 1959), 62.

83. "Que nunca fuera a trabajar para el gobierno le había pedido su padre muchos años atrás. . . ." ". . . se iban desvaneciendo en su memoria casi un instante después de que las pronunciara, absurdas, delirantes, sin ningún sentido. . ."

84. Bakhtin, *Dialogic Imagination*, 345, defines "internally persuasive dis-

course" as the words and ideas of others which are assimilated into an individual's internal consciousness.

85. "Muchos años antes, los años que van de una madurez inútil a una infancia irrecuperable. . . ."

86. ". . . dividido en dos voces, . . . dialogando a balbuceos . . . con la figura triste y desolada de su padre.—Nunca vayas a ser policia—le había dicho."

87. "Lo siento todo más bien como un involuntario diálogo de la traición. . . ."

88. Rodenas, in "¿Texto, *Pretexta* o Pre-texto?" 7, suggests that Ocaranza represents Bruno's "literary father," his model or precursor and the betrayal of the father—symbolic patricide.

89. ". . . nunca trabajaré para el gobierno. . . ." ". . . el recuerdo de haber olvidado a su padre, de haber aprovechado su inocencia madura y confiada para derivar de allí el poder que se finca en la confianza y que procede justamente de todas las traiciones."

90. ". . . los restos de su papá. . . ." ". . . sus huesos en una bolsa de plástico transparente. . . ."

91. ". . . tomó material de sus diarios personales, de sus sueños, y sintió que a sí mismo plagiaba. Sentía que a sí mismo se robaba ideas y frases, que algo de ilícito e inconfesable había en el hecho de usurpar a los sueños realidades que no debían ni siquiera nombrarse. Y con ello vino el inconfundible sentimiento del traidor que circula desnudo por la plaza."

92. "Servir a otros fue convirtiéndose en una actividad natural. . . ."

93. "La ley estaba concebida y hecha precisamente para utilizarse en favor del interés del Estado, pero era la ley la raya, el punto de referencia, el de aquí para allá y el de allá para acá, la coartada de la legalidad que convenía orquestar a todos los niveles, salvar. Todo menos la forma. Todo menos la apariencia; todo era sacrificable. Si la ley requería elementos de juicio, elementos de juicio se le proporcionaban. La forma, por encima de todas las cosas. El crimen incluso no era crimen si estaba sancionado por la legalidad: la norma, el ordenamiento sagrado."

94. Christopher Lasch, *The Culture of Narcissism* (New York: Norton, 1978), 30.

95. ". . . el policía a veces todos lo llevamos dentro. . . ."

96. Rodenas, "¿Texto, *Pretexta* or Pre-texto?" 4, points out that the "doubling" between author and character in Campbell's text echoes the doubling established by Borges in his short text "Borges y yo."

97. This schizophrenic state of the writer is represented par excellence in *El grafógrafo* by Salvador Elizondo (Mexico: Joaquín Mortiz, 1972), 9, when the narrator says: "I write. I write that I write. Mentally I see myself write that I write and I can also see myself seeing that I write. . . ." ["Escribo. Escribo que escribo. Mentalmente me veo escribir que escribo y también puedo verme ver que escribo. . . ."]

98. "Uno puede darse un encontronazo consigo mismo, tiene allí enfrente el esperpento de una actividad inventada, de un oficio asumido sin saber cuándo ni por qué." ". . . no es el ping pong de quién fue primero el huevo o la gallina? No. Pero sí la placentera aventura del soñado y soñante, la cópula consigo mismo. . . ."

99. ". . . en este instante despierto y digo, *me* digo, *le* digo: Se puede tener dos cuerpos pero no dos corazones."

100. Duncan, *Voices, Visions, and a New Reality,* 208.

101. Ibid., 208.

102. Duncan, Ibid., 207, comments that *Pretexta* "indicates how a theory that has become a cliché nonetheless still has considerable vitality in practice, entertaining us with its examples of discourse, its ways of telling a story (which of course it never tells) that suggest future possible directions for narrative."

103. Ibid., 209.

104. Barthes, "The Death of the Author," in *Image, Music, Text*, trans. Stephen Heath (New York: Hill and Wang, 1977), 142–48.

105. Duncan, *Voices, Visions and a New Reality*, 209.

106. ". . . un creador invisible, omnipotente, divino, situado en todas partes y en ninguna."

107. "Creía sin embargo que todo aquel juego de artimañas, giros verbales, referencias irreprochablemente inventadas y peculiares afijos, tendrían más tarde un efecto de bumerang en su contra. Sería señalado: el colaboracionista, el traidor, la pluma mercenaria, el *ghost writer* que tiraba la piedra y escondía la mano, el pérfido."

108. ". . . las palabras clave que lo particularizaban y que más pronunciadamente definían su estilo. . . . Como en las parodias, sabía que las peculiaridades conscientes de un estilo podían imitarse, pero no la impronta inconsciente que era justamente la que se indagaría al hacerse una prueba de paternidad en contra suya."

109. Lima, "Documento e ficção," 4. "A ficção . . . é uma produção direcionada pela unidade (pretensa) do eu. Produção que pode sempre ser percorrida ão revés, por um poeta ão revés, i.e., por um leitor ou analista, que, dependendo do seu talento, poderá ãos poucos interpretar aquilo de que a refração é 'documento'."

110. ". . . debía de andar una especie de método interpretativo paralelo al desciframiento freudiano de los sueños: asociaciones, realización simbólica de deseos, creación de personajes que no son sino disfraces del propio soñante, actos fallidos, omisiones significativas."

111. "Intentar rastrear el destino último de Bruno Medina es un propósito ocioso. Todos preferimos ignorar su paradero. Por lo demás, siempre se evadía . . . y de esa misma forma se ausentaba sin explicación de por medio. . . ."

112. Brown, *Life Against Death*, 62.

113. ". . . obraba por la vía de la representación, por el camino del fingimiento. . . ."

114. "¿No tenía derecho Ocaranza a la ironía, por amarga que fuera? Y si alguien no entendía su sarcasmo pobre de él, él se lo perdía: ese alguien, ese imbécil que por requerimientos de la subsistencia tenía que simular no darse cuenta del carácter satírico de un discurso cáustico y desfachatado." "¿Qué era a fin de cuentas la seriedad? No era ésa la actitud del profesor Ocaranza. Fingía que tomaba en serio las cosas, aparentaba que las tomaba al pie de la letra, a sabiendas, muy a sabiendas de que en aquel subtexto, en aquel subdiscurso, en aquel enunciado más atrás de lo dicho, se estaba literalmente cagando en lo que la historiografía y el buen decir diplomático y académico establecían como propio. ¿No era suficientemente obvio?"

115. ". . . los peligros de su indiscreción irrefrenable. . . ." "Tenía en sí mismo a su peor enemigo. . . ."

116. ". . . medir su voz, evitar la desmesura, no cometer imprudencias, aunque se le antojara hacer guiños al lector. . . ."

117. "¿En qué consiste el juego en el fondo?" "¿Qué significa la seriedad?"

118. Guillermo Cabrera Infante, *Tres triestes tigres* (Barcelona: Editorial Seix Barral, 1970), 264. "Una broma dentro de una broma? Entonces, caballeros, la cosa es seria."

119. ". . . fingía que era clasista a fin de disimular que en el fondo, entrañablemente, era visceral e inevitablemente clasista. . . ."

120. Hernadi, "Clio's Cousins," 248, discusses this perspective of history, where the role of the historian is something of a scientific creator of myths.

121. M. Oakeshott, *Experience and Its Modes*, 9, cited in *What is History?* 16.

122. Lionel Gossman, "History and Literature," in *The Writing of History: Literary Form and Historical Understanding*, eds. Robert H. Cavary and Henry Kosicki (Madison: University of Wisconsin Press, 1978), 18.

123. Adam Shaff, *History and Truth* (London: Pergamon Press, 1976), 100.

124. Ibid., 101.

125. ". . . recortes, fotografías, cartas personales, cuadernos de notas, agendas, directorios, actas de nacimiento, credenciales: la historia toda de un personaje."

126. ". . . la información venía y venía en cantidades que no siempre necesitaba. ¿Para qué enterarse de la hora en minutos y segundos precisos y fracciones de segundo? ¿Para qué tanto detalle sobre la presión atmosférica y la humedad. . . . ?"

127. ". . . una cortina de humo: mucha información (aparentemente diversificada pero en el fondo idéntica) para no informar nada. Se trataba no de aclarar sino de enturbiar, no de hacer visibles las cosas sino de ocultarlas, no de que se viera el bosque sino de que los árboles impidieran escudriñarlo."

128. "Me entero de cosas que no necesito, se decía, y al mismo tiempo nada sé de lo que realmente está sucediendo. . . . Pero la novedad, el placer de comunicar algo que los demás todavía no conocían pervivía en él como un vicio preservado desde la adolescencia."

129. "Empezaba a recomponerse sobre el escritorio como piezas de un rompecabezas, la historia y sus elementos dispares . . . con la fingida objetividad o imparcialidad del reportero. . . ."

130. "Allí justamente, en esos huecos, Bruno tenía la posibilidad de inventar y más cancha para dilatar las acciones y atribuírselas a un personaje u otro."

131. "La uniformidad de la información, los boletines oficiales, los diecinueve diarios matutinos que le entregaban todos los días no lograban uno solo digno de lectura . . . sino una variedad de periódicos que en rigor, bien vistos, eran el mismo pero con diferente título."

132. "Saberse el verdadero autor de la gloria o el fracaso de quien caía en sus manos, sentirse también el creador del fingido cronista que tras el seudónimo asumía una nueva existencia . . . la gratificación íntima y solitaria y obsesiva del espía. . . ."

133. ". . . el ojo detrás de los binoculares o la mira telescópica que penetraba las ventanas encendidas de los edificios o que se aproximaba a los muslos de las parejas recostadas en los parques." "Así procedería, como una fuerza inatrapable y omnipresente, con la dulce irresponsabilidad infantil de quien se sabe invisible y maléfico, devastador, un diablo, un Dios, un hombre de Estado."

134. Danto, *Narration and Knowledge*, 358.

135. "Nunca en sus mocedades imaginó que a la vuelta de la esquina, en uno de los rincones del poder, él, Bruno Medina . . . se iba a topar con las puertas abiertas hacia la creación desinhibida y sin tapujos, sin escollos, sin obstáculos hacia la libertad imperturbablemente inútil que por fin se avizoraba campear en el reino de lo absoluto: el libelo de su propia vida."

136. ". . . lo hacía por dinero, eso estaba claro."

137. "Todos dicen que sí. De putas. Y la incapacidad de decir *no*, la impotencia, el servir para que el otro cobre. . . ."

138. Ramsey Macmullen, *Roman Government's Response to Crisis* (New Haven: Yale University Press, 1976), 15.

139. "Yo de pie y Lauca de cabeza, yo cogiéndola por la cintura, yo de pie y ella cabeza abajo . . . y de un brinco nos volteábamos mutuamente, quedando a cada volteo yo en pie y la Quebranta bocabajo."

140. ". . . era una mujer intangible. . . ."

141. ". . . el hecho de que la Quebranta tuviera a su padre en una urna en el ropero, tal vez. . . ." It seems that la Quebranta, like Bruno, has a conscience symbolized by the remains of her father which she always keeps with her.

142. "De esa manera lúdica vivíamos de noche, dormíamos de día."

143. Carlos Fuentes, "Una literature urgente," in *Latin American Fiction Today:A Symposium*, ed. Rose S. Minc (Takoma Park, Md./ Montclair, N.J.: Hispamerica/Montclair State College, 1979), 10. "Como Cervantes, los escritores de hoy sólo podemos serlo en una forma impura, paródica, mítica y documental a la vez, en la que la ficción, al re-presentarse, se convierte en la forma literaria más cercana a la verdad porque se libera de la pretensión de verdad y la más cercana a la realidad porque mina esa misma realidad con la burla ilusoria de un caballero que dice "créanme" y nadie le cree; "no me crean" y todos le creen."

144. ". . . las cosas no tenían remedio pero al mismo tiempo había que hacer algo por cambiarlas. Su valor, su coraje para oponerse al sistema, su capacidad de indignación . . . eso era lo que lo mantenía en pie y lo salvaba de caer en el estercolero."

145. "Bruno se encontraba del lado inquisidor, aunque furtivo. Desde la otra orilla de los acontecimientos, y en otro tiempo, rehacía y organizaba la historia. Los hombres viven los hechos, se decía, pero yo soy el que los comunica. . . ."

146. ". . . a nadie hacía daño. . . ." ". . . memoria a punto de reventar. . . ." ". . . palabras no pronunciadas. . . ."

147. "Y fue allí mismo en sus sueños donde se vio a sí mismo invadiendo el futuro, no, no el porvenir siniestro que avizoraba o preveía para él como justo merecimiento, no, sino simplemente irrumpiendo en el centro de la ciudad y llamando la atención de todo el mundo."

148. ". . . un pantalón encima del que ya llevaba puesto sobre la piyama de franela, un saco a cuadros del professor Ocaranza, . . . una camisa encima de los harapos que lo cubrían a medias . . . y encima de todo su cuerpo se ponía el gran abrigo del profesor Ocaranza, negro, largo, hasta el suelo."

149. ". . . el profesor, el profesor, ya no está. Ya no está. Ya no está." "Y luego cantaban todos a coro, en bola, en nudo, en can can.: 'So-mos-u-nas-pu-tas-so-mos-u-nas-pu-tas-del-Fo-llies-Ber-gé-res!'"

150. ". . . enmendarse y corregirse o destruirse en su totalidad. . . ."

151. Shoshana Felman, "Beyond Oedipus: The Specimen Story of Psychoanalysis," in *Lacan and Narration: The Psychoanalytic Difference in Narrative Theory*, ed. Robert Con Davis (Baltimore: The Johns Hopkins University Press, 1983), 1051.

152. "A usted lo que lo perdió fue lo de la pretexta. . . ."

Chapter 6. Conclusion: The End of the Story?

1. Fuentes, "Una literatura urgente," 13. "Escribir en la América Latina es apostar a la litertad, decirse intimamente en el acto de escribir que es urgente

mantener viva la cultura del pasado porque sin ella no tendremos verdadero presente ni porvenir inteligible. . . ."

2. Edmundo O'Gorman, *The Invention of America; an Inquiry into the Historical Nature of the New World and the Meaning of its History* (Westport, Conn.: Greenwood, 1961) discusses the experiences of Christopher Columbus, who on "discovering" America had to invent it, that is, to create an identity for it that would correspond to his expectations at the same time as explain what he found.

3. Paz, "Literatura de fundación," Introduction to *Puertas al Campo* (Mexico: Universidad Nacional Autónoma de México, 1966).

4. Friedrich Nietzsche, *The Birth of Tragedy*, 142 discussed and cited in Hayden White, *Metahistory: The Historical Imagination in 19th-Century Europe* (Baltimore: The Johns Hopkins University Press, 1973), 343.

5. Paz, *Posdata* (Mexico: Siglo 21, 1970), 115–16. "La historia que vivimos es una escritura; en la escritura de la historia visible debemos leer las metamorfosis y los cambios de la historia invisible. Esa lectura es un desciframiento, la traducción de una traducción: jamás leeremos el original. Cada versión es provisional: el texto cambia sin cesar (aunque quizá siempre dice lo mismo) y de ahí que de tiempo en tiempo se descarten ciertas versiones en favor de otras que, a su vez, antes habían sido descartadas. Cada traducción es una creación: un texto nuevo. . . ."

6. Louis Minc, "Narrative Form as a Cognitive Instrument," in Canary y Kosicki, 149.

7. Baez et al., *Ficción e historia*, 340. "Es evidente . . . que al cuestionar el contexto sociohistórico del presente, se cuestiona también la visión mitificada de la historia. . . . En la base de todo este proceso crítico hay pues un cuestionamiento decisivo de la historia institucionalizada, que abarca el nivel económico, el político y el ideológico con claro predominio de los dos últimos."

8. White, "Historical Text as Literary Artifact," in *Writing of History*, 43.

9. Frank Kermode, *The Sense of an Ending: Studies in the Theory of Fiction* (New York: Oxford University Press, 1967), 39.

10. Paz, *El laberinto de la soledad*, 94. "History has the atrocious reality of a nightmare; the greatness of man consists in making beautiful and lasting works out of the real substance of that nightmare. Or in other words: to transfigure the nightmare into vision, to free us, even for an instant, from the disfigured reality by means of creation." ["La historia tiene la realidad atroz de una pesadilla; la grandeza del hombre consiste en hacer obras hermosas y durables con la sustancia real de esa pesadilla. O dicho de otro modo: transfigurar la pesadilla en visión, liberarnos, así sea por un instante, de la realidad disforme por medio de la creación."]

11. See n. 9.

Bibliographical Appendix
List of Works on Tlatelolco

Novels and Testimonial Novels

Aguilar Mora, Jorge. *Si muero lejos de ti.* Mexico: Joaquín Mortiz, 1979.
Aviles Fabila, Rene. *El gran solitario de palacio.* Buenos Aires: Fabril, 1971.
de Paso, Fernando. *Palinuro de México.* Mexico: Joaquín Mortiz, 1977.
González de Alba, Luis. *Los días y los años.* Mexico: Era, 1971.
Martre, Gonzalo. *Los símbolos transparentes.* Mexico: Cinco Siglos, 1978.
Mendoza, María Luisa. *Con El, conmigo, con nosotros tres.* Mexico: Joaquín Mortiz, 1972.
Poniatowska, Elena. *Fuerte es el silencio.* Mexico: Era, 1980.
———. *La noche de Tlatelolco.* Mexico: Era, 1971.
Ramos, Agustín. *Al cielo por asalto.* Mexico: Era, 1979.
Sainz, Gustavo. *Compadre Lobo.* Mexico: Grijalbo, 1975.
Spota, Luis. *La plaza.* Mexico: Joaquín Mortiz, 1972.

Documentaries and Testimonies

Balam, Gilberto. *Tlatelolco, reflexiones de un testigo.* Mexico: Tallares Lenasa, 1969.
Barros Sierra, Javier. *1968/Conversaciones con Gastón García Cantú.* Mexico: Siglo XXI, 1972.
Blanco Moheno, Roberto. *Tlatelolco, historia de una infamia.* Mexico: Ediciones Diana, 1969.
Campos Lemus, Sócrates. *El otoño de la revolución (octubre).* Mexico: Costa-Amic, 1973.
de Mora, Juan Miguel. *Tlatelolco 1968: por fin toda la verdad.* Mexico: Editores Asociados Mexicanos, 1975.
Hernández, Salvador. *El PRI y el movimiento estudiantil de 1968.* Mexico: Ediciones El Caballito, 1971.
Martínez, Carlos. *Tres instantes.* Mexico: Ediciones Jus., 1972.
Ramírez, Ramón. *El movimiento estudiantil de México.* Mexico: Era, 1969.

Works Cited

Alter, Robert. *Partial Magic: The Novel as a Self-Conscious Genre.* Berkeley: University of California Press, 1975.

Arenas, Reinaldo. *El mundo alucinante.* Mexico: Editorial Diógenes, 1978.

Arreola, Juan José. *La feria.* Mexico: Joaquín Mortiz, 1963.

Bakhtin, Mikhail. *The Dialogic Imagination.* Austin: University of Texas Press, 1981.

Barnet, Miguel. *Biografía de un cimarrón.* Havana: Academia de Ciencias, 1966.

———. "The Documentary Novel." *Cuban Studies/Estudios Cubanos* 11, no. 1 (January 1981): 19–32. Translated by Paul Bundy and Enrico Mario Santi.

———. "La novela testimonio: socio-literature." In *La Fuente Viva.* Havana: Editorial Letras Cubanas, 1983.

———. "Testimonio y comunicación: una vía hacia la identidad." In *La Fuente Viva.* Havana: Editorial Letras Cubanas, 1983.

Barrios de Chungara, Domitila con Moema Viezzer. *Si me permiten hablar . . . Testimonio de Domitila una mujer de las minas de Bolivia.* Mexico: Siglo 21, 1977.

Barthes, Roland. *Criticism and Truth.* Translated by Katrine Pilcher Keuneman. London: Athlone Press, 1987.

———. "The Death of the Author." In *Image, Music, Text.* Translated by Stephen Heath. New York: Hill and Wang, 1977.

———. *Writing Degree Zero.* Translated by Jonathan Cape, Ltd. Boston: Beacon, 1967.

Bernstein, J. M. *The Philosophy of the Novel: Lukács, Marxism and the Dialectics of Form.* Minneapolis: University of Minnesota Press, 1984.

Bloch, Marc. *The Historian's Craft.* Translated by Peter Putnam. New York: Vintage Books, 1953.

Borges, Jorge Luís. "Pierre Menard, autor de Quijote." In *Ficciones.* Buenos Aires: Emecé Editores, 1956.

———. "Las Ruinas circulares." In *Ficciones.* Buenos Aires: Emecé Editores, 1956.

Braudy, Leo. *Narrative Form in History and Fiction.* Princeton: Princeton University Press, 1970.

Brown, Norman. *Life Against Death: The Psychoanalytical Meaning of History.* Middletown, Conn.: Wesleyan University Press, 1959.

Brushwood, S. John. *Mexico in Its Novel.* Austin: University of Texas Press, 1966.

———. *La novela mexicana 1967–1982.* Mexico: Grijalbo, 1984.

———. "Períodos literarios en el México del siglo XX: la transformación de la realidad." In *La crítica de la novela mexicana contemporánea.* Edited by Aurora M. Ocampo. México: Universidad Nacional Autónoma de México, 1981.

Cabrera Infante, Guillermo. *Tres tristes tigres*. Barcelona: Editorial Seix Barral, 1970.

Campbell, Federico. *Pretexta*. Mexico: Fondo de Cultura Económica, 1979.

Campos Lemus, Sócrates. *El otoño de la revolución (octubre)*. Mexico: Costa-Amic, 1973.

―――. "El testimonio: recuento y perspectivas del género en nuestro país." In Jara, *Testimonio y Literatura*, 333–41.

Canary, Robert H. and Henry Kozicki, ed. *The Writing of History: Literary Form and Historical Understanding*. Madison: University of Wisconsin Press, 1978.

Carr, Edward Hallett. *What Is History?* London: MacMillan, 1961.

Casas, Nubya. "Novela testimonio: historia y literatura." Ph.D. diss., New York University, 1981.

Casaus, Victor. "Defensa del testimonio." In Jara, *Testimonio y Literatura*, 324–32.

Christ, Ronald. "The Author as Editor." *Review of the Center for Inter-American Relations*, no. 15 (1975): 18–19.

Costa Lima, Luis. "Documento e ficção." In Jara, *Testimonio y Literatura*, 22–47.

Culler, Jonathon. "Problems in the Theory of Fiction." *Diacritics* 14, no. 1 (1984): 2–11.

Danto, Arthur. *Narration and Knowledge*. New York: Columbia University Press, 1985.

de Man, Paul. "Literary History and Literary Modernity." In *Blindness and Insight: Essays in the Rhetoric of Contemporary Criticism*. New York: Oxford University Press, 1971.

Dorfman, Ariel. "Código político y código literario: el género testimonio en Chile hoy." In Jara, *Testimonio y Literatura*, 170–234.

Duden (Encyclopedia) 3. Mannheim, Germany: Bibliographisches Institut, 1977.

Duncan, Ann. *Voices, Visions and a New Reality: Mexican Fiction Since 1970*. Pittsburgh: University of Pittsburgh Press, 1986.

Durán, Manual. "Notas sobre la imaginación histórica y la narrativa hispanoamericana." In González Echevarría, *Historia y ficción*, 287–96.

Elizondo, Salvador. *El grafógrafo*. Mexico: Joaquín Mortiz, 1972.

Fell, Claude. "Destrucción y poesía en la novela latinoamericana contemporánea." In *III Congreso Latinoamericano de Escritores*. Caracas: Ediciones del Congreso de la República, 1971.

Felman, Shoshana. "Beyond Oedipus: The Specimen Story of Psychoanalysis." In *Lacan and Narration: The Psychoanalytic Difference in Narrative Theory*. Edited by Robert Con Davis. Baltimore: The Johns Hopkins University Press, 1983.

Foley, Barbara. *Telling the Truth: The Theory and Practice of Documentary Fiction*. Ithaca, N.Y.: Cornell University Press, 1986.

Fornet, Ambrosio. "Mnemosina pide la palabra." In *Testimonio y Literatura*, 342–46.

Foster, David William. *Alternate Voices in the Contemporary Latin American Narrative*. Columbia: University of Missouri Press, 1985.

―――. "Latin American Documentary Narrative." *PMLA* 99, no. 1 (1984): 41–55.

Foucault, Michel. "What Is an Author?" In *Textual Strategies: Perspectives in Post Structuralist Criticsm*. Ithaca, N.Y.: Cornell University Press, 1979.

Fraire, Isabel. "Testimonial Literature: A New Window on Reality." *The American Book Review.* (September-October 1983): 5–6.

Franco, Jean. "The Critique of the Pyramid and Mexican Narrative after 1968." In *Latin American Fiction Today, A Symposium,* edited by Rose S. Minc, 49–60. Takoma Park, Md./Montclair, N.J.: Hispanmérica/Montclair State College, 1979.

Fuentes, Carlos. *La nueva novela hispanoamericana.* Mexico: Joaquín Mortiz, 1969.

———. *Tiempo mexicano.* Mexico: Joaquín Mortiz, 1972.

———. "Una literatura urgente." In *Latin American Fiction Today: A Symposium.* Edited by Rose S. Minc. Takoma Park, Md./Montclair, N.J.: Hispamérica/Montclair State College, 1979.

García, Gustavo. "Federico Campbell: Literatura y poder, una conversación con Gustavo García." In *Revista de la Universidad de México* 39, no. 8 (April 1980): 14.

Garcilaso de la Vega, El Inca. *La Florida.* Mexico: Fondo de Cultura Económica, 1956.

Garro, Elena. *La casa junto al río.* Mexico: Editorial Grijalbo, 1982.

———. *Los recuerdos del porvenir.* Mexico: Joaquín Mortiz, 1977.

———. *Testimonios sobre Mariana.* Mexico: Editorial Grijalbo, 1981.

Glantz, Margo. "Estudio preliminar." In Introduction to *Onda y escritura en México: jóvenes de 20 a 33.* Edited by Margo Glantz. Mexico: Siglo 21, 1971.

González del Alba, Luis. *Los días y los años.* Mexico: ERA, 1971.

González Echevarría, Roberto. "*Biografía de un cimarrón* and the Novel of the Cuban Revolution." *Novel* 13, no. 3 (Spring 1980): 251–63.

———. "*Cien años de soledad*: The Novel as Myth and Archive." *Modern Language Notes* 99, no. 2 (March 1984): 358–80.

———, ed. *Historia y ficción en la narrativa hispanoamericana.* New Haven: Coloquio de Yale, Monte Avila, 1984.

———. "Humanismo, retórica y las crónicas de la conquista." In *Historia y ficción,* 149–66.

Gossman, Lionel. "History and Literature." In *The Writing of History: Literary Form and Historical Understanding,* edited by Robert H. Cavary and Henry Kosicki, 3–39. Madison:University of Wisconsin Press, 1978.

Habermas, Jürgen. *Knowledge and Human Interests.* Boston: Beacon Press, 1971.

Hale, Charles A. "The History of Ideas: Substantive and Methodological Aspects of the Thought of Leopoldo Zea." *Journal of Latin American Studies* 3 (1971): 59–70.

———. "The Liberal Impulse: Daniel Cosío Villegas and the *Historia moderna de México.*" *Hispanic American Historical Review* 54, no. 3 (August 1974): 479–98.

Handlin, Oscar. *Truth in History.* Cambridge: Harvard University Press, 1979.

Hardy, Barbara. *Tellers and Listeners.* London: Athlone Press, 1975.

Hellman, John. *Fables of Fact: The New Journalism as New Fiction.* Urbana: University of Illinois Press, 1981.

Hernadi, Paul. "Clio's Cousins: Historiography as Translation, Fiction, and Criticism." *New Literary History* 7, no. 2 (Winter 1976): 247–57.

Herrnstein Smith, Barbara. *On the Margins of Discourse: The Relation of Literature to Language.* Chicago: University of Chicago Press, 1979.

Hollowell, John. *Fact and Fiction: The New Journalism and the Nonfiction Novel.* Chapel Hill: University of North Carolina Press, 1977.

Iser, Wolfgang. *The Act of Reading: A Theory of Aesthetic Response.* Baltimore: The Johns Hopkins University Press, 1978.

Jara, René y Hernán Vidal, ed. *Testimonio y Literatura.* Minneapolis: Society for the Study of Contemporary Hispanic and Lusophone Revolutionary Literatures, 1986.

Jiménez de Báez, Yvette, Diana Morán, and Edith Negrin. *Ficción e historia: la narrativa de José Emilio Pacheco.* Mexico: El Colegio de México, 1979.

Jitrik, Noé. *El no existente caballero: La idea de personaje y su evolución en la narrativa hispanoamericana.* Buenos Aires: Megápolis, 1975.

Kadir, Djelal. "Historia y novela: tramatización de la palabra." In González Echevarría, *Historia y ficción,* 297–329.

Kahler, Erich. *The Meaning of History.* New York: Braziller, 1984.

Kermode, Frank. *The Sense of an Ending: Studies in the Theory of Fiction.* New York: Oxford University Press, 1967.

Kiddle, Mary Ellen. "The Non-Fiction Novel or 'Novela Testimonial' in Contemporary Mexican Literature." Ph.D. diss., Brown University, 1984.

Lasch, Christopher. *The Culture of Narcissism.* New York: W. W. Norton & Co., 1978.

Leal, Luis. "Nuevos novelistas mexicanos." In *La crítica de la novela mexicana contemporánea.* Edited by Aurora M. Ocampo. Mexico: Universidad Nacional Autónoma de México, 1981.

———. "Tlatelolco, Tlatelolco." *Denver Quarterly* 14, no. 1 (1979): 3–13.

Lemaire, Anika. *Jacques Lacan.* Translated by David Macey. London: Henley; Boston: Routledge & Kegan Paul, 1977.

Lindenberger, Herbert. *Historical Drama: The Relationship of Literature and Reality.* Chicago: University of Chicago Press, 1975.

Lloyd, Genevieve, "Masters, Slaves and Others." *Radical Philosophy* 34 (Summer 1983): 2–8.

Loewenberg, Peter. *Decoding the Past: The Psychohistorical Approach.* New York: Knopf, 1983.

MacMullen, Ramsey. *Roman Government's Response to Crisis.* New Haven: Yale University Press, 1976.

Mailer, Norman. *Advertisements for Myself.* New York: Putnam, 1959.

Martin, Wallace. *Recent Theories of Narrative.* Ithaca, N.Y.: Cornell University Press, 1986.

Marrou, Henry. *The Meaning of History.* Translated by Robert J. Olson. Baltimore: Helicon, 1966.

Méndez Rodenas, Adriana. "¿Texto, *Pretexta* or Pre-texto?: historia y parodia en la narrativa mexicana contemporánea." In *La historia en la literatura iberoamericana: memorias del XXVI Congreso del Instituto Internacional de Literatura Iberoamericana.* Edited by Raquel Chang-Rodríguez and Gabriella de Beer. Hanover, N.H.: Ediciones del Norte, 1989.

———. "Tiempo femenino, tiempo ficticio: *Los recuerdos del porvenir,* de Elena Garro." *Revista Iberoamericana,* nos. 132–33 (July-December 1985): 843–51.

Mendoza, María Luisa. *Con él, conmigo y con nosotros tres.* Mexico: Joaquín Mortiz, 1971.

Miller, Beth and Alfonso González. *26 autoras del México actual.* México: Costa-Amic, 1978.

Miller, J. Hillis. "Narrative and History." *English Literary History* 41 (1974): 455–73.

Mink, Louis. "Narrative Form as a Cognitive Instrument." In Canary and Kozicki, *The Writing of History,* 129–49.

Monsivais, Carlos. *Días de guardar.* Mexico: ERA, 1970.

Narvaez, Jorge. "El testimonio 1972–1982. Transformaciones en el sistema literario." In Jara, *Testimonio y Literatura,* 235–79.

O'Gorman, Edmundo. *The Invention of America; an Inquiry into the Historical Nature of the New World and the Meaning of Its History.* Westport, Conn.: Greenwood Press, 1961.

Ortega, Julio. " *Cien años de soledad.*" In *La contemplación y la fiesta—notas sobre la novela latinoamericana actual.* Caracas: Monte Avila, 1969.

Pacheco, José Emilio. *Morirás lejos.* 1967; Mexico: Mortiz, 1977.

Paz, Octavio. *El laberinto de la soledad.* 1950; Mexico: Fondo de Cultura Económica, 1967.

———. "Literatura de fundación." Introduction to *Puertas al campo.* Mexico: Universidad Nacional Autónoma de México, 1966.

———. Introduction. *Massacre in Mexico.* By Elena Poniatowska. Translated by Helen R. Lane. New York: The Viking Press, 1975.

———. *Posdata.* Mexico: Siglo 21, 1970.

Poirier, Richard. *The Performing Self.* New York: Oxford University Press, 1971.

Poniatowska, Elena. *Hasta no verte Jesús mío.* Mexico: ERA, 1969.

———. *La noche de Tlatelolco.* 43rd ed. Mexico: ERA, 1984.

Pozas Arciniega, Ricardo. *Juan Pérez Jolote, biografía de un tzotzil.* Mexico: Fondo de Cultura Económica, 1959.

Prada Oropeza, Renato. "De lo testimonial al testimonio: notas para un deslinde del discurso-testimonio." In Jara, *Testimonio y Literatura,* 7–21.

Pupo Walker, Enrique. "Primeras imágenes de América: notas para una lectura más fiel de nuestra historia." In González Echevarría, *Historia y ficción,* 85–103.

Rice-Sayre, Laura. "Witnessing History: Diplomacy vs. Testimony." In Jara, *Testimonio y Literatura,* 48–72.

Ricoeur, Paul. *Time and Narrative.* Translated by Kathleen McLaughlin and David Pellauer. Chicago: University of Chicago Press, 1983.

Riding, Alan. *Distant Neighbors.* New York: Knopf, 1985.

Rodríguez Monegal, Emir. *El boom de la novela latinoamericana.* Caracas: Editorial Tiempo Nuevo, 1972.

Rodríguez Vecchini, Hugo. "Don Quijote y 'La Florida' del Inca." In *Historia y ficción,* 105–48.

Rosenblat, Angel. "La primera visión de América." In *La primera visión de América y otros estudios.* Caracas: Ministerio de Educación, 1965.

Sacks, Oliver. *The Man Who Mistook His Wife for a Hat and Other Clinical Tales.* New York: Harper & Row, 1987.

Sainz, Gustavo. *Fantasmas aztecas*. Mexico: Editorial Grijalbo, 1979.

Sarduy, Severo. *Escrito sobre un cuerpo; ensayos de crítica*. Buenos Aires: Editorial Sudamericana, 1969.

Sartre, Jean-Paul. *Nausea*. New York: New Directions, 1964.

Schaff, Adam. *History and Truth*. London: Pergamon Press, 1976.

Schlegel, Friedrich. The 80th "fragment" from the *Athenaeum*. In *Kritische Friedrich-Schlegel-Ausgabe*, vol. 2. Edited by Hans Eichner. Munich, 1967.

Schwartz, Murray M. "Critic, Define Thyself." In *Psychoanalysis and the Question of the Text*. Edited by Geoffrey H. Hartman. Baltimore & London: The Johns Hopkins University Press, 1978.

Searle, John. "The Logical Status of Fictional Discourse." *Expression and Meaning: Studies in the Theory of Speech Acts*. Cambridge: Cambridge University Press, 1979.

Spota, Luis. *La Plaza*. Mexico: Joaquín Mortiz, 1972.

Stanford, Michael. *The Nature of Historical Knowledge*. New York: Basil Blackwell, 1987.

Todorov, Tzvetan. *The Conquest of America*. Translated by Richard Howard. New York: Harper & Row, 1985.

Visión de los vencidos. relaciones indígenas de la conquista. Translated from *nahua* texts by Angel María Garibay K. Mexico: Universidad Nacional Autónoma de México, Biblioteca del Estudiante Universitario, 1972.

Weber, Ronald. *The Literature of Fact: Literary Nonfiction in American Writing*. Athens: Ohio University Press, 1980.

Weimann, Robert. *Structure and Society in Literary History: Studies in the History and Theory of Historical Criticism*. Baltimore: The Johns Hopkins University Press, 1984.

White, Hayden. *Metahistory: The Historical Imagination in 19th Century Europe*. Baltimore: The Johns Hopkins University Press, 1973.

Wilden, Anthony. *Speech and Language in Psychoanalysis: Jacques Lacan*. Translated with notes. Baltimore: The Johns Hopkins University Press, 1981.

Index